UNFRIENDLY NEIGHBOURS

Unfriendly Neighbours

BY

Chilco Choate

The Caitlin Press
Prince George, British Columbia
1993

UNFRIENDLY NEIGHBOURS

The Caitlin Press
P.O. Box 2387, Station B
Prince George, B.C. V2N 2S6
Canada

The Caitlin Press would like to acknowledge the financial support of the Canada Council and British Columbia Cultural Fund.

The cover photo is courtesy *The Vancouver Sun*.
The brand reproduced on the cover belongs to the Gang Ranch.

Canadian Cataloguing in Publication Data

Choate, Chilco, 1935–
Unfriendly Neighbours

Includes index.
ISBN 0-920576-42-7

1. Choate, Chilco, 1935– 2. Cariboo (B.C.: Regional district)—Biography. 3. Gang Ranch (B.C.)—History. I. Title.
FC3845.C3Z49 1993 971.1'75 C93-091226-8

Edited by Dave Speck
Indexed by Kathy Plett
Cover Design by Roger Handling
Typeset in Bembo by Vancouver Desktop Publishing Centre
Printed in Canada

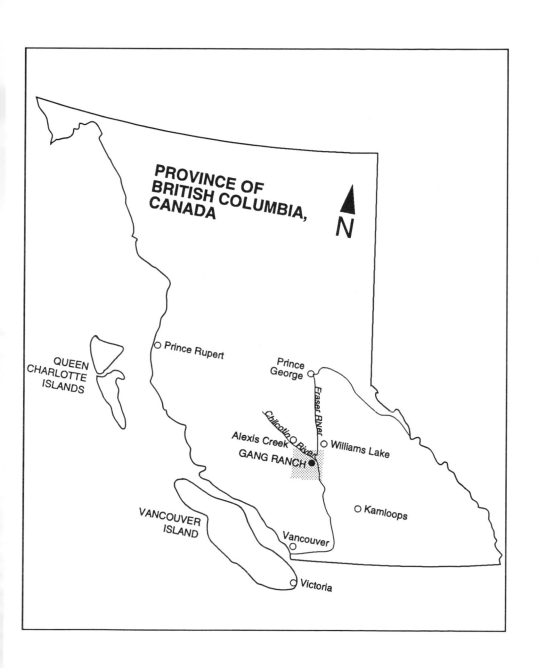

PROVINCE OF
BRITISH COLUMBIA,
CANADA

N

QUEEN
CHARLOTTE
ISLANDS

○ Prince Rupert

Prince
George ○

Fraser River

Chilcotin River

Alexis Creek ○

○ Williams Lake

GANG RANCH ●

VANCOUVER
ISLAND

Vancouver
○

○ Kamloops

○ Victoria

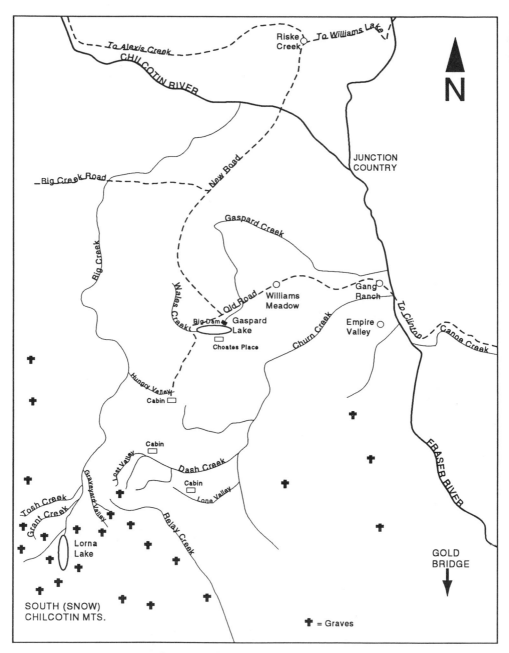

The Range of the
High Country Men

CHAPTER 1

THE GAME WARDEN REARED BACK in his chair, pointed his nose towards a spot somewhere near the centre of the ceiling, and bellowed out, "Hey Shorty, get your ass down here." When he turned to face me, there must have been a strange look on my face, because he started laughing and pointed his thumb back at the ceiling and explained what he had just done. "The fellow I want you to meet lives upstairs and that system of getting his attention is a lot faster than cranking up the telephone and waiting for the operator to finish chewing the fat with some of her friends," he said.

A few moments later a small, wizened, weather-beaten man in a brown western hat walked in the door and I began the first of my long and eventful associations with a million acres of British Columbia, known as the Gang Ranch country of the Chilcotin. The time would have been mid April of 1955 and I had just gone into Game Warden Bill Fenton's office in Clinton to inquire about getting a cougar hound and also to investigate the possibility of being able to qualify as a bounty hunter for the government. In those days the government paid double the normal twenty-dollar bounty for cougars to a few selected hunters who kept specially trained dogs. I was still pretty young but Fenton listened to me for a while and his decision that day steered me into a life that I had wanted since I was eight years old and have never regretted since.

As Fenton introduced me to this new fellow who turned out to be Shorty Watson, he also made a further comment, referring to Watson, "this little bastard is the nemesis of the Gang Ranch." I had no real idea what the word "nemesis" meant, but suspected it might have something to do with ownership, so was immediately impressed. But as Watson and I were shaking hands, he in turn asked a question that added a little more confusion to the situation, and that was, "you ain't by any chance a fuckin' rancher are you?" To that we all had a good laugh, even though I didn't quite understand the joke yet. It would take a while longer for everything to catch up.

It's been over thirty years now, since that introduction and it seems surprising just how vividly clear that it's all still frozen into my mind. Of course it was the pivotal point in my life and it was also to become associated with the changing times of the entire Cariboo-Chilcotin as well, but nobody could have known that then. Thinking back to that time from now, it is obvious that for me that was the beginning of a soul feeling and meaning to describe an old saying that reminds us, "these hills are the hills of home," because that is what it all eventually led to.

My early years had been spent on the family homestead near White Rock, not far from Vancouver. My parents subsequently moved up to Clinton but my life in the lower mainland brings back interesting memories. I remember waiting impatiently to reach the magic age of sixteen when I could legally quit school and head NORTH. My folks had delusions that I would become a lawyer, but it was not to be. By the time I was thirteen and in junior high my thoughts were always outdoors, so it was only natural that as soon as I was strong enough to do all the things that seemed interesting, my body started following my mind. When I was thirteen I was already six feet three inches and about 165 pounds, so the idea of being locked into a building six hours a day for the next seven years became intolerably depressing. The regular school curriculum at that time was about as dull and uninteresting as anything that could be imagined. Luckily, because of my size and agility, sports such as basketball and softball came easily so there were a few compensations for attending school, at least some of the time.

I played hooky on a regular basis and during the fall, and winter months when the duck season was open I often spent two or three school days a week sitting in duck blinds behind Mud Bay which is a tidal flat on the Pacific Ocean. If I wasn't shooting ducks, then I would be tending a line of muskrat and mink traps set up along the Nicomecel, Serpentine, and Campbell Rivers near home. These little extracurricular activities used to drive my teachers to distraction and I spent many an hour sitting in the principal's office waiting for the next lecture. My folks were often notified about my truancy but when they attempted to rectify my ways, it was always possible to neutralize their argument by reminding them, that because of my size and farm upbringing, there would be no problem for me to find a job if I were to hit the road, even before age sixteen. We all knew that this was true, so usually after a few cooling off days, the call of field and forest would draw me back to the rivers, especially on Monday mornings. Oh, how I hated the thoughts of returning to school on a Monday. If ever there has been a hell on earth, then it was just mentioned here.

In those days it was not that difficult to pass through the yearly grades as all we had to do was make passing marks on about four exams a year. This could be accomplished by reading through the text books a couple of times.

Many times throughout my life I have thought back to

3

school days because for me they were often hunting days as well. My school in White Rock was called Semiahmoo High and at that time the principal was a very large, silver-haired man by the name of Murray Sanford. Some of the kids referred to him as "Old Eagle Head," but not to his face. Back then, truancy and several other misdemeanours could get a kid a strapping and Sanford had a reputation of knowing how to really lay it onto unruly kids. Of the three years spent in that school and the many hours I spent cooling my heels in his outer office, strangely enough he never once strapped me or even really threatened to. It often made me wonder why, because he had beat hell out of other kids for less reason than I was giving him. Of lectures, however, I received many.[1]

By the time I was fifteen I was intensely aware that there was a huge and interesting world out there just waiting for me and by God, I was ready for it. I left school a few weeks

---

1   It's a small world. Many years later, my wife and I were attending the annual convention of the B.C. Wildlife Federation when one of our friends came up to our table and said, "There's an old man on the other side of the room who says he thinks he knew you when you went to high school and he would like you to come over and say 'hi.'"

When I went to his table I could hardly believe my eyes: there sat Murray Sanford, just as I remembered him but a lot older. We chatted for several hours. During the course of our conversation, I brought up the subject of my school trunacy.

Murray chuckled, shook his head, and told me, "I knew where you were all the time, but I sort of sympathized with what you were doing and wished that I could be out there with you, but I had a wife and family to feed and just couldn't do it. There were times when I came close to strapping you, but I knew if I did, you would have left school right then and there, so I gambled on trying to keep you there by building up your interest and hoping you might come to your senses before you quit altogether. It obviously didn't work and at that time I don't think there was anything else that would have worked either."

Ted Choate at Maindley Ranch in 1951, with the first moose he had ever seen. It was a big tough one as it weighed in at the butcher shop in White Rock at just over 800 lbs.

after my sixteenth birthday and in early January of 1952, I said so long to my buddies and headed up to Old Jack's ranch. I had met Jack the previous fall when an older friend had taken me moose hunting. While there I became so impressed with Jack, his ranch, and the lifestyle he had built for himself, that I wanted a piece of that type of life, as well.

My mother, on the other hand, felt that I had made a backwards step in that there would be few if any financial advantages to allow me to build a family nest.

Jack Maindley, who is long gone now, was in the second wave of settlers who homesteaded the Chilcotin district and he arrived here about 1912. By the time I first met him he knew almost all the early settlers who lived between Ashcroft and Anahim Lake, a distance of 400 miles. If he did not know a person or family personally, he certainly knew everything that would be worth knowing about them from the moccasin telegraph. People who live in the hinterlands know that this system can glean as much information out of the country as the best police surveillance. It really makes a person sit up and take notice when he starts hearing stories about himself, which sometimes happens. It's almost like suspecting that the neighbours have been reading your personal mail.

Old Jack, as he was known to everybody, had a small ranch about 30 miles north of Alexis Creek, which in turn, is about 100 miles northwest of the Gang Ranch. He ran 125 head of Aberdeen Angus cattle and also took out a few moose hunters each fall. The cattle were his main income and he only took the hunters out to give himself a break from the monotony and hard work of running the ranch. In that three year period, one of the major things I learned from Old Jack was that trying to run a small ranch and make a living out of it required a lot of damn hard work. To make a profit from a small outfit in those days meant that most of the labour was done by hand because there was not enough money to purchase the machinery that today we consider essential. It was also before the curse of government subsidies.

When I went to work for Old Jack I had just turned sixteen, so these were the most impressionable years of my life and I can assure you that I had the most understanding tutor that any teenage boy could ever be lucky enough to grow up with. By the time I met Old Jack, he was already well-known as a great story teller, but was not a bullshitter. The stories I spent three years listening to were probably 90% fact and they were about people, places, ranching, horses, hunting, dangerous experiences, and just about all the other things that any farm boy wanted to learn about. It is hard for me to describe to you now, exactly how Old Jack told his stories, because he was one of those old English farmers who was very observant about everything around him and he could then relay his observations with the driest English wit that you can possibly imagine.

Jack Maindley branding one of his Angus calves at Maindley Ranch.

For me, every breakfast and every supper was flavoured with stories about pioneering people who, in many cases, still existed just as Old Jack described them. Old Jack was either blessed with common sense or he developed it over a long lifetime. It's a pity there is not much of it around any more.

Here are just a few of his beliefs that I hold onto to this day. Take for instance the idea that we must always maintain at least a year's wood supply stacked in the shed, just in case of sickness or injury. How many people do so today? He insisted that all animals, both domestic and wild, must be treated with respect because so much of our well-being is dependent on theirs. His suggestion to make a spoiled pet out of at least one saddle horse ensured that I was rarely left completely afoot. One of his tips that proved to be a real life-saver was his insistence that you should always carry a winter coat after the first of October, regardless of what the morning weather looked like and that has saved me many

7

Jack Maindley in the corral at Maindley Ranch with some of his Angus cattle. Another oldtimer told me in more recent years, that Maindley was also known as "Black Jack Maindley" because he was the only one raising these animals in the vicinity of Alexis Creek.

times from dangerous situations. In the Chilcotins, Indian summer can turn into winter with one shift of the wind. I can vividly remember many temperature swings when I would go to bed at night at sixty degrees Fahrenheit and wake up the next morning with the thermometer reading sixty below. Conversely, in February and March it can work the other way around which is, to say the least, a wonderful surprise to wake up to. These, and the many other skills he taught me, made life in the bush more than just survival but also pleasantly tolerable.

Everything about those three years with Old Jack still brings back fond memories. However all good things seem to eventually come to an end and it was in the late fall of 1954 when I bid Old Jack farewell. All of the good meadows in his area had long since been taken by others so there was not

8

Jack Maindley or "Old Jack" as he was known to all who knew him. He stands beside Maindley Lake that was named for him and here he holds up the first Kamloops trout that were ever caught there. They had been stocked by F&WB but in a later year they all winter killed. (circa 1952 or '53)

room there for me. His stories had whetted my appetite for greener and more isolated places.

Both in and out of school, we had been surrounded by some of the nicest and prettiest girls this country has ever produced. But to me, they were still just very good friends and lots of fun to be around. Subsequently, however, especially during long cold nights on the ranch, I began remembering what I had recently left behind. There were many times when I contemplated going back to the coast for a while to see if I could convince one of those girls into coming back up-country with me, but I never did get around to giving it a try.

In the early '50s there were very few single white women in the Chilcotin and the few there were had enough older suitors after them, that pups like me had no chance. I have never felt the slightest inclination to become queer, so for a long time my companions were other men like myself, dogs, horses, the wildlife that was always part of our lives, and the ever-present guns. Remembering back to those days brings to memory a conversation I had with my mother, which would have been sometime during the winter of '54-'55, when I stayed with my folks in Clinton. We had been talking about God knows what, when I mentioned something about the

9

young female possibilities around the town. There were a few young women in the Clinton area by then, but Mom turned to me and said, "Son, don't you ever get serious about those girls because I never raised you to get married. You have acquired a lot of bad habits that you don't even seem to know about so don't you ever mess up some girl's life with them." When Mom told me that, I thought it was just about the funniest thing I had ever heard, but she seemed to take herself quite seriously about it.

So there I was, a twenty-year old kid looking for work and adventure. Shorty Watson was pressuring me to go to work for him, guiding big game hunters. Fenton, the game warden, sided with him, saying that this was better than heading out into the bush alone. It probably did not take a lot of convincing to get me interested, because of the last three years I had spent in the bush working for Old Jack.

Shorty Watson and his wife, Ruth, were Americans who had moved into here from Castle Rock, Washington. Although they were in their sixties, a couple years earlier they had taken over the Gaspard Lake Hunting and Fishing Camp which was located ninety-three rough miles northwest of Clinton. More specifically, the camp is located right in the geographical centre of the Gang Ranch cattle grazing area. I don't remember how long it took Shorty, Ruth, and Fenton to convince me to work for Watson, but after several days of visiting with them, the decision was made.

Shorty was a great story teller, but his stories were a lot different from the ones Old Jack told. There were also a large collection of photographs of successful hunts taken in the area which told me that this was going to be a totally different type of country, so the operation and work were going to be much different too. One thing that really astounded me was the number of moose their hunters had been killing in this area.

Apparently this camp had been producing between fifty to sixty-five bull moose every year since about 1946.

But what really clinched the deal for me were the pictures of the wide-open, unfenced country which meant the days of back-breaking fence repairs would be over. The only livestock the Watsons had were twenty-five head of horses, so there weren't going to be any cows to nurse or tits to pull. My farming days were over.

So that's how it was decided. We struck a deal on wages and I was to be paid the princely sum of $150 per month until the hunting season ended, which would be about the first of December. When I had worked for Old Jack, the wages had been $70 per month, so the economics were definitely looking up.

One of the reasons Watson wanted me for this job was because I had already served as an assistant guide to Old Jack for long enough to be eligible for a Second Class Guide licence. This would allow the camp to operate since the Watsons were still American citizens, which meant that they could not have a licence in their own name. During the previous two years, they had made a deal with Pete Duncan of Canoe Creek to do what I was about to do, but Pete had died a year ago.

Even though this was a common practice, it did create a strange situation for the owners of the camps, because they became completely dependent on the head guides they had to hire. If the head guide was to quit, then the licence went with him and not the camp. Those non-resident owners must have made it a point to hire only people that they thought they could somehow control. Back then, there were actually two types of operating licences: First and Second Class. There was no real difference in what we could do with them, except the First Class cost five dollars more and required at least six years' previous guiding experience. Someone told me that at a much earlier time the licences were supposed to separate the guides who maintained a lot of special equipment for long pack trips, from the operators, like Old Jack who just hunted close to home. Somewhere along the line the licences became all mixed up, so the government has now scrapped the Second Class licence in favour of the all-encompassing Guide-Outfitter licence.

So sometime in late April of 1955, my future had been resolved. Shorty, Ruth, and I spent the next several days sorting out and repairing some of their equipment and, of course, telling and comparing stories by the hour. Actually, all we were doing was killing time until the road west of Clinton dried up because we wanted to get to Gaspard Lake with a truck. That road then, especially during the spring breakup, resembled the wagon road that it originally was, rather than anything a sensible person would want to force a motor vehicle over.

We also had to pick up the horses from the Canoe Creek Indians who had been wintering them for Shorty, so it was to be my job to drive them the fifty miles home, while Shorty drove the truck with our bedrolls and grub. The trip might take one day or two, depending on the condition of the horses and also the condition of the roads for the truck.

There was another little item that had been cropping up in Shorty's conversation and it had something to do with the possibility of having trouble getting the horses across Gang Ranch land, into the hills beyond. According to Shorty, one of the owners of the Gang Ranch was an absolute son-of-a-bitch by name of Bill Studdert. It sounded like Studdert and Watson were not friends.

I had been taking these subtle hints from Shorty with at least a small grain of salt, because by now I knew he was a top hand at spicing up any story. According to Old Jack, there were always stories floating around the Chilcotin about

neighbour conflicts, but they rarely became violent or destructive. True, there were a few stories about when lids did blow
off but not in recent times. Having spent the past three years
living with and around ranchers and cowboys, I had yet to
meet an unfriendly one. As my mother used to say, she was
from Missouri and had to be shown.

I did too. When I was twenty, I was as strong and bold as
was safe for any kid to be, so no matter what, with my
Winchester in the scabbard, I was convinced that there was
nothing in this world that could stop me from trailing the
horses to wherever I wanted to go.

CHAPTER 2

B<small>Y THE FIRST WEEK IN MAY</small> Shorty and I figured the road west of Clinton should be dry and solid enough to make the trip to Gaspard lake. Early one morning, so as to be on top of the frost, Shorty and I started out in his truck. Our first destination was the Canoe Creek Reserve to pick up the horses from the Indians there. My first introduction to this area was when, right in the centre of the main road going through Indian Meadows, the truck slowly began to sink until the mud reached the floorboards. There was nothing to pull it out with, so while Shorty spent the afternoon visiting and dickering with the Indians over the horses, I spent it digging, jacking, and prying the truck out onto dry ground. By late afternoon we were ready to roll again, but by then it was too late in the day to start moving the horses as the feed along the road was very scarce and Shorty did not know how far it might be to where we could rest them. So we decided to bed down beside the pickup and start at first light the following morning.

That evening the Tenale family corralled our horses beside the truck so I had a chance to look them over. During the past winter Shorty had bought several new horses from an ex-cowboy, turned bartender, turned wheeler-dealer horse trader, named Tom Prest. These horses were now mixed in with his old herd and from the sounds of the squeals and hard thumps from flying hooves, they were obviously not mixing well. These new horses had been sold to Shorty as being good, sound, and gentle stock suitable for hunting camp dudes. As we sat on the fence that evening looking over our saddle prospects, I became a bit sceptical about some of these new horses and I remember drawing Shorty's attention to the fact that three of these horses lacked any old saddle marks. These particular horses were acting real goosey just from being in the corral.

A couple of the young Indians had stayed to visit, so I asked them if they knew anything about these horses as I did know that most of them had been purchased locally. The answer was a burst of laughter and the two men looked at Shorty, said something to each other in their own language, and laughed even harder. About then, Shorty began to get a strange grey look to his face as the probable truth started soaking in.

Reality started descending onto me too, because these were the horses I was to start riding and herding the next morning. As I had been riding for only about three years, there were still a lot of things that I did not know about horses. So far, I had never been on a real snotty bronc so you can be assured that I was starting to sweat.

Some riders are good enough to pile onto any type of horse under any circumstances but in 1955 I was nowhere near that experienced. There were still many things I did not know about handling horses and especially ones that had learned how to fight back. The very first thing all beginning riders should learn is that a horse is much bigger and stronger than we are. It's possible that some of them are smarter too. There's an old cowboy saying that reminds us, "There aint ever a horse can't never be rode and there aint ever a rider can't never be throwed."

One of the Indians, Marvin Tenale, was about my age and as he had his own saddled horse tied to the outside of the corral, I suggested to him that I would sure appreciate it if he stuck around on his horse and maybe help me ride the big sorrel out of the corral, to see if he possibly could be a wrangling horse.[2] A common and safe way of starting out on an unknown or green horse is to use a gentle horse to either lead or follow it out of a corral.

Marvin agreed to it, so I got the lariat off my saddle and went into the corral. Immediately, the big sorrel quarter horse really started tearing around. Even so, I caught him on the first throw and promptly all hell broke loose. That horse did everything he could do trying to shake the rope. With twenty-four other horses in the corral with him, he soon jerked the lariat away from me but he was still doing his double damnedest to cause a riot among his buddies. While he was dragging the rope around the corral that way, I noticed a little character flaw: every once in a while, he would crash to the ground and roll on top of the rope, perhaps trying to crush it to death. I did not need anyone to tell me that this might be a sign of anti-social behaviour and I might be looking at a widowmaker.

Eventually I got my hands back on the rope but even then it took all four of us to get him snubbed up to a post as he

---

2 A wrangling horse is a dependable and valuable herding horse. A cayuse or cayooshe usually describes a horse of unknown parentage. Wild horses and sometimes Indian horses are examples. A horse who is "acting Western" is one that bucks, runs away, or acts berserk. The term is sometimes used to describe a boozy cowboy. A goosey horse is one who is skittish and nervous. If they persist, they end up in a dog food can. A widowmaker deliberately tries to harm the rider. They will actually turn on a thrown rider and use their hooves and teeth to finish the job. Cultus is a Chinook word meaning "bad" or "just no good."

fought us all the way. When I was finally able to throw my saddle onto his back, he threw a real fit and broke the snubbing post off at the ground. Now we had a first class mess: one sorrel was tearing around the corral dragging that goddamn post, banging into the other horses until there was a real danger that from the weight of the herd, they might knock the entire corral flat. We finally tossed another rope onto the sorrel and got him snubbed to a stronger post. It cost us some skinned hands and some of the other horses lost a few patches of hide too.

Meanwhile the Indians thought this entire situation was just hilarious. It was probably the most interesting thing they had seen all winter. Shorty and I decided that the sorrel might not make such a good wrangle horse after all, so we turned him loose. Shorty was not too happy with this turn of events as there now was an ominous likelihood that some of the other new horses were going to be just as difficult since we had all noticed that most of them had been acting quite western as well. This was disappointing because I had wanted to use them for wranglers instead of the old hunting string which showed definite signs of having had a lean winter.

After having spent most of the day getting the truck out of the mud hole, then getting skinned and bruised from fighting that bloody horse, I was beginning to wonder if I might not have started something I really did not want to finish. But when Shorty suggested that perhaps we should use some of the old hunting horses for wranglers and just go slower, I felt considerable relief. These older horses were quite usable; it was just that they were not exactly what we would consider to be fat, like some of the new ones were. I could understand why Shorty made this decision because if the wrangle horses starting throwing fits along the road, we might lose the entire herd. On one thing we were in total agreement: at the first opportunity, we were going to use both the sorrel and the horse trader for bear bait.

After these decisions were made Shorty and I and the Indians all went over to our campfire where Shorty broke out a bottle of whisky, something he always carried in good supply. Along about dark and half-way through the first bottle, the entire afternoon started taking on a different hue and it wasn't long before Shorty and I were beginning to see the whole affair in almost the same light as the Indians saw it. It also helped knowing that I wasn't going to have to ride the new string of horses, at least not for the time being.

By the time we finished the first bottle all of us were all down to real serious story telling. Something I have always noticed at times like this is I have yet to meet an Indian on the ground who ever admitted to having been thrown off of a horse. There are lots of white riders that are that good too. No matter how wild the horse the riders will admit to getting skinned up, shaken up, broken up, almost off, but never all the way off. Around the bars, bunk houses, and campfires, one of the most common cowboy expressions you will ever hear is someone declaring, "I rode that son-of-a-bitch to a stand-still." Before the night was over we had told ourselves a lot of other lies too. The whisky was good for still something else, because before the Indians left for home, Shorty got a promise from them that they would return next morning and give me a hand to start the horses down the road until we knew how well the two strings would travel together. They agreed to ride with me as far as the main village, about ten miles further down the road.

The next morning we started out, the two Indians and myself herding twenty-four horses and Shorty following along in the Dodge pickup. The saddle horse I had picked this time was a bit on the lean side, but he was strong and well-behaved. We just let the herd go at their own pace which soon settled into slow jogs and walking. This suited me just fine as it gave me a chance to visit with the other riders and learn something of the country we were riding through.

Most of the Indians I have ever met are great conversationalists, especially when talking to people who are interested in the same sort of things they are. Under these circumstances there are very few unfriendly Indians. The so-called "silent Indian" is probably just silent while in the company of white men with whom they have little in common. This situation largely results from the difference in language and culture, because make no mistake about it, we *are* different. There are still aspects of our white culture that many Indians have not adjusted to and perhaps don't even want to. In addition, there are too many whites who will not even recognize that the Indian still has a separate culture. In their own way, almost all of the Indians I have ever met have been extremely polite and when they don't understand or appreciate some of our ways and values, they tend to say nothing, rather then offend us — hence the silent Indian. But among themselves or among people who they know how to relate to, the silent Indian becomes a very rare bird. I would venture to say that there are far more silent and anti-social white men than there are silent Indians.

These particular Indians were curious about me as not many strangers passed by this way anymore and furthermore, since the job I now had used to belong to Pete Duncan, who had been their friend (and perhaps even a relative), they were probably interested to see what kind of person was going to take over from him.

The Tenales rode with me as far as the village and then out beyond Koster's Canoe Creek Ranch and by that time the horses had lined out down the road just like they were supposed to. We said our goodbyes and from that point, I was on my own. West of Canoe Creek, the country opened up into the wide open grass and sage brush bench land along the Fraser river. I had never lived or ridden in country such as this, but the weather was clear, the sun was warm, and I was happy. I can still remember the feeling of exhilaration, just to be out of town and heading for the bush again. Riding along the banks of the mid Fraser, we could see the Chilcotin mountains further to the west where I was going to be spending the next eight months with these horses for my constant companions. Maybe people who have learned to depend on the security that city life gives them will find it difficult to understand my pleasure at anticipating such a prolonged period of solitude. But for me, leaving town after too long a stay gives me the feeling that other people must get when they are released from prison. Once again, my world was unfolding just as it was supposed to do.

Shorty said it was about 50 miles from Canoe Creek to Gaspard Lake and if we were lucky we might make the trip in this one day. He was still moaning about the possibility of having trouble getting the horses through the Gang Ranch property which we would begin entering as soon as we crossed the Fraser, just a few miles ahead. This subject was getting a bit stale and I was beginning to wonder if Shorty was afflicted with some sort of paranoia. Before leaving Clinton, I had made a few inquiries about the legality of the roads in the Gang Ranch area and both the RCMP and the Public Works foreman had assured me that the roads were public and they always had been. Therefore I just couldn't understand why Shorty kept worrying himself over the subject.

We soon arrived at an ancient-looking wooden suspension bridge that spans the Fraser river and as home was still thirty uphill miles on the other side, we had to cross it. I had heard many stories from Old Jack about this bridge and the river fording just below it, where the early ranchers had to cross their cattle and wagons. There had also been a ferry here at some distant time, but no evidence of it in 1955. The bridge had become a godsend for these people, but that day our horses refused to believe it and came to an abrupt halt at the threshold. Well, at least they were not trying to get away from us, so we just let them stand there and think about it for a while.

That damn sorrel had used his size and temperament to lead the herd and would not allow the other horses to cross ahead of him. So I tossed a rope onto him and led him to the rear and while doing so, came up with what seemed to me to be a brainwave. I had my saddle gun in the scabbard, so I handed it to Shorty and told him, "Just as soon as I slip the rope off this sorrel, you start shooting out over the heads of these sulky bastards." It worked like a charm. The entire herd took off like they had exploded out from the gun barrel itself and some of those horses were literally climbing over each other in their efforts to get away from those muzzle blasts. I noticed that when Shorty fired the shots, he laid a couple of them about as close to the sorrel's ears as he could, without actually hitting him. By the time the horses got to the west side, that sorrel had fought his way right through all the other horses and was out in the lead again. Because this old suspension bridge was made of wood and wire, it was really limber when that many horses ran on it. When I rode out behind the last horse, the bridge was actually bumping and swaying from the momentum of the horses ahead of me.

As soon as we were across, Shorty drove past and hollered that he would put the truck into the lead and would meet me at the Gang Ranch headquarters which is about two miles further up the hill. He said we had to stop there to get clearance from either the owner or manager and he was hoping the owner would not be there. So we were still on this road access subject.

From many of Old Jack's stories, I already knew a little bit about this road. In earlier times it had been the only wagon and cattle drive road into all of the Chilcotin ranches to the west. There were some big cattle drives pass through the Gang Ranch from the turn of the century right up into the 1920s. In those days all western and northern cattle had to be driven to Ashcroft to be loaded onto the CPR for markets east and southwest. Old Jack had ridden with the last of those long drives and he had good stories to tell about them. By the time the ranchers in the west Chilcotin drove their cattle to Ashcroft, loaded next year's supplies onto their wagons, and reached home it must have been mighty close to snow fly time.

These long cattle drives were shortened considerably when the provincial government pushed the PGE railroad through to Quesnel and also built another bridge across the Fraser River near Williams Lake. Since then, Williams Lake has become, in fact and mentality, cow-town British Columbia.

But that day back in 1955 I refused to worry about anything for I was once again west of the Fraser, which means Chilcotin country and it was just like returning home. Every new turn in the road seemed to be retelling Old Jack's stories of wilder pioneer days. I was in high spirits that day what with the beautiful weather, my innovation for moving stubborn horses, and getting credit from the boss for having done so. It was great to be alive and be at a place like this.

The horses were moving out well, so within a short time we crested the steep hill from the Fraser and entered into a wide, shallow, bench land valley that supported alfalfa fields as far as I could see. About half way up the valley there was a large cluster of buildings which all seemed to be painted CPR red. No question that I was finally gazing at the headquarters of the ranch I had been hearing so much about. The road wound right in among some of these buildings and when I got the horses herded up to that point, Shorty was waiting for

The panorama view from the hills overlooking the Gang Ranch head-quarters. This is where Choate rested the horse herd as he reminisced about his new job and life that began in May of 1955. Luckily, the view is still the same today. This is the real cowboy country.

me beside a large log corral that was built right beside the road. He already had the gate into it open, so he gave me a hand signal to push the horses into it, which we both did.

So I had finally arrived at the Gang Ranch, the place from where at least half the B.C. cowboy stories seemed to originate. As we walked up through the yard that day, it was very noticeable that this was an old outfit — many of the buildings were beginning to sag and lean with the slope of the ground. The only new building I could see was a huge red barn which resembled the barns that I had grown up with in the lower part of the province. There were all those red buildings spread across about sixty acres of land and close to 1000 acres of hay fields within view. To this twenty-year old kid whose entire worldly possessions amounted to one saddle, a bedroll, and several guns, this place looked so impressive that it took my breath away.

We walked over to a large frame building which turned out to be the office, store and post office. When we went through the door, we stepped right into the last century. The front part of the building served as the store and had one of those old-fashioned, horseshoe-shaped counters that kept all the merchandise smaller then a saddle out of reach of the customer. The counter was very wide so there was not going to be any problem of shop-lifting in this store. All of the merchandise that I could see was pure frontier ranch and cowboy gear.

The only person in the store was a medium-sized man who looked to have been in his mid to late 60s and when Shorty began talking to him, I noticed that he addressed him as Mac. A few moments later I was introduced to him and it was then confirmed that this was MacIntyre, or just plain Mac, the manager of the Gang Ranch. I had been hearing stories about Mac ever since I had arrived in the Chilcotin three years earlier. He came to the Gang Ranch as a young immigrant from Scotland and went to work as a ranch hand. From there he graduated to cowboy, then cowboss, and finally all the way up to become manager of the entire outfit. By then, Mac had been on the Gang Ranch for over 40 years, so he had seen and done many interesting things.

Mac was very quiet-spoken and after a few noticeably short and cool words with Shorty, he turned to me and started quizzing me about my background: where I had come from, what I had done, and who I knew. After telling him about my stay with Old Jack, Mac informed me that he remembered him very well from the days of the cattle drives that used to pass through the Gang Ranch country. As the cattle drives did not come this way any more, Mac had lost contact with many people from the Alexis Creek area and he seemed pleased that

I was able to tell him some of the news from over in that area. I remember being extremely flattered by being able to relate so many mutual things to somebody of Mac's stature but at the same time I also noticed that he had cut Shorty completely out of the conversation, which seemed odd.

After we had been talking for a few minutes, the door literally burst open and a big, heavy-set man stepped just inside and hollered at us, "Who in hell put that bunch of crow bait horses into our corral?" As he walked further into the store he noticed Shorty and I standing there and he walked over and said, "By God, is it you again, Watson? I thought they had run you back out of the country." Although we all laughed at these remarks, I noticed that Shorty was beginning to get a hard look in his eye. Shorty then introduced me to this new fellow who turned out to be Jim Bishop, boss of all the cowboys on the Gang Ranch. His actual title was cowboss.

After he and Shorty traded a few more sarcastic remarks, Mac interrupted and said to Bishop in a quiet voice, "This young fellow here has just spent the past three years working for Jack Maindley, up near Alexis Creek," and he then just turned and walked into the back room where we never saw him again.

Bishop also cut Shorty out of the conversation but he and I had a good visit as it turned out that he too knew Old Jack and several other people that I knew quite well. The tension in the store was getting so obvious that it became embarrassing and I was relieved when Shorty finally said it was time for me to mount up again as we still had twenty-eight uphill miles to go. As Shorty led the way out the door, Bishop called after him and asked, "Hey Watson, are you sure you can find your way back up there?" At this remark, Bishop and I both had a short laugh, but I noticed that Shorty didn't even chuckle. As we were walking down the porch, I turned to nod and wave goodbye to Bishop when he gave me the whoa signal and then walked up to me and said in a voice that I suspected was calculated to accidentally reach Shorty's ears, "Ted, when you get tired of playing around up there, get in touch with me and I'll give you a real job in the cow camp."

When I caught up to Shorty at the corral his face was grey and there were tears in his eyes as he turned to me and said, "Someday I'll make that fat bastard swallow his snuff can."

Shorty got into the truck and instructed me to haze the horses after him. He wanted us to travel up to the timber-line (and thus off the Gang Ranch property) before we would eat our lunch. It appeared that we were not going to be challenged about access after all and that did come as a bit of a relief.

It was six steep miles up to where we were going to have lunch. As I rode up those hills that day I can still remember thinking that I had just walked into a very strange situation. No doubt my twenty-year old head was swollen beyond normal, because how many near greenhorn kids had ever been offered the chance to ride and work with people like Mac and Bishop. It was common knowledge that every beginner was expected to work their way through the ranch hand stage before ever being even considered for the cow camp. A long time ago, even MacIntyre had been made to go through that initiation.

So this was my introduction to the Gang Ranch as it was then. Strange and interesting.

CHAPTER 3

Three miles up the hill from the Gang Ranch headquarters, there is a beautiful vista of the ranch below consisting of a twenty mile stretch of the Fraser River valley and most of the hills all the way back to Clinton. Sitting on my horse and gazing across such an expanse, I found as usual that this place encourages contemplation. For any living creature to be able to look across onto that sight and not to be somehow moved by this panorama, they would have to be dead between the ears.

On that particular day as I sat on my horse and rested the herd for half an hour at this place, I reflected on what I had learned about the Gang Ranch. It's the sort of place where history unfolds and for me it began to bring back several recent conversations I had with people who claimed to know about the local history of this area. As soon as I knew I was coming out into here to go to work, I had deliberately made acquaintances with people in Clinton and the surrounding area who had either worked here or were known to have had dealings of some sort with the area or the people in it. Almost invariably the Gang Ranch was mentioned.

Some of the information I had accumulated did not come easy, because I soon noticed that many people were quite reluctant to talk about anything specific, especially about the actual Gang Ranch operation. However, almost all of my informants agreed that it was difficult to figure out how and why this dinosaur continued to exist as it did. At my first question people would usually just smile, shake their heads, and say, "It's huge, maybe a million acres."

Since I had already listened to some of Shorty's stories about access problems crossing private property, or as Shorty said, areas that the Gang claimed were private property, I asked many questions about such access. There was general agreement that access had sometimes been a problem in the Gang Ranch country, but it was not so much that people were being flat-out denied access to the Crown land in the back country. It was more like the ranch was implying that people were only permitted to travel here at the sufferance of the Gang Ranch.

As one neighbour put it, "Whether the Gang Ranch smiles or frowns upon you seems to depend on how long you intend to stay in the area. Travellers that were obviously just passing through with no intention of hunting, or especially home-steading, were usually given a warm reception, but there were lots of stories about how the others were dealt with," he said.

This rancher knew that I was coming out here to work for Watson and he also knew that Watson and the Gang Ranch were not on the best of terms, so he cautioned me.

"I suggest that when you get out there, you should try and locate the actual surveyed boundaries of the ranch's private property, so you always know where you stand on that subject. There are many rumours around here now that say the Gang Ranch are getting ready to put a real squeeze on that hunting camp because they're afraid it might become the foot in the door to other so-called tourist operations out there. My guess is, there

28

might be a lot of bluffing going on, but you would still be wise to learn for certain exactly where you stand on every situation that might crop up on you. And there's something else you should remember, as well. That camp has already had several owners in the ten short years it's been there, so that should tell you something too."

This rancher was much older than I was and had been born and raised here, so his next piece of advice was, in his opinion, the one I should really heed.

"I understand that is a nice country out there, but you may not like the situation, so don't be too proud to pack up and leave, because that is exactly what almost every other settler that went over there ended up doing. Try not to get too involved in your new boss's problems because all you'll have there is a job that I doubt is paying you enough to take foolish risks."

This rancher did not really have a very high opinion of either hunting camps or tourists and this became a little clearer to me as he summed up his own advice by offering that there were lots of better jobs around this country than the one "that Yank has conned you into," and he suggested that I give serious thought about getting a permanent job on a ranch that had a good reputation, because ranchers were always looking for young, willing workers.

Almost everyone who has lived in the Cariboo-Chilcotin for very long seems to have formed opinions about the Gang Ranch and most of these have their favourite Gang Ranch story to tell. The people who have actually lived close to, or worked for, the Gang Ranch seem to have less favourable things to say about it than did those who had never actually had anything to do with it.

The Gang Ranch had been started back in the 1860s by two brothers from Virginia, Thadeus and Jerome Harper, so it is one of the oldest ranches in B.C. As time went on it also became one of Canada's largest ranches. Stories were told of its being the largest ranch in North America, but this was a bullshit yarn because it never was.

The land area that the Gang Ranch owned used to be spread all over the B.C. Interior from Kamloops to Riske Creek, a spread of 200 miles. The closest size estimate I have been able to come up with was that the Gang Ranch, at its zenith, only owned about 60,000 acres, leased another 30,000, and had a provincial government permit to graze their cattle over approximately a million acres of Crown land.

It seems quite possible that, because the Gang was in existence before there were rules and laws governing the use of the open range, they might have actually used more than the million acres, but on that subject all the people who would have known for certain have gone on to the upper range. However, it was the existence of this million-acre grazing permit that prompted the story teller to brag-up this "biggest ranch" baloney. Even with the million-acre grazing permit, the Gang never did have exclusive use of that area because many parts of it were shared with other smaller ranches.[3]

The only sensible way to judge the size of a ranch is to determine how many cattle it is capable of maintaining on a sustained basis. When the Gang Ranch was at its highest peak,

---

3   Even these combined ranches never had control over the other resources on that land (such as water), even though many of the ranchers thought they should have. There has been a lot of bluffing and bravado over this issue.

it was paying taxes on about 90,000 acres and running about 12,000 cattle for a very short time. It did not take all that long for the owners to discover that the area did not really have enough grass for that many cattle and that during long winters they did not have enough hay, so their pyramid collapsed on them. Under different owners and managers this has happened at least three times that I know of.

Still and all, 12,000 cattle was a mighty nice-sized ranch, but even here in B.C. the Douglas Lake Ranch has always been able to sustain about that many, and over in Alberta there are several ranches that run more than that.

In the United States there are a great many ranchers that run as many and some like the King Ranch in Texas used to run 90,000 cattle on 900,000 deeded acres. So against figures like that, the Gang Ranch becomes, in reality, just another fair-sized ranch. The mistake that people have been making around here for almost 100 years, is confusing the Gang Ranch operation with the Gang Ranch country or area, which has become just a vague geographical description of this part of B.C. It appears that all of the various owners and managers of the Gang have deliberately fostered this confusion so as to discourage other potential users of the same land base. There will be much more about this subject later in this story.

When I arrived here that spring of 1955 the ranch was then owned by two Americans, Bill Studdert of Seattle and Montana and Floyd Skelton of Idaho. They had bought it just a few years earlier, but still neither of them had ever lived on the ranch. Studdert was the General Manager, MacIntyre, the Resident Manager, and Jim Bishop was considered to be third man on the totem pole as he only oversaw cows and cowboys. Studdert showed up a few times a year so Mac and Bishop were the ones who actually ran the day-to-day operations of the ranch. At that time several people had met Studdert, but hardly anyone had met or knew anything about Skelton, as he seemed to be just some sort of silent partner and he had seldom been seen at the Gang Ranch.

The stories floating around Clinton in 1955 were suggesting the Gang was at a very low ebb as the cattle herd had been reduced and most of the mechanical equipment such as a D-4 Caterpillar, the power plant, a couple of tractors, and a few old trucks seldom, if ever, worked any more. As I rode along that day I noted that the rest of the outfit was very run down too, as evidenced by holes in the fences, broken gates, and a general air of disrepair. From the looks of any operating equipment I saw, the ranch seemed to be reverting back into a horse and buggy operation as there were several beautiful iron wheeled wagons parked all over the place. Horse drawn mowers and rakes were everywhere, but no sign of a power mower.

For a supposedly million-dollar ranch, this did not make much sense, but it was also interesting and to see all of these historic relics still being seriously used, when most other ranches in the country that could afford to were busy mechanizing their operations. Earlier that day when I was in the Gang Ranch store with Mac and Bishop, I had the sensation that I had gone back a hundred years in time and I was very much aware that I was seeing and talking with the glory of a byegone era. I felt privileged.

I found it easy to relate to the people in a place like this, because I couldn't drive a car either and didn't have much desire to learn. A couple of years earlier I had bought a Jeep but the second day I had it, a tree jumped right in front of it and tore off a front wheel. My head had hit the windshield, but as soon as I came to, I vowed that I was going back to horses. Horses are much more understandable. At least they were then.

The Gang Ranch headquarters was not always located where it is now, but rather about twelve miles further up

Gaspard Creek at a place now known as the "Old Home Ranch" which, in 1865 was first staked by the Harper brothers, Americans from Virginia. I have never been able to find out when it was moved to its present site, but by the age of the buildings it must have been about 1890. Some of the local survey markers are dated 1884, so that might be a closer date.

Up to that time, the Gang Ranch had had four different owners, but all were non-Canadian. It was the second set of owners who were British and they had their head office in London, England and a branch office in Victoria. At that time, those owners were well-connected to various levels of government, which had, no doubt, a strong bearing on how the ranch was able to receive control of so much land so quickly.

An interesting detail can be found on the survey maps of this area; there is a huge, single-surveyed block over near Riske Creek that was given to the Gang Ranch. I have never seen on any other map a lot as large as that one is, since usually surveys are broken down into 160 and occasionally 640-acre lots. While an owner can purchase several of these smaller lots that are bounded together, there are still survey lines that show on the map, showing exactly how many acres there are in that cluster. The large survey over near Riske Creek is difficult to decipher, but it amounts to several thousand acres.

The Gang Ranch that we know today, was originally called "The Western Canadian Ranching Company, Limited." The Gang Ranch came by its present name because it was the first ranch around these parts to use a "gang plough", which was a horse-drawn plough having more than one blade.

CHAPTER 4

THE ROAD BEYOND THE GANG RANCH in May of 1955 was barely up to a jeep road as it was much more suitable for those horse-drawn wagons down in the ranch yard, or better yet saddle horses. Riding through this new country heading for Gaspard Lake, we met Augustine Rosette, an outfitter who lived at Williams Meadow, which was half way between Gang Ranch and Gaspard Lake.

It was around this time that I discovered a rather somber truth: people who live in remote areas can sometimes pay a heavy price for their freedom. It was late afternoon when we arrived at Augustine's place and we found him laid low in his bed with an advanced case of pneumonia. His wife, Lilly, who was crippled from arthritis, was there with him, as were his two youngest sons who would have been about twelve and thirteen years old.

Augustine was in such a bad way that Shorty immediately dropped our camp beside the Rosette house and while I stayed to ride herd on the horses, he turned the truck back towards Gang Ranch where one of Augustine's older sons was working. We were afraid to put him into Shorty's truck since the road was so bad that we were not sure if that two-wheel drive would make it back. It seemed to us that he would be

34

safer staying in the house rather than take a chance having to spend the night sitting in a truck that might become stuck in a mudhole. We needed more dependable transportation and we knew that there was at least one four-by-four truck at Gang Ranch that was still working. As Shorty pulled out of the yard that afternoon, he gave me some final instructions.

"If there isn't a truck back here by daylight tomorrow morning, you catch the strongest horse we have and come back down this road as fast as you can. I don't care if you have to kill a horse doing it, because Augustine is a good friend of ours and we don't want the old bugger kicking the bucket on us."

Just as the truck started to roll he hollered out the window, "If I do get stuck today, I'll start walking towards the ranch, but I ain't much of a walker. So you be damn sure to keep a horse well tied up tonight."

I spent most of the evening sitting in the house trying to visit, but it's a very depressing feeling having to watch a strong man slowly slip away and not being able to do anything to help. I don't believe any of us were able to sleep. In the middle of the night one of the boys saw the headlights of two trucks coming up the road. Within a few minutes Shorty, Willie Rosette, and Augustine Charley were in the house and we lost no time getting Augustine bundled up and into Willie's truck. The last we saw of them, they were heading for the hospital at Ashcroft, a bone-jarring 100 miles and five hours away.

The doctors kept Augustine in the hospital for a long time and it was a very near thing for him. Shorty and I could only guess why Augustine got caught this way, but he probably did not realize, until it was too late, just how sick he really was. By that time he would have been too weak to catch a team of horses by himself and his wife was unable to, so there came a time that they were completely at the mercy of fate. Even

35

though they lived right beside a public road, in our two days of travelling, we had not seen another vehicle since leaving Highway 97 near Clinton. All's well that ends well, but that situation did drive home to all of us how vulnerable we, who choose to live in isolated areas, are.

The Rosette family, who is mostly Indian, go way back in this part of the world. Ever since the Gang Ranch has existed, there have been Rosettes working on it and these men are as capable as anyone else would be from anywhere in North America. Augustine himself had done lots of cowboying, but his real love was hunting and trapping. He was truly an Indian's Indian. Later on, as I got to know him better, I came to the conclusion that he was the most knowledgable hunter and guide in the country.

Augustine literally knew every creek and crack in the ground within a fifty-mile radius of his home. Just figure that out in square miles. For all the years I knew him, he was always great company as are his several sons who are now scattered all over this part of B.C.

The next morning Shorty had me cut some wood for Lilly and then about midday we started for Gaspard Lake again, which was now only about fifteen miles away. The road, if it could be called that, got progressively worse, so we took the truck only a few miles further to where Shorty parked it on a dry downhill slope. We then caught two more horses, putting Shorty's saddle onto one and a pack saddle onto the other. We made up a light pack which consisted of our bedrolls, a few clothes, and a little grub for this horse and we tarped and tied it all down tightly so we could just turn the horse loose to run with the rest. With both of us mounted now and the older horses getting closer to home, there was no trouble keeping them headed into the right direction.

There had been quite a bit of snow that winter and the spring runoff was in full force, so we heard Gaspard Creek long before we got to it. At the point where we came to it, the creek runs through quite a narrow canyon, but there are some gravel banks alongside where there are some cattle trails plus this other track that Shorty kept assuring me was the road. When we rode up to the creek, it looked to be about fifty feet wide and right up to a jumping boil. We could not see the bottom.

I was not very enthusiastic about this situation but all the trails said that this was the place to cross. The loose horses ahead of us had stopped dead in their tracks, not one volunteering to start across. I stopped too, suspecting that we had come to the end of that day's travel. There seemed to be no way to get to the other side as this was not really a creek, but a thundering little river that needed a bridge to cross on. I sat there on my horse taking in the situation and wondering how far down the creek we might have to go to find a bridge or a meadow to hold the horses on until the water receded enough for a safe fording. I was naive.

Shorty rode up beside me and shouted over the roar of the water, "Throw your rope on the pack horse and lead him across and try and make the others follow."

I was hoping Shorty might consider looking for a better place or time, so I shouted back, "That colt with the bay mare can't possibly cross that current; it'll get sucked into those big rocks just below the crossing."

Shorty hollered back, "So what? A colt in a pack outfit is a goddamn nuisance. If it doesn't drown now, we're going to shoot it later." I then realized that in the next few minutes I was going to have to learn to swim a horse, something I had never done before. But Shorty assured me that the only part of me that was going to get wet were my legs.

Shorty then turned and started riding towards the tail-end of the herd to keep them from turning back on us, but as he did so, he motioned me to throw a rope on the pack horse and go. I was, by now, starting to understand a little more clearly what my raise in pay might be for. Considering that these were his horses and not mine, there could be little argument. I thought of the old cowboy adage that says, "We're paid to ride, not to think," and shrugged my shoulders. I couldn't think of any other excuses to avoid doing what Shorty said, but I was really hoping that he was not one of those people who like to live on the edge of self-destruction.

Well, it had to be done, so I caught the pack horse and turned into the creek. The old horse I was riding had probably crossed here many times before, but his balking reconfirmed my suspicions that it might be wrong to do it today. To make him change his mind, I had to lay a few good licks onto his rump with the end of the rope, because the one thing I did know was that it could get very dangerous if he got us half way across and then decided to turn back. If he did this in that current with the big boulders so close, it would be good night for both of us.

He finally made a serious plunge and we were totally committed. My guess was that the water was about four feet deep which meant the horse had his feet on the bottom at least some of the time. The water was every bit as swift as it had looked from shore and we were being swept towards those boulders. When I felt the horse stumble a couple times on rocks he couldn't see, my heartbeat stumbled in sympathy. However, he was a good horse and wanted out of there as much as I did, so he was scratching for all he was worth and he did manage to get us onto the opposite shore with no serious mishap. At some point during the crossing, I felt myself being swept from the saddle, so I slid completely out of it, held onto the saddle horn and the horse's mane, and just floated along on the downstream side of him. I had also dropped the lead rope to the pack horse and by midstream I knew he was still following on his own, but by that time I also didn't give

The spring time road into Gaspard Lake. This crossing is where Choate first learned to swim a horse. The road is now re-routed onto safer ground.

a damn if he was or not. On a couple of the stumbles in midstream my horse had gone completely out of sight except for his head, so that became the part of his mane that I held onto.

I must have floated quite nicely, because even though I was totally wet, I arrived on shore still wearing my black western hat. Just as I got onto dry ground and was staggering around trying to recover my senses, the rest of the horses hit the water at the same time and came across in a big foaming surge. They all made it, even the colt. When Shorty came across, his horse stumbled on those goddamn rocks too and he lost his hat. I was too cold to be interested in volunteering to go look for it and I noticed he didn't either.

Since crossing the Fraser River the day before, we had been steadily climbing and were now about 4,600 feet above sea level with the temperature just a few degrees above freezing. It was the fourth of May and there was still snow in

39

some places in the bush and I do remember that we had been riding in sleet squalls all afternoon. Oh God, but we were cold and we knew we had to do something damn fast, because we knew we could not possibly make the six-mile ride as wet and cold as we were.

We cornered the pack horse and tied him and our mounts to a tree and tried to get a fire going. My matches were wet and useless but Shorty had a lighter. I had my twenty-eight-inch saddle axe that I always carried so as soon as I found a pitch pocket on a tree, we soon had a fire going. We stripped off beside the fire and wrung as much water out of our clothes as we could and then put them back on.

There was no possible way we were going to get dry, even with the fire, but at least we could get warm enough to make a dash for home. The possibility of freezing to death or dying of hypothermia was very real. We called it exposure and we knew we were vulnerable. Shorty warmed up enough to start cracking graveyard jokes about the possibility of getting laid out like Augustine. At times like that, Shorty Watson could be a real comfort.

We knew we had to make the dash before dark and as our tethered horses were trembling and shaking as much as we were, it was time to make the run. Our saddles were soaking wet and starting to freeze. The rest of the horses had already wandered on ahead, but Shorty figured that, because we were so close to home anyway, they would head in that direction and we should soon overtake them.

In three fast miles we came to a log fence with a closed gate and that was where we caught up to all of the loose horses. As soon as we got them through the gate, we could then see the big earth dam that creates most of Gaspard Lake which irrigates the Gang Ranch hay fields twenty-six miles away. That spring, the overflow spillway was booming full and as we rode by, Shorty pointed to what was an almost unbelievable

The shack beside the Big Dam at Gaspard Lake. Jim Russell spent many springs here, as he watched for snags in the spillway. The shack was burned many years ago.

cloud of airborne fish that were trying to jump from the lower creek up into the lake. There were dozens of those rainbows in the air at any one time and I had never seen so many trout in one place before.

A short ways past the dam we came up to a large, rough board shack built right beside the lake and be damned if there wasn't smoke coming out of the chimney. Heat! Warmth! We were saved! Shorty was in the lead and instead of riding over to the shack, he swung his horse up the lake shore and shook his fist at the shack and called back to me, "Gang Ranch, so we aren't stopping." After that scene at the store, Shorty would rather die than ask them for anything. So much for getting saved.

But as we loped past the doorless outhouse, be damned again if there wasn't someone sitting on the throne. It was a man and he sure had a surprised look on his face when he saw us, because up to that moment he had been the only person in the valley. He jumped up and started pulling his pants up, but Shorty called out to him to stay put, because we had to chase the horses to the other end of the lake before dark. That was my introduction to Jim Russell, a long-time ranch hand and fence builder for the Gang Ranch.

As we rode along and between shiver spasms, Shorty said we would come down and visit Russell later. He explained that Russell was keeping an eye on the spillway, keeping the floating snags pulled out of it. For this job he had a very large draft horse on a picket rope right there beside the shack. As the story went, the dam had just been rebuilt a few years earlier and the owners had not constructed a large enough spillway out of it, so if just a few snags got hung up in there it could cause the entire dam to wash out. It had already done that in 1948, so the ranch was still nervous about the possibility that it could happen again. There is a lot of water in this lake when it's full, since it's about three miles long and more than twenty feet deep.

A half an hour later we had circled to the top end of the lake and rode into a circle of log cabins. We had made it, but not by what I was prepared to call easily. We were so unbearably cold that we could hardly tie the horses. We got a rip-roaring fire going in the cook house heater. Our clothes were still frozen, so I pried and twisted mine off as I figured I could get warm faster that way. After I warmed up, I went out into a sleet storm as naked as a jaybird, except for my boots, to unsaddle the horses and cut the pack off of the pack horse. I can still remember being so goddamn cold that my gender was pulled up so tight that a spectator would have needed a magnifying glass to decide if I was male or female.

When we got the packs off and into the cook house, we were surprised and just super lucky to discover our sleeping bags and clothes were hardly wet. Apparently we had the pack tarped down better than we thought. So with warm clothes, the heat from the stove, and a couple good slugs of whisky, we were ready to look the place over. It had been vacant since last November.

We wandered around through the cabins, sheds, and five-acre yard, checking things out. Nothing was missing even though there had never been a lock on any of the doors. The camp was made up of five recently built, rough log cabins and two small sheds made of boards. We were on the west end of Gaspard Lake, right where Wales Creek enters into it. The entire camp was set up on a hill, about fifty feet above the lake. To the east, we looked straight down the lake; looking south, up a long grassy meadow that leads to the mountains; west, up Wales Creek; and from the north, pine forest coming right into the yard. A beautiful setting. I had never lived in a place like this before, but I can remember feeling quite comfortable at settling in.

It's a good thing I did too, because it was to become my home for most of the years since.

CHAPTER 5

WE SPENT THE NEXT SEVERAL DAYS riding around the valley, with Shorty teaching me the trails, meadows, watersheds and generally showing me the lay of the land. In 1955, this area was still recovering from the terrible winter of 1948, when the snow had come early, lay deep, and stayed until the rains of early summer almost washed the Interior Plateau country down the Fraser River and out into the Pacific Ocean. Since '48, rainfall and snowfall were still abnormal, so the meadows were so full of water that, for a stranger like me, there was no way to know whether I was about to ride into a flooded meadow, a pot hole, or a small lake. During the white man's history here and up to '48, the Chilcotin had been known as dry belt country so we were still having a difficult time adjusting to all this moisture.

As we rode around that spring, these meadows were so wet and boggy that many of the trails had become impassable for horses. Several old trails just disappeared into ponds of water and we were left with the dilemma of having to guess if we could wade the horses across to high ground on the other side, or play it safe and ride around the ponds. I began referring to these places as "horse traps" because we bogged our horses down on several occasions. It's a very frustrating

44

experience to have your mount drop to its belly in the mud, right in the centre of a well marked trail. When horses do go down that way, they don't always come out easily and sometimes we had a bitch of a time coaxing or pulling them out. We always carried at least one nylon lariat with us, because sometimes a horse became so mired down that it was impossible to get it out without a pull from the second horse. Before the wet weather was over, some of these horses must have had their necks lengthened by several inches.

That spring it generally rained a little bit every day, but sometimes it rained night and day. All the creeks were flooded up over their banks, which made crossing them on horseback a bit of a challenge. We always made it and there was never a danger to ourselves but as most of the creeks in the valley have mudbottoms, there is always the risk that the horse might get sucked so deep into that mud, it could drown in the two to four feet of water on top. There was also a few known pools of quicksand here and some of the mud holes were close to being so. Even on the trails above the valley floor we found the same problems; it's hard to understand how water can lay on the side of a mountain but it surely does. All of that spring and summer riding any distance almost always meant coming home soaking wet.

One of the things that helped make it bearable was encountering so many moose that were there then. We were seeing forty to fifty every day. On top of this there were the coyotes that often followed our horses, the smaller animals and birds, and the odd bear track. Every flooded meadow had swarms of ducks and usually a few Canada Geese. As both of us were avid hunters, this wildlife certainly helped keep our spirits up.

While out on these rides of exploration, we were always on the lookout for the moose antlers that had been shed the past winter. Whenever we came across a set, we made a game out of guessing how large a spread that bull would have in the coming fall when we would be hunting for him. It did not take me long to start thinking that this might be a pretty nice place to live. From the very first day I had noticed other unfamiliar antlers, but Shorty told me that they were from elk that used to live here, perhaps before the white man's arrival. Shorty said he did not believe there were any left in this area; in the three years he had hunted here, he had still not seen one. He had heard of another outfitter over near Big Creek, about twenty miles away, who had shot one recently, so we assumed that there might still be the odd straggler left somewhere.

As Shorty had lived and hunted all of his life in the western United States, he had hunted elk many times and knew quite a lot about them. He figured that from the size of some or these antlers we were inspecting, there had been a breed of huge elk that used to live here. In 1955 there were so many of these antlers laying around in the meadows that for a long time I half expected that one would walk out in front of us, but that year none ever did.

Those spring days may have been wet and cold but the evenings were long and warm and filled with many interesting conversations about the history of the camp, the area, some of the neighbours — and always the Gang Ranch. I have always been a nosey person who likes to know what's going on around me, and since Shorty was a good story teller, he kept me perpetually entertained. And also there on the table was the omnipresent bottle of whisky, which helped to warm and loosen everything.

As Shorty told it then, he was still considered as being a very recent immigrant to the area, as they had arrived here in 1952, when they went into partnership in this camp with a Canadian ex-cowboy by the name of Sam Grypuik. That partnership broke up in 1953 or '54 and since that time Shorty had been operating the camp under a special permit or license that had been issued to Pete Duncan, who had died last fall. For the past two years there had also been a couple of assistant guides and they had also been used to relocate the camp from its former location below the Big Dam up to where it is now.

Before Grypuik had taken over the camps, he had worked as an assistant guide for Sonny Collins of Cache Creek who had started the operation back in 1943. As I remember the story, Sam had worked part time for Collins and part time for the Gang Ranch, until he was able to raise the capital to buy Collins out. Then for some reason Sam took Shorty in as a partner until the partnership dissolved just previous to my arrival here, so that brought us up to present time.

Because we were located right in the centre of the Gang Ranch's million-acre summer grazing area, this was a contentious issue with the Gang Ranch. The Gang had always considered this entire area as their country and, as Shorty repeatedly told me, they still thought that way. The guiding area allotted to this licence covered almost the exact same geography as the Gang Ranch grazing permit did. There were two traplines that overlaid the same ground too, so it hardly gave anyone exclusive access to the land base. Then to top all that off the hunting camp had recently been issued a grazing permit for twenty-five horses, so that really threw a monkey wrench into the Gang Ranch's propaganda of having a million-acre exclusion.

The hunting camp had always been geared mostly to the large moose and deer population present here and there had never been any problem to find between fifty and seventy bull moose for the clients every year. These hunters had been taking very few of the mule deer and fewer still of the bears or California bighorn sheep. These big horn had a reputation of being smaller in the horns than their cousins over in the Rocky

Mountains. Also they were scarce.[4] Shorty did not think there were very many bears in the area either. It was common knowledge that the Gang Ranch and the domestic sheep herders were keeping the bear population trimmed down, as ranchers and sheep herders considered all bears, both black and grizzly, as vermin and dealt with them accordingly. And anyway, not many of his clients had been interested in shooting them even when they were encountered while hunting other game.

If we were thinking that there were still lots of moose here in 1955, Pete Duncan had told Shorty that he figured the winter of '48 had killed half of them. This was not a new figure to me, as I had heard other ranchers and outfitters propose the same figure for other parts of the Chilcotin too. The brush in these local meadows told us that these numbers could well have been so because in some places it was browsed right down to ground level.

If this figure was even close to being true, then there must have been a hell of a lot of moose here before '48. I sure wish I could have seen it.

There had not always been moose in the Cariboo-Chilcotin country; they only arrived here around the early 1920s. But by the 1940s they were everywhere. Some of the old timers figured the wolves drove them down out of the north country but others suggested that it happened when the early prospectors and white settlers had made projects out of burning the country, and the subsequent luxurious re-growth that followed those fires had much to do with drawing the moose southward.

---

4   A recent sheep count done by the Game Department in 1953-54 had estimated the herd at about 125 head, of which there would only be between five and ten trophy-sized rams. Trying to hunt for five rams in a million acres doesn't assure satisfied hunters; with those odds very few had been interested in wasting their time and money.

How many moose were here before 1948 and how many afterwards? Considering the vastness and ruggedness of the Chilcotin, only a fool would propose a figure and, sure enough, a few did. At a meeting of the Chilcotin Guides and Trappers Association in 1953 two Government biologists stated that there were between 50,000 to 60,000 moose in the area. The Association, led by the president, Eric Collier, disagreed and stated that there were about as many moose as there were cattle. This meant that there couldn't be that high a number of moose. But this didn't stop the wildlife branch from opening the first season on antlerless moose in 1954, right here in the Gang Ranch country.

Shorty and I talked it over for days. We considered what I had seen over near Alexis Creek and what we were seeing here now and agreed that the ratio of bulls to cows might be out of balance, so killing off some of the old barren cows might be a good thing. But what bothered us and others who had lived here for years was whether the expected influx of yahoos from town would know the difference between a wet cow[5] and a dry one. Also there had never been any agreement as to how many moose were in the total herd. How can you set the length of the season if you don't know something like that? And if this wasn't enough of a mess, the cow moose season was being posted in the very late fall and early winter, which would almost guarantee to drive the majority of the moose right down to the roadside. There seemed to be a terrible danger of creating an overkill.

Our evening conversations always ended up going back to the subject of the Gang Ranch and its relationships to everyone and everything else around here. This should not be surprising because the strange situation I witnessed at the Gang Ranch store was also foremost in Shorty's mind. He said it had been

---

5   A wet cow is one who is nursing a calf.

that way ever since he came to this country and he still could not understand why.

"I've leaned over backward trying to get along with those bastards," he said, "and the only thanks we get is like that shit you just saw down at the store. If you think that situation was bad, wait till you meet Studdert, the owner."

Shorty felt more kindly about the hired hands on the Gang. "Most of the hired help are not as bad as what you just saw and that was the worst mood I've ever seen Jim Bishop in, so it makes me wonder what the hell is up this time."

When I replied that I had never met ranchers or cowboys that came across that way either, Shorty said, "I know goddamn well the whole thing boils down to the fuckin' owners who still think they have a God-given right to control everything and everybody around here. Stories old Pete Duncan told me pretty well confirm the whole problem and it makes me wonder what they are really going to do about us," he continued.

"Pete used to be a cowboy here too, so he knew most of the crew and was related to several of them. Well, about a year ago, some of the cowboys suggested to Pete that perhaps he should quit this outfit and go back to work for the Gang or just plain get out of here, because Studdert had put the word out among the crew that they were to have nothing to do with this hunting camp, because one way or another, the camp was going to be closed out. Pete Duncan was a very honest man and he would never lie about a thing like that, because he would know it might cause discord and Pete was not a trouble maker," Shorty emphasized. He was not quite finished.

"When Pete told me this, we did some double checking in Clinton and certain people pretty well confirmed that they had heard the same sort of stories."

I suspected that he might be referring to Game Warden Bill Fenton whom we knew was a personal friend of Studdert and it seemed likely that he might know more than he would actually tell Shorty. As Shorty said on several occasions, "Bill Fenton is a nice guy but we really don't know whose side he's on, or even if he's on any side."

I found these conversations to be very invigorating and was always wishing that I could have met Pete Duncan, because he must have been a treasure of information. Even as young as I was then, I knew that some of the older Indians were masters at collecting and evaluating gossip and making valuable information out of it.

The stories went on and on, night after night. Shorty pointed out that all of the large meadows around here were named after long gone homesteading families who had originally settled in this area in the late 1800s and early 1900s. "Long gone," Shorty explained because, somehow, the Gang Ranch had acquired every one of these old homesteads. But what puzzled him was how they were able to get all of them.

"Pete Duncan and Grypuik had often made comments about some sort of squeeze that had been going on but they either did not want to talk about it or did not know exactly what was happening," Shorty said.

"Apparently it's been common knowledge around here, almost forever, that when these settlers decided that they had enough and wanted to sell, there was no other bidders except the Gang Ranch, because by then nobody else wanted to live beside the Gang either."

By piecing together Shorty's stories I could see how the Gang had made good use of other people's fears, because by 1955 they had acquired all of the deeded land in the area except for the Sky Ranch near Big Creek, the Kalalest homestead near the Old Home Ranch, and a small dry farm in lower Big

Creek that nobody lived on. They had long since got the land out from under Augustine Rosette, as he was now only squatting on Williams Meadow.

One of the stories that Shorty had been hearing was that someone at Gang Ranch, probably the owners, were very angry that this hunting camp was allowed to establish at this late date in an area that they had spent so much time and energy getting other people out of. Shorty had heard that Collins had offered to sell both the licence and the camp to the Gang Ranch at a very reasonable price, but they were not interested as they knew nothing about the tourist industry, and furthermore, did not want one here under any circumstances. It is probable that they felt they were being blackmailed into buying something which they considered had no real value. Shorty believed this story because he too had approached Studdert to see if they were interested in buying now, but Studdert had not even bothered to reply.

"From what we just saw down in the store, I now have a hunch that some sort of real squeeze is about to be laid onto me, but so far I haven't figured out exactly what they might do," Shorty said. "The way I got it figured now is, the Gang thinks that I'm more vulnerable than the past owners, because I'm not a Canadian citizen and they may use that for all it's worth."

He thought he had it figured a bit further, when he suggested, "The Gang Ranch owners, Studdert and Skelton, are Yanks just like Ruth and me, but we ain't as rich as they are and we can't afford to have a bunch of high-powered lawyers scaring everybody away."

As I was soon to be left here alone for most of the summer, Shorty asked me to keep my eyes and ears open for anything that sounded ominous and that might affect him, the camp, and especially the horses. (If anything happened to the horses, there would be no guiding that season.) He said he was not too worried about actual violence towards us personally as he had never heard of anybody getting hurt during the squeezes against the homesteaders, but there might be a move against the camp or horses as the Chilcotin has a history of settling feuds by burning hay stacks and buildings, and shooting livestock or running them off. I already knew this to be true.

Our closest permanent neighbour was Gus Piltz over at the Sky Ranch, about ten miles west of here by saddle horse. Shorty said he had met Piltz only a couple of times and he seemed to be polite and friendly towards him, but he had heard from several other people that the Gang hated Piltz like poison.

"I suspect the reason they dislike him so much is because he is the only small rancher around here that was able to hold out against the squeeze and he had actually built one of the best ranches in the Big Creek area," Shorty informed me.

"Pete Duncan heard that Piltz hated the Gang in return and was known to have made a vow that, no matter what happened, he would never sell his outfit to them. I would like to get to know Gus better, because he must be a mighty strong character, as Pete said Gus had never been known to 'cowtow' to anybody. There are lots of strange stories about old Piltz, so if you get a chance to meet him, try and find out all you can, because I got a hunch he must have the clue to what it takes to survive around here."

There was still another Gang Ranch story that Shorty liked to tell. The Gang Ranch had a post office located in the store and run by ranch personnel. In these remote areas, that was a common practice. Two years before, a party of hunters had arrived at camp, ready to go hunting. Shorty informed them that this was impossible because they hadn't made a reservation or sent him a deposit of $800. The hunters were indignant. They claimed to have sent a cashier's check for exactly that amount the previous spring. After some squabbling as to

53

whether they were going hunting or not, the hunters decided to pay Shorty the full amount, then and there. Shorty continued his story.

"Well, later on, when the hunting season was over, I was driving into town one day, when Bill Studdert flagged me down as I passed through the ranch yard. He had a letter in his hand that he gave to me and said the thing had been laying around all summer. There was the goddamn deposit cheque," Shorty fumed. "Now you tell me what you think, do you believe those bastards deliberately pigeonholed that letter or what? It was a lesson learned, so from then on, I started going all the way back to Clinton, to pick up our mail."

There was no way for me to know, but the way Shorty told the story sure made it look peculiar. Just by mentioning that incident, he had worked himself into a rage.

"It just makes me mad as hell, having to wonder how many business inquiries we never received, because some son-of-a-bitch can accidentally mislay our mail."

One sunny morning Shorty decided I had a good enough handle on the country and the operation, so he was going back to town and leave me for the summer. From our final conversations, I suppose he still suspected that I might not have swallowed the intent of his many Gang Ranch stories.

"You go out of your way to talk to any riders you might meet and especially Gus Piltz. Now, by God, you go right ahead and double check anything I've told you, and I'll bet some of these other people can fill your ear too."

The very last thing Shorty said to me as he was beginning to pull out in the truck was, "I'll be gone for about two months and when I get back here, I hope you are still working for me and not those other bastards."

It was shaping up to be an interesting summer.

CHAPTER 6

My main job was to ride herd on the horses which had been turned loose into the upper end of this valley, known locally as Fosbery Meadow and named after one of the early homesteader families. They are long gone but their 160 acre lots and the abandoned log buildings are still standing today.

The Gang Ranch had "unofficially" taken it over and was using it as one of their remote cow-camps because there was nobody around to say they couldn't. This was not an unusual situation; I knew of other abandoned homesteads all over the Chilcotin, where remaining neighbours took them over until a new owner moved in to take possession again. It may sound strange, but I have never heard of any hard feelings over the practice. In the Fosbery case, Shorty had said that the Gang finally did buy the land about 1950. They then cut the wild hay on the meadow a few times, but since the quality was so poor plus the fact that the rail fences had long since collapsed, they decided to let the place revert into an open grazing area.

The valley itself is about ten miles long and two and a half miles wide with approximately 5,000 acres of natural meadow and swamp land and lays along Wales Creek at the foot of Wales Mountain. One large, continuous meadow follows the creek, while up in the lodge-pole pine forest there are many

A wild flower garden in Hungry Valley.

smaller meadows. Up near the head of the valley, there is another abandoned homestead called "Wales Meadow" after another family who had sold out to the Gang and then left. In 1955, the Wales buildings were still standing and in reasonably good condition, but the fences had become typical Gang Ranch, as they too had fallen into disrepair. The survey shows 200 acres here, so except for the two homestead lots, plus the five acres the hunting camp sits on, the entire valley was pretty well considered to be "open range." This means it is administered by the Grazing Branch of the B.C. Forest Service.

The hunting camp didn't have any fenced horse pasture back then, but there was, and still is, a long Forest Service drift fence that encloses about 5,000 acres into a controlled public range system.

Anytime we were here, we had to keep at least one fast

saddle horse on a picket rope, so we could locate and catch the other horses. It sometimes took us as long as a couple of days of steady riding to locate and corral them. In those days, when the Gang Ranch cowboys stayed in this valley, they lived in the old Fosbery cabin, but their horses were loose just like ours were.

Other than that, my summer's work was going to be pretty well what I wanted to make it into. My hours of work were my own to set and for a twenty-year-old kid, that can sometimes be a problem to control. It's oh so nice to be able to lay in bed until the sun warms everything up, but common sense reminded me every morning that it was time to check on the welfare of the wrangle horse and get cracking on the chores. Luckily, I have never had a problem with getting away from bed when I should (although later on, after marriage, it became different). The one never-ending job was cutting fire wood. When we arrived here, there was barely a two-day wood supply in the house, so it became an immediate project to start building up a stockpile. The chain saw was broken, so it was back to the cross-cut saw. My Dad had started me on wood piles when I was four; he gave me my own personal swedesaw. During the three years with Old Jack, I had cut all the wood for a large house with a cross-cut saw too, so this was not a new experience for me.

Another sort of chore I had agreed to was to try cutting some wild hay with a scythe. Shorty had a permit to cut up to five acres of it, but so far had never done so. The obvious machine to use was either a horse-drawn mower or a machine powered one, but Watson had never acquired either of them. When we had made my first inspection of the place, I had spotted a very old scythe hanging in a tree. I made the mistake of mentioning to Shorty, that as a kid, I had been taught to use one. Since Shorty had no intentions of investing in a mower, he immediately propositioned me into trying the scythe again. The lack of hay for the horses had been much in our conversations, so for my four-footed buddies, I agreed to give it a try later in the summer. If it ever quit raining.

Shorty had in the past brought hay in over the terrible road, but the distance and economics said it was not practical, so the wild hay seemed to offer an answer to a long standing-problem. A single truck load of grain would still be a needed supplement, but in cold weather, horses need more than that.

After Shorty left, it took me a while to establish and settle into a routine. When I had worked for Old Jack, the longest stretch I had ever been alone was ten days, so this was going to be something different. I am a voracious reader and I especially enjoy books on historical topics. On several occasions I have read where early explorers, trappers, hunters, and outlaws have commented on the problems of living alone, especially for the first time. Every survivor suggested that the answer was to get into a total work routine in order to completely exhaust body and mind.

O.K. partner, I am now going to lay something onto you that I have never read or heard another person suggest. As I write these words, I have spent many months in the Chilcotin bush alone and in the wintertime, which can be the very worst time for loneliness. In the harshness of winter there are sometimes long periods when it becomes almost impossible to create make-work projects, so cabin fever becomes a very real enemy. This insidious mental condition has killed people and you better believe it! Make-work projects are good and valuable, but they tend to end when the project cannot be artificially expanded any further. There becomes a limit as to how far you can con yourself and really make yourself believe in the project.

The real key to living in isolated places is entertainment.

You must be able to entertain yourself and if you are with a partner, then you are absolutely obliged to be able to entertain each other. If you can't do this, then don't go because you are going to crash and that can mean serious trouble.

There is a well-known phrase for people who fail the test and it is called "bushed." This term is often used and taken lightly by people who don't understand it, but it's every bit as real as getting cabin fever, and is often the final phase of that fever. There are many cases where those who became bushed never again regained their original personalities and some became dangerously violent. The major difference between make-work projects and entertainment is that work becomes dull, but entertainment has no limits and goes on forever. Work out a good combination or you run the risk of mental damage.

There was no way for me to know if I would have company that summer, so one of my first decisions was to deliberately get away from camp almost every day. The nights in the camp would be long enough, but if I stayed around throughout the days too, then I knew I would end up boring myself, so almost every day saw me many miles from home. One of my first diversions was to go wandering around through the two old homesteads. The early people who lived out in these meadows had obviously spent many hours carving their names, birthplaces, and dates into the walls of the buildings. I spent many hours at those walls reading those names and wondering what had become of all those people. Obviously most of them had been Gang Ranch cowboys and other such drifters, but as I wandered around through these places, I can still remember trying to figure out why they had all left. When they were here, they were on the ground floor to do whatever they wanted to do in this area, so why didn't some of them stay and do their thing? I had never before seen or heard of an area that at one time had many people living in it, but had now, to all intents and purposes, become depopulated.[6] It was a question then and it's still a question today, that may not have ever been completely answered.

Several days after Shorty left, my first visitor did arrive and I more formally met Jim Russell, a long-time Chilcotin ranch hand and fence builder. At the moment, Russell was doing another stint on the Gang Ranch and they had him watching the spillway of the Big Dam and repairing some of the drift fences near there. As we were living only three miles apart we began visiting back and forth quite often that summer.

Shorty had told me a few things about Russell. He mentioned that many people on the Gang had come to the conclusion that perhaps he might have spent too many months in the bush alone because he seemed to have acquired a few peculiar quirks that others should watch out for. Shorty especially warned me to be cautious of Jim if he had been drinking. Jim Russell turned out to be much older than I was, but he was still as strong as a bull and he seemed to like nothing better than showing off his strength. He was one of those people who, when he worked, liked to use the biggest axe, hammer, shovel, or fork that he could find and he could really make the chips fly. In some ways he was one of those people that every Chilcotin ranch needed more of.

But Shorty may have been right about Russell. He would regale me with his accounts of going into town, tanking up, and becoming a very tough hombre. After listening to his stories of physical and sexual exploits and then witnessing that strength, I made a mental note to keep out of his way if booze

---

6   Later on I asked Gus about this. He shook his head in disgust and said, "You would have had to know most of these people and then you would understand why they ran." Obviously most of them were below his standards.

was around. Even though we were neighbours and did visit quite often, in many ways we had nothing in common except that we both lived in the same valley.

Apparently Jim had been working on the Gang for quite a spell this time and in the process he had come up with a very low opinion of the owner, Bill Studdert, but he had nothing but glowing remarks for Bishop and MacIntyre. I believe Jim's major reason for disliking Studdert was because Studdert had declared the ranch "dry," even though he was such a heavy drinker himself that he often had a nurse travel with him whose job it was to keep him sober.

Another reason that Studdert was disliked by many of his crew lay in the fact that he often refused to pay the men their wages for months at a time. The crew referred to this problem as "the Gang Ranch Compulsory Banking System," but this was not quite correct since, in this case, the banker always neglected to pay the depositors any interest on their savings. In those days the manager did not have cheque writing authority, so the crew had to wait until Studdert returned to the ranch, which could mean a wait of three to six months. On top of this, the Gang also had a reputation of paying some of the lowest wages in the country, so I was surprised at the crew's loyalty. In retrospect, I think the crew was loyal only to the manager and cowboss; the outfit was incidental.

One day in late May when I was out riding, I met a herd of cattle being driven down the valley from the west. There were two riders with a pack horse, driving about 200 head. After a few minutes of conversation with them, I knew that I had finally met Gus Piltz, but I forget the younger fellow's name, a hired hand. As they were driving this herd to Sheep Flats in Lower Churn Creek, not far from the Gang Ranch headquarters, they still had a long ways to go, so I invited them to spend the night with me. We just dropped the herd on the meadow, and as they had already been driven ten miles that day, we knew they would not stray very far before next morning.

That night I fed my guests a big feed of rainbow trout that we caught in the creek right beside the cook house. They said that for them, this was a real treat, because they were getting tired of a winter of tough beef, beans and frozen potatoes. Personally, I was becoming tired of the fish, which had been my main diet for the past two weeks. Other than fish, I had been eating straight out of tin cans. The young cowboy looked over my food supply and commented that, compared to what they had wintered on, I was feasting like a king.

Gus and I spent the evening pumping each other for all the local news. As it turned out, Gus was a German and had arrived here in the early 1900s, as a young man speaking very little English. He was now well into his sixties, grey haired, rather tall, perhaps handsome in a way, and was still sporting one of those little "cookie duster" mustaches that were popular with the Brits and Germans in those days. By now, Gus could speak very good English, though with a thick German accent. He was also very polite, which out here in the bush becomes noticeable.

It did not take long for our conversation to steer onto the subject of the Gang Ranch, and once there, Piltz didn't need much goading to carry us into the small hours of the morning. If I had missed meeting Pete Duncan, then I had now located another source of history that just couldn't wait to share his knowledge and opinions. Gus Piltz was one of those Germans that it just doesn't pay to argue with because when he said he was right, you couldn't budge him. In answer to my questions referring to the Gang Ranch "squeeze" that Shorty had alluded to so many times, Gus concurred completely. At one point during our discussions, he must have sensed some scepticism from me, because he declared, "If you don't believe there's been a squeeze play against the small settlers in this area, then just tell me why there haven't been any new settlers come in to replace them as has happened everywhere else in B.C.?" It was a good question.

Gus Piltz also had interesting little stories about neighbours with long ropes who had reputations of "accidentally" branding their neighbours calves. Suggesting or accusing someone of having a long rope is a subtle way of suggesting that person is stealing calves, or if you want to put it more bluntly, he is a cow thief. According to Gus, these were cute tricks that a rancher had to watch out for and according to him, in this game, the larger ranchers had the advantage over the smaller ones because they could hide these "accidental" brandings in a wider range and larger herd. He really felt that he was at a disadvantage living next door to the Gang Ranch because he was quite certain that they had more and longer ropes than he did. I found his explanation hilarious, because I had already heard many stories about the length of Gus's rope too. After many hours of listening to Gus's stories and both of us playing word games with our questions and answers, it left me with another sort of haunting question. Could it be that Gus Piltz's system of survival here was simply being able to out rope his big neighbour? Somehow I believe it was, but to this day I can't be certain.

There can be no question that Gus had been a tough and resourceful settler, because in spite of everything, he did build a successful ranch at one of the highest elevations of any ranch around these parts. Gus told me that he had had a tough time around here during WW I, because he had settled in what was mostly an English ranching area and there were several neighbours who disliked him because he was "too" German.

"In those days, the English storekeepers around here were not offering Germans like me any credit," he said, "so I just learned to try harder and do without things that I couldn't pay cash for."

He must have spent those years immersed in building fences, buildings, and perhaps just keeping out of sight as much as he could. Cash money had been hard for him to come by and the little he made came from trapping furs and catching and breaking the wild horses that abounded in the area then. All or most of those jobs he had done alone.

From earlier conversations with Jim Russell, I recalled him saying that Gus set the leanest table in the country and wanted the longest hours of work. Russell did admit that Piltz paid about half again as much as other ranchers, so there was a bit of a trade off. Gus, in turn, admitted that he had always had a difficult time keeping hired hands on the place. After I spent that night visiting with him, I suspected this might be because he was so tough himself that he expected everyone else to come up to his standards as well.

But his toughness and resourcefulness were legendary. Even when he was getting on in years, he was still breaking his own colts. Early one spring, while starting a big colt in the corral, it fell on Gus and broke his leg. At the time, he was on the ranch alone, so he splinted the leg himself, then roped that same colt to the fence, got on, and then rode for twenty miles to a neighbour's place where he received help.

Gus had far more horses than a 300 head cattle ranch needed and in 1955, hardly any of his horses were broken. This was largely because they were a strain of their own. The type of horses he had bred up were crossed with work horses and the local wild cayuses. Most of them were large for saddle horses, weighing probably between 1,300 and 1,500 pounds. The major difference between Gus's horses and those of his neighbours was that somehow he had got some bad blood into his herd and they were extremely hard to break.

Gus had a standing offer out to anybody who wanted to try breaking these horses for him. When I first saw his horses that year, he figured that there were at least thirty head of them aged three to twelve years, that had never felt a saddle. When he had been a younger man, he could handle broncs like these himself, but nowadays there weren't many horse breakers who wanted to fool around with them. He was able to get the odd one to come out and try, but since they were working by contract to make the horses dependable, it just took too long to bring them around to that point, so they all gave it up. One of the last riders to try breaking Gus's horses was an older man who had a lot of experience, but this time he met his match. When he had one of these big colts down to where he was beginning to trust it, the knothead threw another fit and bucked so hard, that even though the rider did ride it to the proverbial standstill, the rider's guts were so twisted up, that he died a few days later.

The next morning the three of us rode out together and gathered the cattle up and started them down the trail again. Gus was going to keep these cattle down in lower Churn Creek where he owned a 320 acre pasture. When he was describing this pasture to me, it really seemed to be warming his soul, when he gleefully said, "The Gang Ranch hate that pasture so bad, it just chokes them every time I use it, because it's right in the centre of what they consider to be their 'home ground'." The way he explained the situation to me, it sounded like it was just making his day and it was obvious that he could hardly wait to get there. I helped them along for a few miles and then returned home.

CHAPTER 7

Not too long after that the Gang Ranch cattle began arriving in the valley on their way to summer ranges in the high mountains. Jim Bishop dropped in to visit, so I finally had a chance to meet with a pure cowboy.

One of the first things I noticed about him was that, even though he was dressed in the traditional and useful garb of a working cowboy, his body was not really built to be one. Jim was about five foot ten and he weighed around 230 pounds, being much bigger in the middle than he was at the ends. Nobody with a body like that can be an easy rider and it made me wonder why he stayed with the job. Later I learned that it had to do with his love of horses, cattle, and life in the open. There was, and still is, lots of others like him around here. He and I spent the entire afternoon discussing cows, ranching, horses, and cowboying. Jim Bishop was the first person I had ever met who had actually spent most of his life in the saddle, like about twelve hours a day for 350 days of the year.

His many stories fascinated a kid like me. It was a sort of strange situation for me because when I remember those days and conversations, I can still vividly remember identifying more to being a ranch hand/cowboy type than to being the professional hunter that I was then being paid to be. I can still

*Jim Bishop in Hungry Valley,
1956. Bishop did not look like
the stereotype cowboy as he was
built in a strange shape for a
working cowboy. As you can
see, he was bigger in the middle
than he was at both ends, which
made him a "humpty- dumpty"
rider. In truth, he was a hard
rider on a horse, but even so, he
was cowboss on the Gang
Ranch for about 10 years.*

remember that afternoon with Bishop and the many left handed remarks he would drop about people who wasted their time chasing a bunch of goddamn wild animals around the hills, when they could just as easily be doing something more useful.

I was not totally ignorant about what he was hinting at, but in those days all cowboy types used to pride themselves about their loyalty to their employers. There was never anything wrong with quitting one outfit and going to work for another, but they never left an employer at a critical time and, if possible, parted friends rather than enemies. When we negotiated our jobs, it was done during the quiet times. Then, whatever happened, we would see it through until branding or haying was over. Any cowboy that pulled out during a late roundup would have told the world what he was really made of, and I don't mean just to employers either. It was a sort of code that I now find hard to explain in the light of modern labour practices.

As Bishop mounted up to leave that day, he told me that we now had about 1,000 cattle in the valley for company and he would be leaving one rider with them. He and the rest of the crew were returning to the low country where they would gather up another herd to bring up here and they would then take most of the combined herd into the mountains for the summer. He would see me again in about two weeks when they would be sorting the two herds and leave a few yearlings and one rider here in this valley until late summer.

The rain continued to fall so the trails and old roads just got worse. When the sun finally did come out, it was blazing hot. The grass grew and so did the mosquitoes. That is a combination that is impossible to separate. In this part of the world every rancher and outfitter is dependent on the wild forage so that we can ride across the country with "grass up to our stirrups." We pray for the rain and the sun to come at the right time and in the right amounts and when it does happen that way, it gives us a warm and glorious feeling. But the goddamn flies that come with the moisture and grass we prayed for reminds us that nothing in this world comes entirely free. There are meadows in the Chilcotin that have been known to grow flies in such huge swarms that no hooved animal can stand to feed in them until the frosts of early fall finally dispatches the flies. I have seen flies so thick that they will make a white horse appear to be dark grey. I have almost been run over by moose and deer that were running berserk, trying to get away from those hellish flies.

At that time of year and during the worst fly years, the lower valleys become almost devoid of large wild animals, as they leave for the high ridges where the wind of the glaciers tends to keep those flies in check. Out on the small pocket glaciers that dot these mountains, we often came across moose and deer that had dug holes in the snow so as to keep the flies off them during the day. In the cool of the nights, they then go down into the alpine basins to feed. If there is such a thing in this world as a curse, then the physical side of it could be best described with one word. Bugs!!

A few days after Bishop left, I was sitting in the cook house watching the rain come down and the creek come up and congratulating myself that I had a job which did not require me to be out there getting my feathers wet. I hate being wet. A very faint knock on the door jolted me out of my warm dream and when I opened it, there stood the wettest and most forlorn looking young woman that I had ever seen. She was not very tall and had a dark olive complexion, dressed in jeans and a western hat. The hat was soaked and hung like a rag, almost down to her shoulders. A few yards away, her horse was tied to a tree and she appeared to be alone, so I invited her in.

She came in and went straight to the stove and then turned back to me and said, "Hi, I'm Clara." As I went to fetch her a cup of coffee, she started wringing her hat out, over the wood box. We were eyeing each other up a bit and after she shed a very leaky slicker, I noticed she was much older than me, perhaps thirty or more. She was not really pretty, but not the other way either. Perhaps just plain. Makeup or womanly clothes might have brought out something else; it was hard to tell.

As it turned out, this was the rider that Bishop had left with the cattle. Clara had been around the Gang off and on, for several years, so she was well known to the rest of the crew and neighbours. Jim Russell and Gus Piltz had both told me a little bit about her, but still in 1955 "cowgirls" were not yet common in this part of B.C. so her appearance at the door did sort of startle me.

Anyway, on that particular day Clara was very angry. She was staying in the old Fosbery cabin, which still had its original sod roof, so of course after all this continuous rain, it had been leaking for days. "You should come over and see it, inside that cabin it's raining mud," Clara said. "When I first arrived there the other day, I hung a small tarp up over my bed and now even it's leaking. Just think of it, this is supposed to be a million-dollar ranch, yet half the buildings still have dirt roofs on them," she ranted.

Considering that the plight was hers and not mine, I thought her situation was quite funny and made a few comments to that effect. Clara burned my ears over that, so I gallantly suggested that we should go over and get her gear and move her into one of the cabins here, at least until the rain let up. That was not exactly what she had in mind, as she was hoping we might have a waterproof tent or even a better tarp that she could put up inside her slushy cabin. As it was, there was such a tent here that she could have. When I offered to come over to help set it up for her, she informed me that she was quite capable of doing it herself. Apparently this little wet hen was very independent.

Clara stayed most of the day and steamed beside the stove while we visited. She was a Swiss girl who had been in Canada for quite a while and she now spoke perfect English with only a slight accent. She was obviously a loner, but she also liked to visit when such a mood overcame her. This soggy weather for the past few years was really beginning to take its toll from her as she kept mentioning that she might soon quit the Gang and go to work for an outfit where the roofs don't leak. Gus Piltz had offered her a job at some time, so she was now humming and hawing about perhaps this would be as good a time as any to look into that possibility. Clara had already heard about Piltz's lean table, but she said that would not bother her, because if she took the job, she would rather batch. By the time she left, late that afternoon, it sounded like she had convinced herself to go over and see what the Sky Ranch had to offer.

A few days later, Jim Russell came to visit again and we discussed Clara at some length. Russell seemed surprised that Clara had stayed to visit for so long, as she had a reputation of barely speaking to other men around the ranch, with the exception of Bishop and MacIntyre. Whenever Clara wanted a job, the Gang Ranch always had one for her because she was totally dependable. When they sent her out into a cow camp, they knew she would stay there without getting drunk on hunters' booze, or sneaking off to town for the rodeos. Of course there was always a bit of a problem for her since she was the only white woman out here in mountains full of men. Although she remained aloof a few men had figured she might be a handy type of bush partner to have. Russell admitted that he had been one of the ones that tried, but after receiving no encouragement whatsoever, he had given up on her. Quite recently, a new ranch hand had tried using a little force on Clara, when he discovered her cleaning a stall in the barn, but all he received for his effort was a dose of blood poisoning from being stabbed with the manure fork. After that, the word travelled the moccasin telegraph fast, that Clara's love was for horses only.

The next time I saw Clara was only about a week later when she again arrived at the cook house even angrier than she had been last week. This time she was just spitting mad. She was so upset that for about ten minutes she just stomped around the house, cursing sometimes in English and sometimes in another language.

After she cooled down a little, she told me about her job "interview" over at the Sky Ranch. When she arrived there, Gus was home alone, so she stayed for lunch while they discussed the prospective job that was still open for her. At some point Gus broached another subject to Clara, when he started complaining about getting to be an old man now and that he had never been lucky enough to find a woman that would marry him. What was really bothering him now was that he had accumulated quite a sum of money along with this nice ranch, but he had no heir to leave it to. It was beginning to look like his entire life's work was going to end up with distant relatives or something much worse, like the goddamn government.

"He was practically crying on my shoulder and I was even beginning to feel sorry for him," Clara said. "Can you guess what that dirty old bastard came up with next?" she asked me.

I hadn't a clue what Gus might be up to, but the story was getting real interesting so I quite naturally replied, "No, what did he say?"

By this time Clara was beginning to get worked up again. She was actually trembling and her eyes were just snapping, when she blasted out at me, "That old son-of-a-bitch propositioned me with ten thousand dollars if I would have a baby by him!"

I don't remember if Clara told me exactly what she told Gus in reply, but considering how angry she still was after a ten-mile ride, I'm surprised that he survived. By the time she had finished her story, I was in stitches. I guess it was a mistake on my part not trying to console her a little, because she then turned on me and sort of hissed, "So you think it's so goddamn funny do you? Well, let me tell you something mister. I can now see that you aren't a goddamn bit different from all the other bulls and studs around here!"

When she said that, I realized what she was referring to all right, but up to then I had been under the impression that she was tough enough to handle the situation. I guess it embarrassed both of us a bit, because she didn't stay long that day. After finishing a second cup of coffee, she quietly went outside, climbed on her horse, and rode away.

As the summer wore on, the rains did let up somewhat,

but it still remained a very wet season. The cowboys had passed through, taking most of the cattle up into higher country, except for the three hundred yearling heifers that Clara was to ride herd on, until fall. Then they would be picked up by the returning mountain herd and would all be taken to the ranch for winter feeding. Jim Russell had left the valley as Mac had sent him off on other jobs, so Clara and I were the only human residents of the valley throughout July and most of August. Shorty had returned once for an overnight stay and to bring me a grub supply.

Clara used to come over to visit once in a while and to borrow some magazines that Ruth Watson had left here. As I remember, most of those magazines were Hollywood scandal sheets and I often wondered what Clara got out of them. Occasionally we met up in the meadows when she would be checking on the cattle and I would be up there doing the same for our horses. I don't remember ever going riding with Clara and don't know why we didn't, because their cattle and our horses were often mixed together. I guess she just preferred to be alone with her own thoughts most of the time.

Sometime in early August, I decided it was time to try making some hay with the scythe. As the meadow where the hay was to be cut was still extremely wet, with about six to twelve inches of water laying on it, the hay was going to have to be cut and then forked up onto higher ground for drying. The tall, coarse grass I was cutting is called "sugar cane" because of its very sweet juice and its height, sometimes four feet tall. It's easy to cut with a scythe.

The major problem with this project was having to wade around in the water all the time; I kept falling down into holes, going over top of my rubbers, and sometimes taking complete belly flops which meant all of my clothes were soaking wet. On days when the sun did shine, it became extremely hot and muggy, which made this job very heavy work. After a couple of days sweating in that swamp, I had a brainwave. It seemed like the job would become just a hell of a lot easier if I peeled my clothes to start with and just worked in the buff except for a pair of low rubbers that were needed to protect my feet. It turned out to be another Choate innovation, because during the hot sunlight hours when the mosquitoes were down, it worked just great. With a brisk wind, it was downright comfortable.

One day while cutting hay during a wind storm, I heard something behind me. Here, about fifty feet away, was Clara sitting on her horse. My clothes were on a rock about 100 yards away and there was not so much as a bush or tree on that meadow. I soon discovered that a scythe handle does not really cover very much, no matter what angle it's held. There didn't seem to be much I could do but just stand there, although I believe the thought of sitting down in the water did occur to me. But by then the damage seemed to be irreparable, so I didn't bother. I also discovered that it's damn hard to make conversation at a time like that.

Clara started guffawing. She laughed until she began getting the dry heaves and for a few moments it looked like she might actually fall off of her horse. When she did start to slide that way, I can remember trying to decide in my own mind if I should go over and catch her or not do it. However, she did recover enough to catch hold of the saddle horn so it saved me further embarrassment. Along about then I began to laugh a bit too and started walking towards my clothes, but Clara turned her horse and began riding away. As she did so, she turned in the saddle and called back to me, "Keep on working and I'll see you later, but you better be real careful what you cut with that scythe."

The rest of the summer was uneventful. Shorty and Ruth moved out to camp about mid August and together we finalized things for the coming hunting season. We were only going to have twenty-two hunters so Shorty had not hired any other help except an old man who was going to do the cooking for us up in the higher camp. Shorty and I were going to do all of the guiding ourselves. Ruth was going to stay at Gaspard as she said she was getting too old to enjoy riding horses through the muskegs any more.

Once the hunters started to arrive, time went fast. One of the things I remember about that first fall was that we started hunting close to home and on opening morning we saw thirty-four cow and calf moose on Fosbery Meadow, but not so much as a single bull. After that we moved the operation up into Hungry Valley, which is right at the foot and beginning of the South Chilcotin mountains.

We did get some very respectable bulls that fall but we had to work for them, as the weather remained miserable as the summer rains gave way to sleet and wet snow. In the higher country which was still new to me, I was having to learn the area as we hunted. This meant that we spent a lot of time trying to locate the safest trails for the horses as every trail was flooded and some had reverted to pure muskeg. Several times we bogged a horse down and lost hours of hunting time, while we wrestled them out of the mud. One time, the old cook and I were leading a string of eight meat-laden pack horses back to Gaspard Camp, when six of them became mired, right in the centre of what was supposed to be a road. No vehicles of any kind got into Hungry Valley in 1955.

I had never hunted under these conditions before, but I soon learned that hunting can sometimes be damn hard work. Considering that we were always losing time and wearing ourselves out on the bad trails and meadow conditions that fall, we should have had another hired hand to at least help with the wrangling and packing.

As it was, I did all the wrangling and most of the packing

for all the hunting parties. We took them out in parties of four for a week at a time. Shorty would take two of these hunters and go hunting each morning, just as I did, but when his hunters knocked something down, it then became my job, that night or next morning, to go out and help pack their game into camp. Shorty certainly helped at this too, but he was not as big as a packer should be and he was getting up in his years too. I still believe the reason we got through that season as well as we did was because I was young, strong, and stupid.

By the time we were finished hunting, which was about mid November, we were all mighty weary and I was glad to be able to sleep past four A.M. again. Even Shorty admitted that it had been the hardest work and hunting that he had ever been up against. We ended up placing most of the blame on the weather, which was right where it belonged. Not all of our hunters had bagged the game they came for, but most of them did. That year I made a notation on the wall of the bunk house that says I guided hunters to seventeen moose and four deer.

Ruth, Shorty and I were busy cleaning out the camp, getting ready to leave for the winter, when Shorty asked me what I planned to do for the rest of the year. I told Shorty that I had no plans, other than going into Clinton to visit my folks and look for some interesting work. Shorty reached into a box and pulled out a half full whisky bottle, poured us all a good sized shot, and then said, "Ted, sit down. We got a proposition for you. Instead of going looking for another job, why don't you just stay right here and hunt coyotes and cougars this winter? You can use the camp, the horses, all this grub, and keep whatever hides you get," he offered. This took me by surprise and I was slow to answer as I hashed the idea over before committing myself. This pause brought an unexpected bonus; Shorty voluntarily sweetened the pot by adding,

"The best job you can expect to get for the winter is freezing your ass while feeding someone else's cattle, so we'll toss in ninety dollars a month from now until green grass time, if you promise to keep the camp from being burned out and keep those dumb gunsels from shooting our horses." Wow, that was the best proposition I had ever heard of, so this time I agreed in a hurry, before he or Ruth decided to change their minds on their ninety-buck offer.

So now I was finally going to get my chance to really spend an entire winter out in the sticks alone. While laying in the bunk house that night it took me a long time to get to sleep, because I knew this was going to be my first real challenge to find out if I could hack the solitude. I really did not believe that it was going to be much of a problem. My mind was brimming over with the anticipation of all the wonderful winter hunts that I wasn't going to have to share with anybody. I just couldn't wait for the cowboys to get the cattle cleared out of the valley so it and all the Hungry Mountains would become mine and mine alone for the next six months. Ohhh, what wonderful dreams!

The next day we all went into Clinton as originally planned, as even I needed a break from the bush. By then I had been in it for almost seven straight months and there does come a time when a person should take a break and talk to people about things other than hunting, horses, and cows. I visited with my folks for a few days and then made a quick trip to Vancouver where I spent much of my season's wages to buy a new Remington pump 30:06 rifle equipped with the best Leopold scope made at that time. Previously, I had been a straight 30:30 man and while those rifles are light and dependable, accurate they aren't. I now had a rifle that could accurately shoot as far as it is sensible to shoot at anything. The coyotes were sure going to catch hell in the coming winter.

77

A few days later I was back in Clinton, bidding my folks farewell for the winter and climbing into Sid Elliott's Gang Ranch stage, which was a five-ton truck that he used to deliver mail and supplies to the ranches west of Clinton. When the stage arrived at Gang Ranch, which was its turn around point, I would take off from there to Gaspard Lake on foot, as the road beyond the Gang was by then snowed in.

Shorty, Ruth, and Mom came to see me off and they all wished me luck on the winter hunt. The Watsons told me that they were heading south to the States for the winter, where they hoped to locate a buyer for the camp because as Ruth had said several times that fall, "We're getting too old for this kind of fun".

The last thing that Shorty offered as we waved goodbye was, "I hope you don't break a leg or let anything do you in out there, but I'll come out and check on you, probably sometime in early May." I never saw Shorty or Ruth again.

CHAPTER 8

THAT WINTER AT GASPARD LAKE was the coldest one I have ever lived through. Even though the lowest temperature I recorded was only - 58F on February 15, what made some of the days almost unbearable was the goddamn wind that blew in those mountain valleys. When I lived up near Alexis Creek with Old Jack, we had temperatures that went lower than Jack's -62° thermometer could record, but at least there was almost no wind to contend with. Gaspard Lake is located right at the foot of the Chilcotin mountains and when the storms build up in those mountains, they vent their energy by blowing themselves out into those lower valleys. A person has to experience that kind of cold to understand what it's like. It continues to amaze me how the large animals like moose, deer, horses, and cattle are able to survive these temperatures, but so far, I have never found an animal that I figured had died solely from freezing. Cattle seem to suffer the worst, but other animals seem to thrive in that kind of weather.

I must admit I was apprehensive about the upcoming winter. Would it be as exciting and interesting as I predicted or would I arrive at a point where I would have to admit that it had been a wasted effort? There was also that slight feeling of doubt as to whether I could handle the solitude as well as

I thought I could. I do not believe the doubts were ever very strong, but I still remember wondering if I could come out in the spring without being noticeably "bushed." I already knew from experience that there were different levels of bushed ranging from mild to severe. The mild cases can only be detected by others, providing they had known the person before they became afflicted. Considering that there is no cure for this disease, many severe cases have been taken care of by self-inflicted remedies like twelve gauge slugs. It was something that had to be taken into consideration.

It was to become an interesting winter, but in many ways it turned out to be nothing like I thought it was going to be. From here on, this story will become much more accurate in dates, counts, weather patterns, and conversations because, beginning on December 9th, 1955 (and up to the present) I began keeping a diary. For long stretches it's a daily account of events, but sometimes the notes become more like weekly summaries. It's interesting to sit here at Gaspard Lake reading these diaries and have my memory jogged into reliving, day by day, the encounters and situations that comprise that thirty years of my life. I'd like to be able to relive some of those experiences again, but it's not likely to happen because, try as I might, I have still never figured out the way to part the waters.

The winter hunt was not all that successful, as the only animals that fell to my new rifle were coyotes. Over a period of six months I did not see a single wolf or cougar, even though there were a pack of wolves that passed through the valley, about once every two weeks. I soon discovered that even during the deepest part of the winter, those wolves still remained very nocturnal. During the days that the wolves did visit the valley, they would spend the daylight hours camped up on Wales Mountain and serenade every thing else that was living here.

When they did this, the entire wintering moose herd would move right out into the centre of the valley with the horses and even though I was often up there too, those moose would not leave the open valley and hide in the timber like they normally do. I believe that many of those moose realized that I was some sort of safety net between themselves and the wolves because several moose would often follow me through the meadows, perhaps a quarter mile behind. It was a nice feeling to have them trust me that way; they must have the intelligence to understand that man is not a danger to them all year round.

Up to that time I had not killed a wolf, but I wanted one in the worst way. Wolves are very vocal on moonlit nights, so several times when it was full or nearly so, I went up into the high meadows and sat under a tree until the cold drove me home. Moose, coyotes, and horses would come within a few yards of my ambush, but never one of those moaning wolves.

Ever since arriving in this valley, I had been studying the habits and trying to locate the migration routes of all the animals that lived there. Part way through that winter I finally realized that I was not going to find any cougar close to home either. In this area of B.C. the main diet of the cougar are the mule deer, most of whom winter in Churn Creek and along the breaks of the Fraser River. The Fraser is over thirty miles from Gaspard Lake and the closest place to where Churn Creek comes to it is about fifteen miles, so after putting all of this information together, I quickly lost interest in cougar hunting.

A long, hard day on snowshoes gets you only twelve to fifteen miles and if you use a saddle horse in winter, it must be fed both hay and grain, as the old grass under the snow does not have enough nourishment in it to work a horse on. The fall hunts had already used up my entire summer hay project, so the use of horses was out of the question. I did give some thought into snowshoeing over to Churn Creek and dragging a hand sled with a few days supplies on it, but by that time in my life I had already slept under the stars a few times when the temperature was forty below and had come to the conclusion that situations like that are not really enough fun to repeat unless it was absolutely necessary. There is a limit to everybody's stupidity, even mine, so that winter I decided to hunt within range of the home cabin only. The comfort of knowing that I had that ninety bucks a month coming in, no matter what, may have had a lot to do with my decision.

Most of my time was spent cutting firewood with the cross-cut saw and trying to keep the cabin warm. For some reason Shorty had not had the chain saw fixed. The cabin was only two years old and it had been chinked with moss, but now that the logs were drying out and shrinking, that moss was beginning to come loose. One night when it was only thirty below, a sudden hurricane-force wind ripped through the cabin and within minutes, the moss and flying snow were whirling throughout the room. Since I was already in bed, I tried to ignore the situation until daylight, but it didn't work. The sleeping bag I had at that time was a twelve-dollar war surplus affair that had probably been intended for the troops in North Africa. I finally got up and relit the heater. After putting all of my winter clothes on, including a toque, I kept that box heater cherry red for the rest of the storm. Even at that, I had to sit downwind of the heater and by daylight I discovered the end of my nose had frozen. The wind dropped just after daylight and by then there was two inches of snow on the cabin floor and everywhere else in the cabin too. The only place that didn't have snow on it was the heater and about a two-foot circle around it. Just as soon as I was able to heat up some coffee and warm up a degree or two, I gathered all of the paper I could locate from all of the other buildings and

One of the guest cabins at Choate's Place on Gaspard Lake. This is the same cabin where Choate froze the end of his nose while sitting down-wind of the heater during the winter of 1955-56. Today, the cabin is a bit tighter.

began rechinking the cabin. It was going to be tough on Clara next year because most of that paper turned out to be Ruth Watson's collection of those Hollywood scandal sheets, but I did salvage a few warm looking pictures of some girl named Terry Moore. There was still a lot of winter left on the calender and I didn't want to take the chance of forgetting what life is all about.

After spending the entire day sweeping the snow out of the cabin, I realized that all I was doing was getting ready for the next windstorm. At times like that, it became somewhat more difficult to rationalize the decision to stay and put up with those conditions, but quite possibly ego had something to do with it as well.

The winter turned out to be expensive for the Gang Ranch. They had a very poor hay crop the previous summer, so they gambled by leaving almost half their cow herd on Fosbery Meadow until the fourth of February. They paid an atrocious price for doing this as over sixty of them ended up as coyote feed. There was still lots of grass under the snow, but the snow soon built up to over a foot deep and in many places it had wind crusted too much for cows to root through with their noses. Cattle will not paw through snow the way horses and wild ungulates will, as they have been domesticated for too long and have forgotten how to fend for themselves completely. Some of the cattle did become wise enough to follow close to our horses, which did paw through and open the snow, but as there were over six hundred cattle and only twenty-five horses, there was never enough grass getting exposed, so the weaker cows just got weaker. It did not take an expert from the Department of Agriculture to point out that this was an expensive way to raise cattle. If they lost sixty here in this valley, then by the time the herd was moved out, there was an equal number that had become so sickly that they would never live to see the green grass of spring.

While the cattle were still here, Jim Bishop used to drop in to visit from time to time. He had left two Indian cowboys to ride herd on the cattle and after early January, the boys started getting rebellious about having to stay too far back in the bush for so long. I believe that the Gang actually intended to leave the herd here all winter, but at the half-way point even they finally realized the futility of it. When Bishop did come to visit, I noticed he was becoming a little more persistent with hints about the possibility of me changing jobs and this became especially apparent after the two cowboys had threatened to quit.

When he wanted to, Jim Bishop could be very sarcastic and he used it often when he would wonder aloud why I still wanted to waste my time working for a hunting camp. To that old cowboy, my three-year apprenticeship with Jack

Maindley was just being squandered, because there were not many young white men who were taking up the cowboy trade any more. However when it came to sarcasm, Bishop was not having it all his own way, because I was acquiring a sharp tongue as well. I was not working for Bishop and my boss had many times told me, "You don't have to take no shit off them bastards on my account," so I was free to lay it back onto him. We used to have some real good bouts with it, and it certainly helped break the monotony of a long winter. At that time of year, there was no incentive for me to leave here because the job he had to offer paid exactly the same as I was already making. Thus the thought of trading a warm cabin for a frozen saddle had little appeal and I stayed put. But just to keep the conversation going, I did agree to consider the offer for next year.

We had not planned my grub supply very well; by mid February the dried apples and raisins had run out. I was eating two meals a day consisting mostly of meat and barley stews flavoured with dried Lipton soups and garlic cloves. The stew pot stayed on the heater all winter and when it got below the half-way mark, I'd chip some more meat off of the moose quarter that hung outside from a tree and add it to the pot. A couple more pounds of barley and dinner was ready for another week. Once in a while for a treat, I substituted beans or rice for the barley.

My diary says that on February twenty-seventh I had a bath, but I don't remember if it was the only one I had that winter or not. Considering that the low temperatures meant that all water had to be melted from snow or ice, it might have been. The entry from March second says, "I baked some biscuits and they are fit to eat, but that's all."

One morning I woke up to the sound of dogs barking. Be goddamned if there was not a dog team and sled arriving in the yard! I had never seen a working dog team before and the whole affair really astonished me. Up to that day, I had never known that anyone in the Chilcotin used dogs this way, because after all, this is horse country. I soon discovered that I had a neighbour that I knew almost nothing about. "Bill the Trapper" had a trapline that started over near the Sky Ranch and it was laid out south and west of us, towards the Taseko country, but he was still one of our closest neighbours as his home cabin was only ten miles away. As soon as I got all my clothes on and went outside to inspect this new outfit, Bill gave me a demonstration of what three big dogs can pull. I believe those three dogs were capable of pulling as much as one big draft horse. Amazing!

Bill the trapper had heard that there was a strange kid at Gaspard Lake who liked living in the bush alone, so he had come over to see if I might be interested in buying his trapline and entire outfit. Trapping was something I had always been interested in; I had started setting my first squirrel traps by the time I was eight years old. Although I was still interested in trapping, it was already a well-known fact that the fur market was on the rocks and had been for some time. It was an interesting offer, though, because Bill was offering me his dog team, two sleds, three fully equipped cabins in the mountains, 200 new traps, and loads of other gear, all for $500 cash. He figured he had at least $5,000 invested in it, but was becoming fed up with waiting for the fur market to change and he just wanted out. Ohhh, it was tempting, but I was sceptical of the market, and I let the opportunity slip by me. Later on, Bill was able to sell the dog team, but just walked away from the trapline itself. In those years there were lots of other trappers who had to leave the bush as well. Times were changing.

So the winter dragged on. The horses were doing just fine and I never did see any signs that they had been hassled by wolves. I suspected that the horses could do quite well here

86

without me, since this entire area used to support many herds of wild horses. Bishop told me that the ranchers had killed the last band of true wild horses in Hungry Valley in 1943, but the trail networks that those horses had created were still very evident in the '50s. He also had interesting stories about a pair of brothers named Kane, who had been the horse exterminators for the cattle industry in this area and they had been very efficient at their business.

There is a large meadow near Gaspard Lake that is still named after them. However, even if the four-legged wolves were no bother, as Shorty had said, there was still the danger from the other kind, so I continued to keep watch.

I often went up through the meadows on snowshoes and would wander around all day. I was curious about game numbers, locations and travel corridors so I started recording these observations in my diary. That winter the average number of moose on Fosbery Meadow during the daylight hours was twenty. Often on a really cold morning you could count as many as forty. There were obviously many more moose in the general area, but it was impossible for me to count them accurately because I couldn't cover enough ground fast enough on snowshoes before different bunches mixed up and would get double counted.

On March 5th I received a surprise visit from Augustine Rosette's oldest son, Alex, and two Yanks, Tex Braatz and Don Kempf. They waded and staggered through knee-deep snow looking for a hot cup of coffee. They had started into here from Gang Ranch on a Ford tractor that was equipped with tracks, but had buried it in a big snow drift down at Big Dam, three miles away. The real surprise and big news they brought me was that Tex had just bought this outfit and at the same time had bought out Augustine as well. From now on, Alex and I would be working for the combined operation to be known as "The Gang Outfitter." In its thirteen years of operation, Tex had just become this camp's fourth owner.

It did not take me long to discover that Tex Braatz was a breed of cat that I had never met before. He was the first person that I had ever encountered who had been able to deliberately shape his life to the high, fast road of total adventure. Before that first night was over we were entertained by his stories of how he had put himself through college by racing motorcycles and then when ww ii had over taken him, he volunteered to go to China with the Flying Tigers. When they were later disbanded, part way through the war, he had stayed over there and supervised the building of small airfields along the India-China border. While he was doing this, he was able to find the time to shoot his share of Indian Tigers and God knows what else. When the war was over and he had to tame down a bit, he became involved in a whitewater rafting business in Idaho, as well as hunting for very elusive game animals in B.C. and the lower forty- eight states. The stories seemed to go on forever.

A few weeks later, Tex introduced us to another one of his wartime buddies when he brought Bill Light up here to become second in command and second cook, that almost led to the mutiny of the crew. Bill Light had recently mustered out of the 82nd Airborne Infantry, so he also had lots of interesting wartime stories to tell.

It was very noticeable to those of us who never had the opportunity to get into WW II, that after the war was over, many of these men were having a hard time slowing down to civilian life. Bill Light could have been a classic case. Before arriving here to work for Tex, he had tried his hand at being a gambling shill and a taxi driver, but I never did find out how well he made out at either. When it came to dealing cards though, he sure showed us hicks a few things and it didn't take him long to relieve me of pretty close to half my winter's wages. After that I hung the name of "Slippery Slick" onto him and it stuck for all the years I knew him afterwards. Looking back on it now, it was a name that described him completely.

Slippery Slick must have been a better paratrooper than he was a cook. I have always prided myself at being able to eat anything a wolverine can eat, but Slick's meals told us that he wouldn't be allowed to cook for a zoo. For those of us at the Gang Outfitter Hunting Camp, Slick's cooking became one of our endurance tests. The only thing that Slick knew how to cook that resembled anything familiar was corn bread. With anything else, we knew we were gambling with our lives. According to him, there was no such thing as tainted meat, as long as he had a good supply of cayenne pepper and chili powder. After a month, he had us all breathing and farting jet fire. The only reason we survived those times was because Tex himself was first cook and anytime he was around, the crew insisted that he damn well do it because his meals were a lot better than Slick's. Tex's cooking pride was in his stews. Don't ask me what was in them, but they were pretty good food.

Tex had a lot of plans on what and how he was going to do things with the camp and it sounded like it was going to become a big operation. There were plans to build a whole new string of cabins throughout the guiding area as well as setting up huge tent camps. He had just bought the entire stock of a war surplus store in Eugene, Oregon and we unloaded tons of army gear: field kitchens, several really big tents that weighed over 400 pounds, McLellan saddles from WW I, and hundreds of other things that I have now forgotten about. Some of it was going to be useful and some of it was junk.

One expansion to the business that Tex planned to get into was whitewater river boating on the Fraser River. This was many years before it actually did become popular. He had brought two large wooden river boats along with a twelve man inflatable life raft that he asssured us would be suitable for use on the Fraser as well. After viewing one of his promotional films he had taken on the Salmon, I became very enthused about getting started with the project here. Up to that time, we had never heard of anyone else having even tried the Fraser this way, so we were heading into a "first." I was chomping at the bit to go because having recently immigrated up here from the salt water, I still had boats in my blood.

There still remained one small problem with the boat business that we had to solve first. Tex figured that before we tried a trial run, we needed at least one more strong man on the oars and two more would be safer yet. Even though by this time Tex had a crew of six men, there were no other volunteers but me. The only other one who came close was Steve Johnson, who was only seventeen and not very big, but Steve had never had an oar in his hands in his life, so we were still casting around for likely candidates. Slick said he would not cross a pond with us if Tex was going to be captain. When he told us that, it made me wonder if perhaps the paratroopers do not take swimming lessons.

One time when I went into Clinton with Tex, we tried recruiting some of my young friends into coming along but they all turned out to be dryland boys too. I never realized before that I knew so many people who could not want to take advantage of such an exhilarating experience. Just think, we were going to become the first people who ever took a boat through Hell's Gate Canyon. I had never even seen the place, but we knew it was the main challenge of the river, so Tex had photographed it from the road and said he had it figured and we could take it in a snap.

Regardless of his opinions or how easy it was going to be, we still needed that extra oarsman. There did not seem to be any way to fill the slot and I was getting worried that our boat rides were never going to happen. When I mentioned this to Tex one evening, he assured me that we would be taking the first run no later than September when several of his old friends from the Flying Tigers were due to visit.

"Just wait a while until those guys get here because then we will have a crew that will make that boat fly. Those are the kind of guys that will never let a buddy down," he promised.

God, I was going to be travelling with grand company.

In the meantime, we had started on the building programs by cutting and peeling logs for the new cabins. It seemed like we were doing that day and night as Tex had several building sites going at one time. He never planned or did anything in a small way. However, after about two months of this building frenzy, I began to perceive a flaw in this project and I really didn't care for it. The entire crew worked with a will on the first cabin and it went up quickly, but by the time we moved onto the next site, there always seemed to be less people cutting logs. More people began spending more time looking for stray horses. Finally it got down to the point where only Tex and I were doing any heavy work.

By the end of the second month of this, I figured I had enough; there just had to be greener pastures elsewhere. Two of the crew had already quit and Slick had decided that he was allergic to manual labour. Tex and I parted good friends, agreeing that perhaps I might come back later in the fall during hunting season. It was a small "might" in my mind, but I didn't say so.

CHAPTER 9

I LEFT TEX AND HIS CREW at Gaspard Lake; I was heading into Clinton to visit my folks for a while before job hunting again. But something else was in the back of my mind and that was, with the green grass and smell of a new summer perhaps this would be a good time to take Jim Bishop up on his offer to try the life of a full time cowboy on the Gang Ranch. Tex had agreed to drive me into town but by the time we arrived at the Gang headquarters, I had decided to hell with town and had him let me off right there. Bishop was not there that day but he was expected that night or next day, so I decided to bunk into the ranch until he returned.

This was still early summer and big things were happening on the Gang. The cattle had earlier been turned out onto their spring pasture and the crews were getting ready to gather them up again and start hazing them towards the mid summer range at the foot of the mountains. It was also a few weeks before branding time and this was the job I hoped to get.

Something else had recently happened that had the ranch in a turmoil. Old MacIntyre had quit and gone into unexpected retirement, so there was no ranch manager. For that matter there was no store keeper or postmaster either, although

Bishop had been filling in on that latter job when he was around, which was not often. The scuttlebutt around the ranch had it that Bishop was in line to become manager. He had been cowboss for eight years and since other cowbosses before him had gone on to become managers, it was considered an obvious move. Most of the crew at the headquarters were wandering around in a comfortable daze because there was not even a straw boss to assign them jobs. There were men asleep in the sun almost everywhere I looked. However, the holiday ended about mid afternoon when everything seemed to happen at once.

Jim Bishop rode in from an outlying cowcamp and started putting everybody to work but before he got to me, a small plane buzzed the ranch and landed on the nearby airstrip. There was a one-ton jeep truck that was still working, so Bishop invited me to hop in and come along and meet whoever was in the plane. He hoped it was going to be one of the owners, Bill Studdert.

I was still there as a tag–along as there had been no time to talk about jobs, so under these circumstances and in those days it was standard practice for a man "on the tramp" to do chores for his room and board. Anybody who was job hunting was considered to be "on the tramp" and as long as he was prepared to do light work, no rancher or outfitter would ever turn them away. The idea was we could stay until a paying job came up or simply rest a few days before moving on. When I say rest up, I really mean it because during the 50s, there were still lots of hired hands who had no means of transportation, so it was not uncommon to see them trudging up and down the roads. When you consider the distances between some of the ranches and camps, then there was often a damn good reason for a traveller to need a rest.

Some of the jobs that were usually left for these "on the

tramp" types included wood splitting and re-educating forget-ful horses. The whole idea was to impress the boss that we were worth hiring.

However there were other types of men who moved around this way too; ones who refused to work under any circumstances. These were the true hobos: bums and dead-beats. Although sometimes called tramps, they would never be referred to as being "on the tramp." There were other more explicit names for these types too, but one thing was certain; they were not socially accepted by anybody but themselves.

When we pulled up beside the plane, there were three men standing there waiting for us. The youngest one was the pilot and an older, grey haired man turned out to be Bill Studdert. So I finally met the man who was the subject of all those mean stories. But when Bishop introduced me to him, he came across as a sort of fatherly type and didn't seem to fit the picture that had been painted of him.

The third man was about my size but much older, although it was hard to tell exactly how old. He was an ordinary looking person, although some might have considered him to be on the handsome side. He was a quiet spoken man and since Bishop had not introduced us, he never offered his name either; we didn't exchange names. He didn't act as though he was shy but he did project an image of a person square on whatever he did say.

Perhaps because of our size, he and I seemed to have been delegated to move the baggage from the plane to the truck. After we had done this, we sat on the tail gate waiting for the others to finish their business. Finally the pilot climbed back into the plane, waved goodbye to everybody, and took off. Bishop walked over to the truck and, while he was waiting for Studdert to get in, he turned to my work partner and asked us if we knew each other yet. We just grinned and shook our heads at which time he introduced me to Gary Cooper, the movie star.

Gary Cooper was quite well known around the Gang Ranch as he was a long time friend of Studderts and on several occasions he had been up here on hunting trips. The bunkhouse stories had already noted that he had no qualms about moving into the remote cowcamps with the cowboys and becoming one of the crew. My immediate impression of him suggested that the bunkhouse stories were probably dead accurate. Later I found him to be completely unassuming; he would talk to anybody if spoken to, but would rarely start a conversation himself.

Marcel Bourgeois, the Gang Ranch mechanic, was driving, so Bishop and Studdert got in the front with him, while Cooper and I rode in the back of the truck. When we arrived back at the ranch, Bishop took Studdert and Cooper into the store/office to talk business. I went with Marcel back up to the shop, which was his private domain, and began sweeping the shop floor just to make a job for myself.

After a while Bishop came up to the shop and invited me down to his private room, which was built onto the side of the cook house. He told me he had a bit of a problem and was hoping I might help him out. I was all ears.

"Studdert is an alcoholic who usually has a nurse travelling with him to keep him away from the bottle, or look after him if he gets hold of one. The problem right now is that the bloody old fool has deliberately ditched his nurse and has arrived here with a case of scotch so he can have a party. If I know Bill, he's going to overdo it, like always," Bishop continued.

"Ted, you would be doing me a real favour if you would go along with him and Cooper up to the Tyee House and just stay right there with them to make sure that Studdert doesn't hurt himself or do something really stupid.

"Cooper won't be any problem," he added, "because he hardly drinks at all."

I did not really need the next incentive that Jim tossed out, when he suggested, "If you stay there with them and say and do the right things, there could be a damn good job in it for you."

Oho. Now here was an opportunity that I had never dreamed would come my way. I was being offered the chance to get right beside the man that was the subject of so many stories in the Cariboo-Chilcotin area. Not only that, I would have him virtually all to myself. Would I volunteer? What a question! Gary Cooper was going to be an unknown bonus, but my entire focus was aimed squarely at Bill Studdert.

We moved all of their gear, which wasn't much, up to the Tyee House, which was an old English-style mansion located two miles up the road from the main ranch headquarters. It was a huge frame building with many rooms and if anyone ever tried living in it during the winter, they must have found it as easy to heat as a barn. It had been built long ago by the Prentices, a wealthy English family. It was normally vacant during Studdert's reign except for the times when he brought in guests such as Cooper.

Bishop had been right about Bill and the booze. The first thing Studdert did was to swear me to sobriety and appoint me the bartender. It turned out to be an easy job as the only liquor they had was the case of Black & White Scotch and Bill drank his with only a little water. Cooper did too but I noticed that he could quite happily nurse a single drink for hours.

It did not take me long to figure out that my real job was going to be that of a straight man, asking the right questions at the right time and agreeing with Studdert's philosophical convictions. And let me tell you, he had some doozies.

For some reason, Studdert and I hit it off real well together.

In the two and a half days we were together, he lay tons of what he considered to be good fatherly advice onto me. This visit was turning into nostalgic reminiscing about their earlier lives. They didn't realize they had in front of them the most interested listener they could have hoped for. By the time the first bottle was half empty, we were all on a first name basis. To Bill, I had become "Ted, my boy" this and "Ted, my boy" that. We referred to Cooper as Gary and sometimes "Coop."

Cooper was a good listener but he too had lots of interesting stories. Both these fellows had travelled widely, so they had stories about people and places that I had never even heard of. They had both been in China, but not together, so there were lots of Chinese anecdotes. Studdert had actually met and knew Chinese warlords and pirates and I came to the conclusion that he considered them as peers except, in his stories, he was always the smarter peer. Perhaps he really was. Sometimes the stories became a contest in one-upmanship, but they were so well told that I can still vividly remember many of them. They had me laughing till my guts ached.

There was no question that both of these men had lived interesting lives. I have no way to know if all of their stories were true or not, but I did take note that neither of them ever suggested that the other might be a liar. Cooper and Studdert had known each other for a long time, I believe they said since college days. Looking or remembering back to those conversations, it is now interesting to realize, that when it came to emphasizing story telling, Studdert had it made in spades over Cooper, even though Cooper was a professional actor.

This was turning out to be as cosy a bull session as you might want to imagine. When Bill had drunk too much, he would go to sleep on us for a few hours. When he woke up the drinking and story telling took off again too. He enjoyed deliberately fostering the image of himself as an arrogant, "don't give a shit for anybody" type of millionaire.

After listening to several of his "China" exploits, I asked him if there was such a thing over there as a "land pirate." He replied that he was sure there had to be, because they had every other kind of pirate there could possibly be. By this time I was getting a bit bolder and that's when I suggested that if there were, in fact, land pirates, then that's exactly what Bill Studdert was.

When I said that, Gary spilled his drink and almost fell off his stool. Studdert started to laugh too, but as he was laying on the couch, he almost choked and it took Gary and I a few minutes to get him breathing properly again.

When I look back and visualize Bill Studdert, I'm always reminded of a character from the old L'il Abner comic strip. Studdert resembled and behaved exactly like General Bullmoose.

He often talked about money: its blessing and pitfalls. When, in my youth and innocence, I suggested that money could not buy loyalty, Bill came up with a lecture I remember to this day.

"Loyalty is the easiest and cheapest commodity to buy there is," he assured us.

"All you have to do is make your first million, let the world know you have it, and every shyster there is will come sniffing around, offering their 'free' services but hoping they can skim something off your bundle. The trick to keeping their loyalty is making sure the nest egg is so well-secured that they can never actually get their hands on it. But as long as they know it's still there, they'll never leave you. In the meantime, a wise man (such as himself) will be using their talents to make more money off them than they do off you," he hammered at me. "If you don't win everything, then you've lost and that could mean you are headed for the scrap heap. So you better decide which end of the table you want to sit on."

The old boy was a good educator and he would often leave me with my head spinning.

Cooper hardly ever talked about Hollywood or actors and actresses. When he did talk movies, it was mostly about the technical side of it, such as how they faked things for the cameras and how good some of the trick riders were. Cooper was already known on the Gang as being a good rider in his own right. Bishop stated that he could probably handle any green broke horse on the ranch.

One time when Studdert was sleeping another one off, Cooper and I took the truck out for a drive and to get some fresh air. I never went anywhere without my new rifle and once when we were parked on a hill soaking in the warm, green summer, he admired it so I invited him to try it out. If this fellow was supposed to be a good rider, then I soon discovered that he was also a very good marksman as well.

Our diet was not all liquid. Every once in a while Cooper would drive the truck down to the cook house and have old Lem, the Chinese cook, make us up some grub, but Bill never left the Tyee House except to stagger out the back door to have a piss. Of course my job was to stay with him, which was certainly necessary because he was becoming quite helpless. Physically helpless that is, but his mind and mouth continued working until he would pass out on us.

I had hoped to get a lot more information about the Gang Ranch out of Studdert but as it turned out, he didn't really know very many of the details of its past either. He confirmed some of the stories that Shorty, Augustine, and Piltz had told me but Bill said he left the nitty-gritty stuff to people like Mac and Bishop. When I brought up the phrase "squeeze" that I had heard so often, he got a bit defensive.

"If some goddamn homesteader comes to the ranch and wants to sell me his 160 acres for $5,000, then I'll sure as hell buy it, but I'm not remotely interested in why he might want to sell it," he said.

"If these goddamn homesteaders feel that they are being squeezed, it's only because they're not big enough to look after themselves and should never have been allowed to have that land in the first place. There is no goddamn way any rancher can make a living off such a small acreage. One way or another, they're going to lose that land to somebody else," he said, building up a full head of steam.

"It's about time that this country understood that every-body would be better off if outfits like the Gang Ranch are allowed to put large land areas together under one roof, so the land can be used properly," he defended, by this time having worked himself into a small rage.

I didn't improve his disposition when I brought up the topic of the "new" hunting camp that Tex had just taken over.

"Why in hell this stupid goddamn government went and issued those people a license to move into here and screw up this ranch, I'll never understand," he fumed.

"Shorty Watson had gall enough to try selling me that outfit for $25,000 and he didn't even own an acre of land. He tried telling me he was selling a tourist business that doesn't need any deeded land. Now, can you imagine anything more stupid than that? All that son-of-a-bitch had up there was a cluster of shacks that we don't need and some type of licence that says he has the right to guide hunters across our range land. What the hell do I want with a business that caters mostly to a bunch of goddamn drunks?" he raged.

These words came out of the mouth of Bill Studdert as he lay on a couch, so hopelessly inebriated that he couldn't stand up. He was still not finished with the subject.

"It will be a cold day in hell before I ever pay a dime for something like that, but it really scares the shit out of me when I think of what kind of can of worms this stupid government may have opened up. Letting people like that on this land is somebody's idea of a sick joke. No one is going to blackmail the Gang Ranch," he warned us.

To a kid like me, this was all mighty heady stuff, because I was at an age when my opinions and beliefs were beginning to solidify. At the time I felt that I had two of the world's best teachers from which to draw advice, so I asked the ultimate question.

"All I own in this world is three rifles, a shotgun, a saddle, and my bedroll, so how in hell do I grab a chunk of action that is going to make me my first million?"

Studdert answered first and admitted that it was getting harder to do all the time because of governments, taxes, and a lot of nosey people who keep interfering with a person's business.

"If I had to start over again in this part of the world, I'd make an effort to try and locate a valuable mineral deposit because it seems like there should still be some unlocated ones around here someplace," he advised.

"And if that doesn't work, then a person should always keep their eyes peeled because every once in a while, we meet rich people who aren't all that bright and sometimes, by using sharp bold strokes, you can relieve them of some of their burden," Studdert guffawed.

"But if you ever try that route, be goddamn careful, because when they finally realize that they've been had, some of them can be dangerous."

Cooper had some different advice. He figured that a young man should try going to Miami Beach to find a rich widow, preferably an old one.

One day Studdert told the story of how he became rich. It sounds a bit far-fetched but, as it fitted his personality to a T, I'll pass it on to you.

"People think I inherited my money, but by God I can assure you that I made my first million all by myself, when I was exactly the same age as you are now," Studdert said.

"It was right before they brought in this goddamn income tax and I went to Alaska looking for something interesting to do. Well, while I was bumming around the docks up there, I met this real pretty little Indian girl and talked her into shacking up with me.

"After the honeymoon wore down a bit and we started talking to each other, I discovered that her tribe had fish trapping rights on the river there. We helped some of her relatives catch salmon in these traps but I realized that they were catching only enough to feed themselves and their dogs, so it was easy to figure out that they were missing the boat, completely.

"Well, I was able to borrow some money and paid some of the Indians to rebuild some of the traps bigger and better than they ever had been.

"That was a good year for both salmon and prices because we caught over a million fish and the cannery paid us a dollar a piece for them. Well, as you know, those poor simple bastards don't know how to handle that kind of money," said Studdert, laughing, "So I packed up and moved back to Seattle and took it with me."

The party was winding down as Marcel and Bishop came to tell us that a car was coming out to take Studdert and Cooper to Clinton, as there was some business that Bill had to attend to. It would also give him a chance to clean up, as he had not washed or shaved since arriving here. As I was rolling up my own bedroll and saying goodbye, Cooper gave me a couple of phone numbers and said, "Ted, if you ever get down into the L.A. area, get in touch with me and I might be able to set something up for you." Studdert was standing by the door listening to us and he had the last word.

"Hell, Ted. You just stay right here and you might learn something a lot more worthwhile."

CHAPTER 10

JIM BISHOP DID NOT GET the job as manager of the Gang Ranch. For some reason, perhaps his lack of education, Studdert bypassed him and the job went to a totally new fellow brought in from Vancouver. It didn't really affect me and, after leaving the ranch for a short holiday, I returned to the Gang and finally started working as a full time cowboy in Bishop's cowcamp.

The new manager's name was Bob. I can't recall what his last name was but I do remember that he was a big man. To the Gang Ranch crew, he became "Big Bob." He had been an office manager before Studdert shanghaied him into taking on this chore and was a total greenhorn to ranching but he was a quick learner. Personally, I had very little to do with him but the few times I saw him in action it was obvious that he could understand what we were doing at a glance and then find better ways of doing it.

One of Bob's strongest points was his ability to get along well with the other people on the ranch with a couple of exceptions. Bishop did not like him for the obvious reason of his job bypass, but I never did hear if Bob's opinions of Bishop were reciprocal. The other exception was a crazy talking French Canadian that we naturally called "Frenchie."

Over the years there have been many French Canadians working on the Gang Ranch and they had all picked up the handle of "Frenchie." One exception, however, was Marcel Bourgeois who was the ranch mechanic and handyman, a position he had held for over 30 years. Not once have I ever heard anyone refer to Marcel as "Frenchie;" to every other person on that ranch, he was just Marcel. Shorty Watson once told me that Marcel was probably the best person on the ranch and, after having worked with him, I am in total agreement. Marcel never did get involved with the petty politics of the ranch and that is probably why everyone respected him.

Marcel was responsible for keeping all engines operating and all equipment with wheels rolling. In the 1950s this meant that Marcel had to keep an old Dodge Power Wagon, two Jeep trucks, a D-4 Caterpillar, and several old motorized buckrakes functioning. He was also expected to repair the big iron-wheeled, horse-drawn wagons too, but they were very durable and seldom needed repairs. When one did, it usually meant that it had been involved with a runaway team of horses, which resulted in the wagon being smashed to bits. Out behind his "shop," Marcel kept a stock of all the salvageable parts from those wrecks and when he had some spare time, he would puzzle out how to make mismatched pieces fit into a new wagon. Some of his rebuilt wagons looked a bit strange but they worked.

Marcel's biggest headache was trying to persuade Studdert to buy parts for the motorized equipment. Studdert had a strange maintenance system; he wouldn't buy a part for anything until the last vehicle had quit running. Then there would be a great flurry of repairing everything all at once, even hiring the stage driver, Sid Elliott, to come out for a few days to help Marcel. This was a strange rationalization that made sense only to Studdert.

During hay time if any of these machines quit, then they

had to be replaced with horse-drawn mowers, rakes, and hay slides. Since all of these had to be kept ready to roll as well, Marcel had to be very versatile. A work delay of more than a day meant hay not made, which affects the condition of the brood cows come calving time. When Big Bob took over the running of the Gang Ranch, it did not take him long to appreciate the fact that Marcel Bourgeois was as sacred as the cows.

When I became a Gang Ranch cowboy, the first job Bishop assigned to me was to help three other riders with the spring horse roundup. In those days, nobody knew for certain how many horses there really were on the Gang. They had a herd of the best draft and saddle horses in this part of B.C. so our job was to locate and bring in as many as we could before horse thieves beat us to the slick colts. The area where we were horse hunting was an unfenced range covering about ten by twenty miles in size. It was two-thirds timbered, the rest being open benchland or natural meadows. The horse herd was spread throughout the entire area and we were quite sure that some bands had strayed or had been driven further afield by horse thieves, than the range we were ordered to search for them in. For several days we hazed all the horses we found into what was once the "official" horse pasture about eight miles from the ranch. This had become a typical Gang Ranch pasture, as there were holes in the fences almost every mile which explained why the horses were now ranging as far as they wanted to go. It did not take us long to realize that for every ten horses we put back into the pasture, we lost at least three of them before the next day.

As the junior cowboy in the bunch, I was soon taught that on the Gang Ranch it was considered to be below a cowboy's dignity to get off of his horse to fix a fence. That job was left for fence builders like Jim Russell and if there was no one assigned to that area, then to hell with it. I'm not sure what the score is on this subject today, but there was a time that if the boss told a cowboy to fix a fence, it meant that he was fired. Thus fences on the Gang Ranch seldom got fixed.

We worked on that "ten horses in, three horses out" project for about ten days. By that time we had so many horses in the holding pasture that we became worried that they might hit us with a mass escape, which would mean we would have to start all over again. When horses that have been used to being loose on the open range are corralled, it takes them a while to settle down to confinement again and, if they do get away within the first few days, they have a habit of running for many miles before stopping. I had some sympathy for them because it sort of reminded me of my school days.

Early one morning, just before we were to mount up to go out on the daily search again, one of the older cowboys rode in from the holding pasture and told us he could sense that our captives were getting restless. He suggested that perhaps we should run these ones down to the ranch right now while we still had them. We all agreed because we knew if we lost them, it would be somewhat embarrassing to have to explain to Jim Bishop how we had squandered ten days of hard work.

We quickly rolled up our gear and tied it to a pack horse. Our strawboss assigned an old Indian to lead the pack horse down to the ranch for us, which would mean that he would miss out on the wild run that everybody seemed to be so enthused about. On several occasions, the rest of the crew had told me that I was damn lucky to have been chosen to come out on the annual horse roundup on my first year here, because this was considered to be about the highest honour and achievement that a Gang Ranch cowboy could ever hope for. Every time somebody told me that, my head swelled up a little bit more. The old Indian was a bit grieved about being chosen to be the tail-end Charlie because he felt the job should have gone to me, since I was the youngest in the crew. Even though the old man did not have many more horse roundups left in him, I still did not volunteer to take his job.

One of the boys opened the gate and we were off. Most of the old brood mares had been through this before, so they knew exactly where we were headed. All we really had to do was haze the herd from behind to make sure none of the smarter ones tried doubling back and out onto the timbered range behind us. I had never been on such a ride in my life! It was eight miles downhill at a wide open run. We tore through those gullies, rock piles, and out across the open benches and my heart was in my throat all the way. Most of the time I just let my horse have his head and prayed that he wanted to live as much as I did. At times like that, religion can come back to a person real easy. If anyone had been watching from one of the hill tops, they would have witnessed a piece of cowboy heaven because it would have been the most wonderful sight to behold: 300 blooded horses streaming down out of the hills, with every mane and tail flying straight out and then three riders laying flat against their horse's necks, with never a stumble or a tumble. When daydreaming of rides like that, it's easy to imagine that at some distant time, God may have been a cowboy too, to let us get away with such a reckless run.

When we pulled up at the ranch corral, I almost fell off my horse because my knees were so sore. When I dropped my pants to find out why, I discovered that there were sores on the inside of my knees the size of dollar bills. I can still remember making a half-hearted vow to myself that the next time I was lucky enough to go on the horse roundup, I'd let the old Indian earn himself another feather. Maybe.

After the horse roundup was over, we joined Bishop and

some other cowboys and began the summer cowcamp in earnest. Our first job was to round up the cattle on the spring range and brand the calves before herding them into the mountains. It took us about three weeks to locate 1,200 brood cows and brand their calves. This was not all the cows on the ranch that summer, but it was most of them. The rest would stay behind and get brought into the ranch on the last roundup, late in the fall. Bishop figured we were leaving behind as many as 300 head, but considering the size of the range they were hiding in, it might take us another two weeks to locate even half of them and we just did not have the time. There was enough grass left there that feed would be no problem for them.

A little incident at one of the branding corrals really raised my curiosity. On this lower spring range, the Gang Ranch had to share the area with small ranches from the Big Creek area. We were operating short-handed, so many times when we located a herd of cows, they would be intermixed with cattle bearing several different brands. As there were not enough riders to hold and separate the brands out on the open range, we would begin driving the small herds toward the corral. As we drove them along, the idea was we would drop the strays from the herd, one by one, before we arrived at the corral.

Well, several times we were not able to get the strays weeded out in time, so they got corralled right along with the Gang Ranch cattle. Every time that happened, I noticed that we branded every calf in the corral. I knew that this was not quite right. But I was told that we simply gave the rancher one of our unbranded slicks later.

This answer made sense, so I didn't give it any more thought until many years later when I was talking to one of the Big Creek ranchers whose calves I knew we had branded. When I brought the subject up, he listened to me for a while and then just shook his head and said, "If the Gang Ranch has ever given somebody around here a slick calf, then I've yet to receive my first one."[7]

When most of the calves had been branded, we gathered up the entire herd and started hazing them towards their summer and fall pastures in the mountains to the south and west, a distance of seventy miles. We would be taking the herd up there in stages, as newly branded calves can only be driven ten or twelve miles a day. Even at that, we tried not to move them more than two days in a row. When young calves get tired, they have a fatal habit of sneaking away from the herd and finding themselves a nice cosy place to lay down and sleep. When they awake, their mothers are several miles further up the trail and a calf will never search forward for its mother; instead it will go back down the only trail it knows. I estimate that about eighty percent of the lost calves are found by their mothers; the rest are discovered by coyotes or bears.

What saves this situation from worse losses is the mother up ahead. When she realizes that her calf is no longer trailing with the herd, she lets us know about it.[8] A cowboy must learn to distinguish which of those cows has really lost her calf and then let her slip back down the trail to locate her wayward brat.

---

7   Rustling is a subject that few ranchers want to discuss with outsiders. People here make a distinction between "rustling" and "making a mistake." The words stealing and rustling are only used when a person who has no cows on a range is caught taking or branding one on it. It can't be explained away and is looked on the same as if he had stolen your poke. But if someone does own cattle and brands another's, it's always possible that it's a mistake.

   When it comes right down to it, I believe that the most successful rustlers are simply neighbours with long ropes.

8   Some of the younger cows do not have a strong mother instinct and it's their calves that usually get "had" by something.

All of this meant that we had to keep doubling back on our tracks to bring the re-united families back up with the main herd. There were only seven men in our trail crew, so it meant that we had our work cut out for us. For the rest of the summer it was going to be ride, cowboy, ride.

In most ways it was a great life, but it also left us mighty weary by the end of a day, as the heat, dust and flies took their toll. While we had been working at the branding corrals, one of the Chilcotin Indian cowboys had his wife doing the cooking for the crew, but on the trail, Jim Bishop took over that job and he also drove the big iron-wheeled chuck-wagon that also carried all of our loose gear.

For the first forty miles of this cattle drive, we followed very rough wagon roads for which our chuck-wagon was well suited, but by that time there were also a few damn fools who were beginning to drive their trucks and four-wheeled drives over the roads too. But that summer we were lucky and never met up with any of them, so we had the hills pretty much to ourselves. Bishop was a good cook and the rest of us tried to keep him at it permanently, but every few days he would climb back onto a saddle horse and delegate the cooking and chuck-wagon job to somebody else, usually me. I often wondered how some of the other men had survived so long on their own cooking. Some of them did not even know how to put together a stew or make a pot of coffee without screwing it up somehow. I mean we were travelling with some of the worlds worst cooks.[9]

---

9   Personally, I am a very good coffee maker and my pet recipe is simple. You put enough coffee in the pot to make what you know will be a good brew and then add half again as much. This guarantees that nobody is going to complain about having to drink weak horse piss. Out in the bush no one is more despised that a cook who is chintzy with ingredients.

Part of Jim Bishop's cowboy crew at Hungry Valley, 1956. From left to right: Jack Cade, Orie Hance, Bill Sanford, Jim Bishop, and Wayne Haas.

The long days in the saddle soon took the glamour out of our life. Bishop expected to have to replace at least half the crew, because he felt that some of us were not going to be able to cut the hard work and low wages. Most of the crew had been promised ninety dollars a month and grub, which, even in those days, was still on the lean side. Our work day began at daylight when the wrangler went out to chase in the horses that we would be using that day. As soon as they were corralled, the rest of us would saddle up before breakfast and go to the creek and wash up, which meant splashing water on our faces. As soon as breakfast was over, we stepped straight into the saddle and would be gone for the day.

A working day might be anywhere from six to twelve hours. We normally packed a lunch of some sort, usually a piece of cold meat and a can of juice or tomatoes. Often there was no bread so most of the time cold pancakes served in its place but they didn't carry all that well. After five or six hours bouncing behind a saddle, those pancakes were often reduced to something that even a dog would have to be coaxed to eat.

We were expected to work seven days a week, but once in a while, one of the crew would be so weary that he would just say to hell with everything and take a Sunday off, to lay around camp to rest up a bit. When one of us did this, Bishop would dig out his "time sheet" and put a mark beside that person's name, indicating that there would be three dollars deducted from his pay cheque (if and when he got one). I can't remember a time when the entire crew took the same day off, but whenever someone did, the rest of us would refer to him as the "three dollar cowboy." His usual retort to that remark would be, "What the hell. With this outfit, we probably won't get paid anyway."

The Gang Ranch Compulsory Banking System was a continual topic of conversation any time two or more riders came together. I heard stories about how some of the men on earlier crews had worked for months at a time only to have Studdert flatly refuse to pay them anything. Some of them became so frustrated that they finally just rode away with nothing for their labour except bad memories. Bishop did not like to hear his crew discussing this type of campfire story and he always tried to play down the possibility that it would ever happen again. As for myself, I felt pretty secure because Bill Studdert and I had become good tillicums.

This problem of ranchers refusing to pay their hands was not that uncommon; there used to be many other ranches besides the Gang that pulled the same trick. The problem was that there were no labour laws that covered farm or domestic help, so they could do with us pretty much as they pleased. The only legal recourse we had was to go to town and hire a lawyer to collect the wages due. Even that was no assurance of a fair settlement because some of the ranchers had acquired a profitable habit of lying about how long the hand had been working. I had never met any cowboy who had tried collecting his wages through a lawyer, as most cowboys have a rather contemptuous feeling for the rule of law. Usually they left quietly, licking their wounds.

There was another reason why a hired hand would not hire a lawyer. Anyone who tried the lawyer route would damn soon find himself blacklisted throughout the ranching industry. Ranching is not a large industry and that type of information would travel quickly.

Some of the men I worked with told me that when they had been cheated by ranchers, they had their own collection system but when I asked them what it was, my answer was always just a laugh and shake of the head.

Some of the larger ranches provided a company store for their crew which, if abused, could lead to further hard feelings between themselves and their employees. On the Gang, as on some of the others, most of the crew lived in a cashless society. The company store, however, provided every hand with an account book, so he could draw items from the store in lieu of money. Since most cowboys who work on these places only do so because they were flat-assed broke in the first place, they are at the total mercy of the ranch store keeper. Some of those account keepers were very handy at padding the books in order to keep the hired help perpetually broke. The unscrupulous employer not only made money off them but he also knew that a man with no money finds the road beyond the ranch gates is a very hungry place.

The company store has worked fine for some ranches, but for others who probably overdid it, it created a great deal of hard feelings, which sometimes came home to roost on them.

The problem was that if you think you are being cheated but you can't read or write, no one can tell you otherwise. So some of the hands made up their own accounts by pilfering ranch equipment. The ranchers would have been far better off if they had paid us in cash, and then we would have had to lay it out on the counter.

CHAPTER 11

THE GANG RANCH HAS a string of rough log cabins spaced about twelve miles apart throughout their range area, so we seldom had to sleep under the stars. These are the true cowcamps and while some of them had a small, fenced horse pasture, at others we still had to picket a wrangle horse every night. The further into the mountains we went, the harder it became to keep the forty horses from straying. On some days we spent our entire time just hunting for those horses. In a cowboy's life, working cattle is a chore but hunting or chasing horses is considered to be fun, so there were more than a few times when the horses were encouraged to leave for a while. Riding off to search for them in the wrong directions could make a pleasurable day too.

That was a beautiful summer to be up in the Chilcotin mountains, as the rains of the past eight years had finally stopped. Now with the sun coming out most of the time, wherever we rode, we were always swishing through the proverbial "grass up to our stirrups." In many places it was a damn sight higher than that, too. Anyone who works with livestock will understand what I mean when I tell you it was a grassland paradise. We were in cowboy heaven. In those years, the grass grew in quantity all the way up to the 7,500 foot elevations and since these mountains are mostly great big open rolling hills where cattle can easily climb to the top, our 1,200 cows had found their summer heaven too.

Shortly after we had arrived at the last cowcamp in the mountain range, I noticed that we still had about thirty head that bore the brands from some of the Big Creek ranches. They were now a long way from their home range, so I asked Bishop what we should do with them because I knew some of those ranches were very small outfits and they must have already missed this number of cows by now.

"Just leave the goddamn things right here when we roundup in the fall and maybe next year those people will learn to keep their cattle off of our range," he said.

I pondered this for a while. I knew there was a very slim chance that those small ranchers would ever think to come up this far looking for their strays, so they were being set up for a dead loss because no cow could ever survive the winter up in these mountains. None of those ranchers could afford a loss like this very often. (There were no government bailouts in those days.) This situation reminded me of conversations with Gus Piltz when he was talking about small ranchers getting squeezed. If this was a common practice, then it was easy to figure out that over a period of a few years, it would break a small rancher.

Some of these mountains and valleys are beautiful beyond description so we often positioned cattle up into places where there was no real need to put them merely as an excuse to go there. One of these places is Graveyard Valley, so named because of a small cluster of Indian graves located out in the centre of the valley. These are fairly recent graves as they contain the bodies of a group of Chilcotin hunters who were wiped out in the flu epidemic of 1919. When we were there in 1956, there was still clothing scattered around on the grave tops, even though each burial site also bore the Christian Cross.

The Indian graves in Graveyard Valley. At the time of this writing, the woodwork that you see here has now rotted completely away.

Perhaps in 1919 the relatives who buried these people were still uncertain of which religious road to follow so they had played it safe and paved the way in both directions. Why not?

One afternoon when Jim Bishop, another cowboy, and myself, were having lunch at the Graveyard, we were admiring the super lush blanket of wild timothy grass that absolutely covered most of the valley bottom then. In the course of our conversation, Bishop figured that there so much rich grass there that we should make better use of it, other than just letting the cows eat it up with their summer grazing.

Graveyard Valley is at a 6,000 foot elevation and very often in the past when an early winter engulfed the area, the cowboys had to pack up and leave before all the cattle were rounded up. All of this was because there was no way to get hay into such a remote area. But if we could cut some of it here, then over a few years it would save the lives of a lot of cows.

He was really getting serious when he began asking us our opinions about the possibility of being able to cut up a horse-drawn mower and rake, so we could pack them into here on pack horses. While this conversation was taking place, I was beginning to feel queasy. I did not like the direction this project was taking and just as we were getting ready to mount up again, all my suspicions were confirmed. Jim had obviously made up his mind and announced, "Next time I go to the ranch, I'll find out if Marcel knows how to cut that equipment up, so we can put it back together up here, and then when Choate has some spare time this summer, he can make some hay for us."

What a buddy.

One of my problems was that everyone in the country had learned that I had scythed that three tons of hay for Shorty Watson. Apparently nobody else around these parts used a scythe anymore, or at least were not admitting it. So when I had voluntarily done it, I became destined to be something different from all the other yahoos around here. There is a well-known name for such fools; they are known as "volunteers."

My Dad had always warned me about becoming a volunteer because he had also assured me that, "Once the world knows that you have done it the first time, it expects you to keep right on doing it." He was right, just like he most always was. Another problem that compounded all of this lay in the fact that I am also a slow learner.

Later that same day, we rode up into a small side valley near there and be damned if we didn't ride into a huge band of domestic sheep. This was not their range Bishop assured us and he then proceeded to really blow his stack. When he got carried away that way, he had a temper that would sometimes turn his face beet red. Luckily for the herders, they were not at their camp, so we turned around and rode back down to our cabin at the lower end of the valley.

Meeting those sheep did not really surprise me, since I had already known that they were in the general vicinity. When I had been working for Tex, we had run into them in the mountains a little further to the east. But Bishop figured these sheep were coming down too low into the valleys.[10] This time there could be no question that these sheep were being poorly managed; the hillsides behind them were completely denuded of grass and small bushes. The herders were simply not moving their flocks fast enough.

Bishop and I had a mutual dislike for sheep herders but for different reasons. The year before, when Steve Johnson (from the time of Tex and the "Great River Rafting Scheme")

---

10 The sheepman–cattleman agreement stipulated that sheep graze the high ridges and cattle graze the valley bottoms. Sometimes this worked and other times it didn't because both sides were always accusing each other of cheating on the agreement.

and I were guiding hunters, we met one of the herders and we had a long visit with him, which gave us considerable insight as to how they operated.

When our conversation got around to hunting, he started telling us stories about how the sheepmen had a vendetta against all the larger carnivores, especially bears. He bragged about having actually shot ninety-two bears in the previous three summers and that his partner, who had another band of sheep, had killed more than he had. Most of them had been black bears, "But we killed lots of grizzlies too," he assured us.

This sheep herder then went on to describe how they "indirectly" killed many more meat eaters than these bears he had boasted about. He showed us a large supply of strychnine that he said all the herders carried. Anytime they located a sheep that had been killed by predators or died from eating poison weeds, they laced the carcass with strychnine, because anything that might come back to eat on it was considered to be no good for anything anyway.

While we were visiting with this fellow, we had been sitting in his camp eating our lunch that we had brought with us. When we got up to leave, Johnson still had two tins of sardines left over and was about to put them back into his saddle bag, when the herder asked him if he could have them.

"I can put them to damn good use," he said.

Sardines at that time, cost only nine cents a can, so Steve tossed him both the cans, both of us wondering what the herder was going to use them for.

He set both of the tins on a block of wood, took his jack-knife, and proceeded to cut a small V-shaped hole into each can and folded the flap up. He then reached into his coat pocket and brought out a large vanilla bottle full of strychnine and dolloped what looked to be a half teaspoon of "sweetener" into each can. He then folded the flap back down and seemed to be finished with then.

When I asked him what he figured he was going to kill with those little bombs, he replied, "Tomorrow I'll be leaving this camp for another range, but I'll leave these two cans here as a reward for anything that wants them. Any critter with teeth strong enough to bite through that tin, deserves what's inside."

In those days I had a mighty callous constitution but I can still remember being taken back a notch or two by this old bastard's bloodthirsty attitude towards wildlife.

Later on in that same year when I was visiting in Clinton, I checked some of this out with other people who knew the herders better than I did. All of the information I was able to glean out of them, said the same thing: all sheepmen had much the same viewpoint.

Game Warden Bill Fenton suggested that the only way we could ever expect to put a stop to this type of slaughter was to somehow get the sheep completely out of the mountains.

"The laws are vague that cover this problem, but common law has always said that a farmer has the right to protect his livestock, using any methods he wants to." He shook his head and added, "If those sheep are up there, the herders are going to protect them and you also know goddamn well that the cattlemen do very much the same things for exactly the same reasons."

I knew this to be absolutely true because with my new rifle, I had actually become part of the problem, so Fenton was beginning to pierce my conscience a bit. His final words on the subject were: "Someday this country may have to make a final decision as to what we most want up in those mountains, because in the end, I doubt if predators and livestock can really co-exist up there."

A few days after the encounter with the sheep in Graveyard Valley, Bishop and the rest of the crew packed up and returned back down to Hungry Valley where we had previously dropped about half the summer herd. The Graveyard cow-camp is located in beautiful mountain country, so this time I very willingly volunteered to spend the summer there alone. My job was to keep these cattle from straying back down the trail before they were wanted at the lower end.

For me, it was like having a paid holiday. No boss hollering, "Drop your cocks and grab your socks," at 4:00 A.M. every morning. At last I was again back into a job that allowed me to set my own hours of work. Bishop would soon discover if I was doing my job or not, because if I got lazy, some of these cattle would start showing up down in the lower valleys, and as he very explicitly informed me, that would tell him what I was or was not up to at the Graveyard camp. It was going to be fun, but there was considerable responsibility that came with it.

I was left with my pick of four horses so that I could not only alternate saddle horses but also use the others to pack block salt. Part of my job was to distribute salt blocks into a few key areas. We used this salt as much for controlling cattle as feeding them. Wherever the salt is dropped on the open range, it tends to keep the cattle congregated in that general area, rather than have them wander into places where they were not wanted. It's not a totally effective system, but it was good enough to be considered useful. My grub supply was a bit on the skimpy side, which was typical of Gang Ranch cowcamps, but there were some very large Dolly Varden trout in the creek right at the cabin door, and red meat on the mountain if I could catch it. At that time, all Gang Ranch cowcamps were expected to live off the land as best we could, so there was almost always a deer carcass hanging in a sack from a tree near our camp site. In the cowcamp we rarely ate beef.

A few days after Bishop left, I rose quite early, caught myself a trout for breakfast, and was cooking it when a small plane buzzed so close to the cabin that it almost knocked the tin stove pipe off. By the time I ran outside to see what the hell was going on, the plane was making another run at the cabin, but this time someone was leaning out of the passenger door and threw a loaded gunny sack at me. The sack missed me and the cabin but it hit very close to where I had my wrangle horse picketed. It spooked him so badly that he hit the end of the rope at a full run and pulled out the picket stake. Down the trail towards Hungry Valley he went at a full gallop, dragging the rope and stake. The other three horses had been grazing off a ways, but they saw it all too, so they took off running in the opposite direction. Holy Christ, I was afoot!

It did not make much sense to curse that goddamn plane and whoever was in it, but I did it anyway. The three loose horses had no hobbles or encumbrances of any type, so I quickly decided that my best bet was to follow the wrangle horse that was dragging the rope. I grabbed my hat and immediately took off after him. This was an emergency and breakfast was going to have to wait. Although I was quite certain that the horse would soon tangle himself up, I also knew when he did so, he would probably throw another fit and break the rope or halter. If that happened, there would not be the slightest chance of ever laying my hands on him until he got to the Hungry Valley camp, eighteen miles away.

I was desperate and began jogging after the drag mark that the picket stake was making and I soon found that jogging in a pair of riding boots equipped with full western riding heels can be a wobbly situation. The trail that the horse was following ran through heavy timber, but do you know, that son-of-bitch was able to go ten miles before I finally did locate him, all loved up to a small spruce tree. The tracks there told me that he had tried to pull the tree or break the rope, but luckily for me, everything held. After I untangled him and calmed him down a bit, I made up a war bridle from the picket rope so I could ride him back to camp bareback. His name was Star and he was a well broke horse, but after his morning's ordeal, he remembered all his coltish tricks of bucking, and he sure as hell wanted nothing to do with going back up that trail. He dumped me, not once but twice, so I ended up having to walk and lead him the ten miles back to the cabin.

I was twenty-one years old and had just walked and jogged twenty miles with no breakfast, so by the time I got home, my belly was warning me of the possibility that my throat might have been cut. As I turned the corner of the meadow to where I could see the cabin, there, not thirty feet from the door, stood my other three horses. Thank God for small favours! After re-picketing my wrangle horse, I swallowed a few cups of cold coffee and ate my half-cooked breakfast fish. By that time I had cooled down enough to retrieve the goddamn gunny sack that had ruined a beautiful Chilcotin summer day.

I was expecting my summer groceries and mail to be in the sack, but all it contained was two slabs of bacon, a five-pound can of coffee, and five boxes of 30:06 cartridges. There was also a very short note. All it said was, "The sheep are still up in Little Graveyard. Shoot as many as you can." It was signed Wm. S.

This was not much groceries for two months and the note hardly replaced the mail I was expecting, but it sure did open up another very interesting proposition. I didn't have any qualms about doing what the note instructed, but it was too late to do it that day, so I slept on it for the night.

The next morning I was up and off shortly after daylight to ride the nine miles or so to where I had last seen those sheep. I decided to approach the area from behind a long high mountain shoulder. It seemed like a wise idea to locate the herder first in case he had any objections to my shooting his sheep. The fact that every sheep herder I had ever seen carried a rifle every bit as good as the one I had suggested that perhaps a little discretion should be observed.

When I finally crested the ridge at the head of the valley, I could not see a single sheep. After sitting there for a few minutes, I decided to ride down to where I figured the camp might be, but all the way down the mountain there was not a sign of man or beast. I knew they had been there because the valley was eaten completely out of feed.

When I got down into the timberline along the head of the creek, I located a very recently abandoned camp site. The ashes were still hot, so I knew that the herder had just broke camp that same morning and all the horse and sheep tracks told me that they had headed out through the head of the valley. Bishop had already told me that the area on the other side of that mountain was considered to be sheep country, so I decided to leave well enough alone. I was still tired and footsore from the day before, so I located a nice warm slope and slept most of the day away. That evening Star carried me and a hundred unfired cartridges back to our own camp.

I spent the majority of my summer riding and exploring the watersheds along the heads of Big Creek and Relay Creek, which is quite a large piece of real estate. In most parts of the world, creeks the size of these ones would be referred to as rivers, so that might give you a better idea of the size of the area.

It remained a beautiful, sunny summer and I must have ridden well over a thousand miles. I spent my time hazing cattle back into the high basins after the snarly summer storms had chased them out, laying on mountain sides, daydreaming the time away, talking with my horses, visiting the huge marmot colonies that are scattered all over those hills, trying to get as close to hundreds of other larger wild animals as prudence would allow - and above all - being glad and thankful of being able to be there. If there is such a thing as heaven on earth, then I had found it.

As all good things must come to an end, so did my summer at Graveyard Valley. Late into the summer a message came up the trail telling me that my folks would like me to come and visit before winter. Bishop had already decided that I had been there alone long enough and he had located two other cowboys who would finish up the rest of the season here, so I packed up and headed out to take a break in civilization. As Bishop said one day, "I don't want to be held responsible for you becoming any more bushed than you already are."

As I passed through the Gang Ranch headquarters, my luck was still holding because Bill Studdert was there with the cheque book. This time he was living in the small house beside the store where the store keeper and manager lived and after supper he invited me in to have a visit. Marsh Brown, the store keeper was there and be damned if Bill didn't pour us both a good sized drink, something unheard of to do for a hired hand on the Gang Ranch. We all had a good visit, mostly reminiscing my summer in the hills and a few other cowboy stories.

When the conversation got around to the sheep herder incident, I found out why I never found those sheep in the valley. Studdert had dropped them a note at the same time, warning them that the entire cowcamp was coming up for them.

This time Studdert was not drunk but he did have a good glow on. Our conversation must have really warmed the old bugger up because he got out the cheque book and paid me off at the rate of $125 per month.

He didn't charge me for my store bill or the five boxes of rifle cartridges either.

CHAPTER 12

I HAD BEEN STAYING in Clinton with my folks for a couple
of months, but by early December I decided I couldn't winter
there. There was just nothing there for me. I had tried a few
other jobs that paid a great deal more than cowboying, but
other than the money, nothing seemed to fit.

It was a strange time in this part of B.C. Up until then the
ranching industry had been the major employer, with very
few jobs outside of it. The tourist industry was just beginning
to develop and consisted of seasonal jobs in hunting camps,
fishing lodges, and dude ranches. These new operations paid
almost double what the ranchers did and because the type of
work was, in many ways, quite similar, so they lured quite a
few cowboys and ranch hands away from their old jobs. Many
ranchers resented this development and became antagonistic
towards the tourist industry.

Most of those ranchers flat out refused to raise wages to
compete and this created another side-effect that further
angered them. Many of the men who stayed with the ranchers
did so only because they were not mentally or socially suited
to dealing with the public, so the ranchers got left with a high
percentage of strange social misfits. Don't get me wrong,
because a lot of good men stayed; only the percentages

changed. Since most of the "bushed" hands had no choice but to stay, they became much more noticeable.

The logging industry was getting into second gear about then too and it, in turn, paid about double what the tourist industry paid. So by this time, the ranchers were really beginning to lose most of their best hands, especially true of anybody mechanically inclined. There were a few construction jobs that were paying fabulous wages, but most of those went to the union halls down in Vancouver. We heard stories of how some of the B.C. Hydro jobs paid as high as $1,500 per month with cooks serving up the type of food that we had never even heard of before.

We were living in changing times and few could avoid being affected. It's never easy to leave the comfortable old ways and embrace the new but during the mid to late '50s, these decisions had to be made. There were lots of jobs available and any able-bodied man that claimed to be unemployed for more than three days was simply not looking for work. I can still quite vividly remember hearing about the first men who were drawing unemployment insurance during this boom time. They were held in total contempt by the rest of the community. Hell, they were even shunned in the Clinton pool hall. Times change don't they?

Jobs for men were so plentiful that sometimes we had to hide to avoid jobs that we didn't like. Many times when in Clinton, Kamloops, and Williams Lake employers would stop me on the street and ask if I was looking for a job. A man without education or training could still get in on the big buck jobs. All he had to say to the employer was, "I don't know anything about this kind of work, but I'm sure willing to learn." Those were the only words the boss wanted to hear and a moment later they would be recording our vital statistics.

If there were lots of jobs for men, it was not the same for women. Young women without an education were almost completely relegated into domestic help or slinging hash in a restaurant and you know what that pay amounts to. Looking back on it now, it still seems strange why women were so rarely offered the chance to draw top dollar wages while learning a job like the men were.

Like everyone else, I became caught up in these changing times but being single left me with many more options than married men my age. I vowed then and there I sure as hell was not going to get caught into a marriage I could not afford and the best way to avoid the temptation was to head back into the bush and try locating a new lifestyle that would offer more financial rewards than being a cowboy. It was a great life for the young and healthy but you couldn't ignore the fact that the job burns you out and ages you prematurely.

About this time, I finally made the decision to strike off for the real north country, possibly all the way to the Yukon. The way I had it figured, the following spring would be a good time to start, so I bought a pair of good sound horses because I was going to go by horseback and slowly prospect my way north. Mom and I collected all the government maps that we could locate and spread them out on the front room floor where we pored over them for days. At the speed I wanted to travel, it looked like the trip might take as long as two years, but I knew it was going to be fun and not only that, it would probably end up being the adventure of my life. We knew the ride could be done because fifty-five years earlier, a Chilcotin rancher by the name of Norman Lee had driven a herd of cattle right to the edge of the Klondike country. If he could make it with a herd of cattle, then sure as hell, I could make it with two or three horses.

After making a deal with a rancher to winter my horses until spring, I went back to the Gang Ranch to feed cattle for the winter in order to add more needed dollars to my bundle for the coming northward journey.

The ranch I came back to was sure different from the one I had left two months earlier. Big Bob, old Lem the Chinese cook, and Marcel were all gone. Jim Bishop had finally received his coveted job as manager and so was now at the top of the Gang Ranch heap. A horse breaker by name of Jim MacDonald was now cowboss and Wiley Holt was the new mechanic. We now had a woman cook, Bessie Zimmerly, and she was as good as they could possibly come. Her son Charley was there too as a feed or ranch hand, the same as I was. Some of the old hands like Jimmy Rosette, Jim Russell, Louis Johnson and his two sons, Antoine Billy and Don (Blackwater) Woodward, and a few others were all going to be my winter work partners.

I arrived a few days before Christmas, just in time to get ready to help feed 1,500 brood cows and 250 five-year-old steers. I don't remember how or why the latter were being held in the main headquarters area; they should have long since been driven up the forty miles to the "Steer Ranch."

However, they were there that winter and stranger still was their age, because five-year-old steers were almost unheard of since most animals then were slaughtered at the two-year level. Keeping them longer, especially in Canada where the winters are long, meant that the cost of feeding them hay over an extra two or three winters, made very questionable economics. Up to that time, there had been a very small and specialized market for commercial sized meat cuts, sometimes called "man sized." While they were not all that common, many restaurants still had several sizes of steaks on their menus, ranging from eight-ounce breakfast steaks up to thirty-ounce dinner steaks. One time when I was on holiday in Portland Oregon, I saw a seventy-two-ounce steak actually listed on the menu. These huge steaks would be hard to cut off of a two-year-old carcass, so there had been a limited market for large steers.

As it turned out, it was a very risky market too, because suddenly the market bottomed out on them and that was why we ended up having to feed them for yet another winter. Studdert, certain the price for them would go up, left instructions with Bishop to keep these oxen fed right up. He was gambling that the market would recover and then we were to ship them so the ranch could make a bundle.

I was assigned to feed brood cows, so that's what my work partner, Antoine Billy, and I did all winter. At that time, the ranch was again at one of its low ebbs, as all motorized equipment except for one Jeep truck had broken down. This winter everything was going to be done with honest horse power which suited most of us just fine. Out of a winter crew of about twenty men, I don't believe more than four of them knew how to drive a mechanized rig anyway. The entire outfit slipped back into the 1880s and most of us thought that it was the way it ought to be. Everybody in the crew was horsey or we wouldn't have been there.

Antoine and I were given a team of beautiful sorrel Clydes and a big hay sleigh which we used daily to feed out three loads of loose hay to 500 cows. In the headquarters crew there were four sleighs working and Jim Russell, along with Dave Gilpin, were feeding another herd up at the Old Home Ranch, twelve miles up Gaspard Creek. Jim MacDonald and his cowboy crew were still out gathering in the strays and they were scheduled to be doing that, off and on for most of the winter, as the late roundup on the Gang Ranch was never really over. It seemed like there was always another stray or bunch of them, showing up some place, so this was the time of year that a cowboy really earned his money.

The range is so vast that it is impossible to locate all the cattle before the snow becomes too deep. Those cows remaining will not come out of the gullies and canyons without manmade encouragement. Older cows that have been to the feed yard before, become quite wise about heading for the haystack in the late fall but yearlings, who have been fed only once, are quite stupid about wanting to winter alone. Bulls are the most witless of all cattle, as I have watched them actually heading uphill when the first winter storms hit.

About half-way through the winter, it was becoming obvious that we were going to be short of hay, especially if those steers remained and continued to consume two loads a day. We could still be bailed out, however; the Gang owned a large hay ranch near Cache Creek where they had a thousand tons of hay that they were trying to sell. Bishop wanted that hay either hauled up to the Gang Ranch or the steers hauled down to the hay stack, but Studdert would not authorize anyone to do the hauling.

Jim Bishop had been born just across Churn Creek in Empire Valley and he had been a livestock man all his life, so it must have been out of sheer desperation when he ordered us to cut the feed to the brood cows in half. The Gang Ranch had always had a reputation for being niggardly cattle feeders, so these new rations became a starvation diet. Jim must have known that, if it went on for long enough, there would be a hell of a price to pay during spring calving time. He must have been gambling on an early spring or a mid winter thaw, so he could turn some of the cattle out onto the rich bunchgrass range that the Gang used to be famous for.[11]

However, it turned out to be a long cold winter with too much snow and the reprieve never came. About two-thirds of the way through the winter the cows began to die. It began slowly: the first week after it started, only a few of them perished but, by the end of the second week, two or three

---

11 One of the qualities that makes Bluebunch wheatgrass such valuable forage lies in the fact that, even when it is frozen and snowed over, it still retains a very high food value.

went every day. It became so bad that it became one man's job just to haul dead cows out of the feed yards and take them to the dump two miles away. And still we pumped two loads of our best hay into those fat steers, every day. One very cold morning we found a registered Hereford bull, dead and frozen against the outside door of the horse barn. It took four of us to clear it from the door so we could enter the barn and get our teams.

One evening when I was in the store visiting with Bishop and Marsh Brown, the store and time keeper, Studdert phoned up to see how things were going. The telephone was one of those really old fashioned "blower" types that could be heard all over the room, so I stayed and eavesdropped. Both Bishop and Brown pleaded with Studdert to either start trucking hay in or steers out, but it was still no go. Old cowboys do not like to be seen crying, but I believe Jim was, because he went into the back room for a while and then, when he did come out front again, he bid us good night and went straight to his room.

Things were falling apart in other ways too. Recently, the food wholesalers who supplied the ranch had cut off their credit. No grub bill had been paid in a year. Studdert had put them on the Compulsory Banking System too. It was getting very depressing for all of us, but it must have been much more so for Jim Bishop. As the manager, all of this was sure to somehow reflect onto him.

As the regular grub was running low, Bishop finally did make a decision to do something about those big fat steers. We started eating them. We tied into those animals with a relish and we ate the hind quarters from two of them every week. I don't remember what we did with the front quarter but that wet silage fed beef was the finest I have ever eaten in my life. Bessie fed us huge steaks for breakfast and lunch and for supper we had our choice of steaks or roasts. There were several other young men at that table, so between us, we had the appetites to indirectly balance out some of the hay problems. Sometimes even now, I dream of eating those platter-sized steaks.

It must have been about the first of April before the winter began to release its deadly grip on us and that is late for the Fraser River benchland. The old grass reluctantly started to show through the snow in a few spots of bare ground, so we knew that spring had to come soon. Studdert finally relented and started the hay trucks into the ranch about the same time as the roads began caving in from the spring breakup. By that time a third of the brood cows were dead and the ones that survived were in such poor condition that many of them would be too weak to nurse their soon-to-be-born calves. Those cows would be lucky to save their own lives.

Bill Studdert appeared with the first baled hay. But this time he arrived in a black mood: cold sober but short and snappy with everybody. Many of the winter crew had had enough and wanted their wages so they could just get away from the place. It had become so depressing that hardly anybody was able to laugh or tell a joke any more.

One evening Studdert did get out the cheque book and started writing out the wages. After he had written cheques for half the crew, he said he was getting tired and would settle up with the rest of us first thing in the morning. That was no problem because, since the stage was not due for two more days, nobody had any way to leave unless they were prepared to walk. A couple of the Indians had their own horses there, so they saddled up that night and left.

At five A.M. the next morning, just as the "wake-up bell" started bonging, we all heard the plane start to warm up and five minutes later Studdert and his cheque book were airborne, leaving no word about when he might be back. It might not

One of the piles of dead cattle (about 450 head) that died on Gang Ranch during the winter of 1957. It was Bill Studdert's doing, but Jim Bishop took most of the flak over it.

be until about mid summer, considering how he usually spaced out his visits to the ranch.

As it turned out, about half the crew was hooked and I was one of them. Our choice was to either stay until Studdert returned or leave with nothing, as others had done before. Bishop thought it was quite funny and I believe to this day that he had something set up with Bill to keep me too broke to leave. I had probably made a mistake by telling everybody about my northward plans because it is quite possible that Bishop had other plans for me.

The more I thought about it, the more I was sure of it and it really pissed me off, so I decided to quit right then and there. I refused to work the next day while waiting for the stage and I spent most of it wandering around soaking up the spring sunshine and taking a few pictures of the ranch. I also photographed the dead cattle where they had been rolled over the cliff near the mouth of Gaspard Creek into the dump. In that particular pile there were at least 450 carcasses and in another pile near the ranch there were fifty more. I had no particular use or intent for those photos. I took them as some sort of memento of a very strange winter and set of circumstances. How often does a person see a herd of cattle squandered that way? I knew my folks would be interested to see, as well as hear, what had happened. Furthermore, if I found a nook in the north country, I might never see the Gang Ranch country again and so I wanted a reminder of these days.

One smart thing that I did do that day while wandering around trying to cool my temper down, was to ask Marsh Brown, the time-keeper, to give me a time sheet. When he was making it up, he laughed and told me that he had never made one for someone not being paid on the spot. He also told me (perhaps as advice) that he had never heard of the Gang Ranch ever mailing anybody their wages, as it had always been a cheque on the counter or nothing. I already knew this but I was still hoping to meet Studdert in town and get him to issue payment there, so I wouldn't have to come all the way back out to the ranch. I was still planning to start my ride north in early June, so I was sure hoping Studdert would show up somewhere around the district before then, because I needed that $600.

Neither Marsh, Bishop, nor I realized it then, but that single sheet of paper represented a turning point in the history of the Gang Ranch and, to some degree, the cattle industry of B.C.

CHAPTER 13

THE SCUTTLEBUTT IN THE COW COUNTRY had it that a cowboy who sicks a lawyer onto the cattle industry will never punch cows again. But I was so mad that I didn't care at this point. I wanted to go north right then, so I said to hell with their cowboy jobs and I chose the lawyer route.

That might sound like the quick and easy way to justice, but this was British Columbia in 1957 and when it came to labour laws, Old Lady Justice had not found this part of the world yet. The lawyer in Ashcroft that I hired agreed to collect my wages for a fee of fifteen percent, but after he located a judge that would issue the garnishee, we discovered that the Gang Ranch bank account was empty. At that time, I was staying in Clinton with my folks again and my situation began attracting more than a little attention because I was the first person that they had ever heard of who had tried collecting wages from the Gang Ranch in this way. Some figured it might even be the first time anybody had collected wages in this way from the entire cattle industry. Some ranchers in the area were rather cool towards me and we realized that not all of them were really all that well disposed towards what we thought was fair play.

The lawyer turned up some interesting information about

how Studdert and the Gang Ranch did business. It appeared that he would come up to Canada to pay bills only when he absolutely had to, and even at that, he would only deposit enough money into the bank to cover current cheques.

When Dad suggested to the lawyer that he should slap a lien against the cattle or some equipment, he refused to do it because he felt that the amount of money owing was not large enough to warrant such an action. His advice was to wait until Studdert banked some money, or forget about it like everybody else had been doing. That was his opinion and not mine but he was the only lawyer in the district, so it appeared that I was going to have to wait my problem out, whether I wanted to or not. A long time later, a mutual friend told me that Studdert and the lawyer were personal friends, so that might explain why he was so reluctant to get the account settled as quickly as I thought it should have been.

I hung around Clinton and stewed in my juices for a few weeks, trying to figure out what to do next. Even a town as small as Clinton was then, can be an expensive place for a young person to kill time in, so I knew I had to find another job away from the temptations of urban living. My frustrations made me so goddamn angry at the cattle industry that I promised myself that, only as a last resort, would I ever work for ranchers again.

One evening there was a knock at my parents' door and it turned out to be the local R.C.M.P. corporal who wanted to talk to me. He had learned that I had some interesting pictures and he would like to see them. Of course the ones he wanted to see were those I had taken on my last day at the Gang Ranch. He looked them over and then asked if he could borrow the negatives for a while. At that point we realized that trouble was brewing, but it wasn't ours to worry about, so I had no objections to him taking them.

Mounties aren't that open about their intentions, but in a

little town, news can't be corked up for longer than an hour or so, and speculation ran rampant. Within a few days the Mountie brought the negatives back and did volunteer the information that he and a representative of the S.P.C.A. had flown out to the Gang to verify the information and take some pictures of their own. Within a day or so, a warrant was issued in Studdert's name to come and answer to charges of animal cruelty, but he was living in the U.S. and it was not the sort of charge that he could be extradited for, and he refused to come back to B.C. at that time. Later we were told that his lawyers had one of his other buddies go into court and proxy for him and the Gang Ranch was then fined the ruinous sum of $100 for neglecting their livestock.

Even though some sort of justice had been meted out to the Gang, it still did not put my wages into my pocket. Without that money my folks and I decided that my assets were too lean to finance my northward journey, so I decided to put the trip off for a year. I was still smarting and angry at the legal fortress that I had bumped up against, so rather than go back to work for anybody else, I decided to gather what outfit I already had, go back into the mountains of the Gang Ranch country, and spend the following summer prospecting and living completely on my own. The Gang Ranch country is located in a gold-bearing region and there are traces of other minerals too, so this plan had possibilities.

Mom could hardly wait for me to get started, as I had made a promise to mail her, whenever I could, a daily account of my travels. I often suspected that if she had been twenty years younger, she would have volunteered to come along. She had originally been raised on a farm and loved the land, but Dad had tried logging, fishing, and farming, but had never liked any of them. He was much more of a social person, who enjoyed the camaraderie of living in a town.

However, we were all in agreement that for the next few

months I should go back to the Gang Ranch country. I persuaded one of my friends who had a one-ton truck that looked like it could make the trip, to haul my summer grub supplies to the end of the last road, where we cached it out of sight. Then it was back into town with him and up to the ranch where my horses had been wintering. After collecting these summer companions, I headed back into the area where I had been riding and hunting for the past two years. It was like returning home.

Some things were going to be a great deal different though, as I was now going to be living completely out in the open, or at best, under canvas. The tent I had was very small and the weather had turned mostly wet again, so it was going to be a cold, damp life with no heated building to dry out in. But I was young, strong and stupider than I am today, and as far as I was concerned, my immediate future was going to be paved in gold dust and wildflowers. This time I came better prepared. I had maps that could take me much further into the mountains than I had ever been before, and I was anticipating true high adventure.

When I started out, what I knew about prospecting could have been written on the head of a pin with a large cold chisel, but I had a geiger counter, a gold pan, and a couple of good books on the subject, so it was "learn as you travel." The books had been given to me by Lawrence Frenier, an experienced prospector in Clinton who had befriended our family. Frenier was well known in central B.C. as he was the discoverer of several paying ore properties. He assured me, that with these books along with what he had already taught me from his rock samples, I should be able to start identifying the more obvious mineral showings. He was right. Within a week or so, I astounded myself by what I was able to recognize from those books and his brief teaching. Perhaps my school

Choate's prospecting camp during the summer of 1957.

teachers had been right about the value of instruction books.

Once I got into the higher hills where the ground was broken open by gullies, creeks and old quake cracks, I began prospecting in earnest. Within a few days, I knew that I was correctly identifying different types of rocks and mineral showings that needed further checking out. This entire region had been continuously prospected for over a hundred years, but all prospectors have rainbows in their eyes, as they dream of finding the big one that the others may have missed.

For me, it was a wonderful summer of riding, roaming, and generally just doing as I pleased. One thing about prospecting, you really learn the country well. When we had been hunting or cowboying, we would often ride up onto high points of land to look over the area below, but prospecting took me right down into the bottoms of the roughest ground I could find, hoping it was the type of land that the oldtimers might have bypassed. I was carrying a watch that had a luminous dial and several times when I forgot to leave it at camp, the readings on the geiger counter set my adrenalin on fire.

After a month or so in the bush, I decided to ride down to the Gang Ranch to find out if Studdert had returned yet. There was also my promise to Mom that I would send out word, from time to time, telling her how things were going. There is a post office at the Gang and Mom had given me several pre-stamped post cards for this purpose. I didn't want her imagining the worst, so it seemed like a good idea to reassure her that nothing had gotten me yet.

From where I was then camped in upper Churn Creek, it took me two easy days of riding to arrive down at the ranch headquarters. As I rode into the yard that day, I had a slight case of butterfly stomach from wondering just what sort of reception I would get when I arrived right into the centre of the lion's den.

There was nobody around the yard when I rode up, so I tied the horses to the hitch rail and headed for the post office/store. I was lucky to find it open because in these small country places, they are often closed for days at a time. I was happy to see that Marsh Brown, who I was hoping was still my buddy, was still the store keeper. Marsh's mouth showed his surprise when he saw me walk through the door, so I tried my best to brazen out the entire visit, as if I didn't care a bit what anybody thought about anything. In a way, it was not all an act. After a few minutes of discussing the weather and a few local topics, I figured I had a good handle on the situation, so I started pumping Marsh for information.

I don't think that Marsh was intimidated by me, but he did know my problem from the beginning and, being a decent sort of person when Studdert wasn't around, he finally did open up and told me what he knew. Some of what he passed on would have got him fired on the spot, if the wrong person ever learned about it.

He told me that when Studdert had found out that I had hired a lawyer to collect my wages, he blew his plug. That much I suspected anyway. Even so, Marsh did not believe Bill had made any definite plans as to how he was going to deal with the situation, other than leaving word with Marsh not to sell me anything out of the store.

Marsh also warned me not to expect any assistance from the rest of the crew because they too, had orders to shun me. We came to the conclusion that the only plan Studdert probably had up was to try and starve me out of the Gang Ranch country so I wouldn't become a bad influence on their hired hands. Marsh made one comment that had a real ring of truth to it.

"My guess is that Old Bill figures he has to make an example of you and I bet he'll do everything he can to avoid ever paying you. He has enough money and influence to stall you off in the courts, almost forever," he warned.

These were not brand new thoughts to me, but now, hearing someone else suggest it, made me angrier the more I thought of it. However, I had long since made the decision to carry this thing through, no matter what the consequences might be, so I was committed. I think that stubbornness and determination are natural traits for those of us that are some sort of British/Krauts, so the old Irishman and I had set ourselves onto a collision course. By this time the money itself was becoming more and more incidental.

After an hour or so visiting with Marsh, I could see that he was getting nervous about having me in the store for so long. By then some of the other hands had passed through and knew I was there, and there was always the possibility that someone might blab to Studdert when he returned, about how neighbourly Marsh had acted towards me. His job was not a well paying one, but at sixty-five, he would have trouble finding another. Cowboys are not known as blabberers, but somebody might decide that by doing so, he could get a bonus or at least a paycheque the next time Studdert passed through. So rather than compromise Marsh any further, I decided to leave.

At the last minute when I remembered to mail one of Mom's post cards, he seemed quite surprised that I would still trust the Gang Ranch to send it on. Then he suddenly remembered that there was a letter for me somewhere in the back and he went to find it. Marsh seemed quite embarrassed since he knew damn well that I knew, he had orders from Studdert to either pigeon hole it or lose it altogether. We must have exchanged looks over that letter, but I do remember that I kept my mouth shut about it, which was a wonder in itself.

After I had packed the few extra groceries that Marsh had sold me on the sly onto the pack horse, I mounted up and turned our heads back towards the hills, which by then had become my home both physically and mentally. I had only ridden up the first series of hills when I spotted another rider coming across a side trail to the wagon road and pretty soon he caught up to me. It turned out to be Jim Bishop, who was still manager, but as he said that day, "Sometimes I like to get away from the ranch yard and make some of those dumb bastards think for themselves for a change."

We rode along together for an hour or so, but Jim was not his usual sarcastic self towards me. During this ride he laid on a mighty heavy lecture.

"It's a terrible thing that you have done to the Gang Ranch and your old friend Studdert," he said.

"You knew goddamn well that Bill would have eventually paid you off without going through all this lawyer bullshit. From here on, you had better be damn careful what you do around this part of the country, because the Gang Ranch cannot possibly let you get away with this. Otherwise, every two-bit ranch hand will be trying the same thing on all of the other ranchers, every time they think they have some little grievance."

When our trails parted that afternoon, the last thing Bishop said was, "You young bastard, you think that you're pulling a smart trick on us, but you're going to learn that you cannot treat millionaires like Studdert and Skelton this way because they just aren't going to let you get away with it".

The two-day ride back to my camp in the low mountains gave me a lot of time to contemplate the day's conversations and the entire situation itself. Jim Bishop was probably right; the Gang was almost certain to make my life more interesting but I couldn't see any way that they might be able to do me any harm, short of flat out shooting me. Other than these two horses and the gear that was tied onto them, I had nothing of value to be taken. I had no fear whatsoever for my life because, of all the squeezing stories I had ever heard, nobody around here had ever been shot.

There was still most of the summer left, so now that I had at least a month's experience in learning travelling and camping skills, I decided it was time to ride to the end of my maps and perhaps even beyond. I needed to really test myself by going into completely unknown mountains and crossing bigger creeks and rivers. I realized that there were many such situations waiting for me when I finally got all my act together and started for the Yukon, so it was imperative that I learn as much about these things as possible so that I could not only make the ride but survive it as well. This summer the south Chilcotin mountains were going to become my training ground.

After picking up the rest of my camp from the centre of

the Gang Ranch range country, I started a leisurely ride southwest towards the Taseko mountains, always present in the distance. Locally, these mountains are also known as the "Snow Mountains of Big Creek." There was no hurry because I had absolutely no time objectives or particular places to reach. There was at least three months' grub on the pack horse consisting mostly of dried apples, pancake flour, sugar, dried soup mixes, rice, pot barley, and a few spices. In those days my "Free Miner's Licence" allowed me to kill wild meat, so I was home free until snow-fly time.

I lived every day just for itself and when I went to bed at night, I seldom had any specific plans for the following day. Many of those days I never bothered to move camp, sometimes because of bad weather, but other times because either the scenery or wild animals around me made the place so interesting that moving on made no sense at all. It was the sort of summer that every kid who wants to should have the opportunity to experience at least once.

Sometime that summer the life of roaming, looking, and learning eventually overpowered the desire to hit paydirt. I did locate gold colours in several of the creeks, but Lawrence Frenier had told me that these traces had been noticed a long time ago. The object was, he said, to locate the real pay streak that nobody had yet been able to find. These colours come from somewhere, he explained enthusiastically and he was certain that such a bonanza existed in this area. He was sure that if and when it was ever found, it would probably be by a greenhorn relying on pure blind luck. The way he had it figured, the Chilcotin or Taseko gold deposit must be covered with either glacial or volcanic overburden, but someday someone was going to stumble onto it.

When Lawrence talked about these things, his eyes got bigger every time he explained what he thought was a new probability. After knowing Lawrence for years, I began to realize that he had contracted and continuously suffered from a rare disease. It's called "gold fever."[12]

As that summer wore on, my enthusiasm for discovering a recoverable ore body in these mountains seemed to wane with every new day. Mining, especially exploratory mine assessment work, is the most destructive activity that can happen in these high altitude areas. Even the slight possibility of having to watch these beautiful mountains and alpine valleys being torn up to extract questionable amounts of gold, seemed to me like it was getting mighty close to criminal intent. Roaming these hills for over four months that year convinced me that long term green would have far more value than short term gold. I believe that was also the year that I decided I never wanted the responsibility of becoming rich. The fact that I was somewhat on the lazy side helped quite a lot in making that decision.

I had many interesting experiences that summer. How about the day I tried crossing Churn Creek when the water was too high? I could see some interesting looking prospects on the opposite side of a crossing that I had never forded before, so they had to be checked out. This creek is another one of those misnamed mountain rivers, especially in the early summer, such as it was then.

The horse I was riding was young and strong and he never hesitated when I started him into the water. About ten feet out from shore, the bottom seemed to drop out from under all that swift running water and I suddenly discovered that the force of it was far more than I had reckoned with. Things

---

12 The bonanza not only eluded me that year but also to this day. I was able to locate two other mineral showings that looked good, but the assays said that the percentages were nowhere near commercial value. Over the years since then, we have spotted other showings that, on the surface, looked interesting but have never amounted to anything.

happened fast because at that instant, the horse was swimming and touching bottom only occasionally, but we both understood that there could be no turning back, so I gave him his head and hoped for the best. There was not even time to pray and I can assure you that in cold mountain water it becomes hard to even think.

About half-way across, the horse stumbled over what must have been a large rock and we both rolled over in what must have been five or six feet of churning Churn Creek. We both surfaced intact, but by then I was out of the saddle and floating free on the lower side of the horse. There was a big water chute not far below that crossing and we were being swept right towards it. I can still remember seeing those whitecaps and the boiling wave up against the canyon wall. It was like looking at the black hole in the wrong end of a gun barrel. In a situation like this, time itself seems to stand still.

The water was far too swift to even think of swimming so I put my entire effort into keeping my head above water and trusting to fate. The horse was a lot stronger than I was and he wanted out of there too, so he was lunging for all he was worth and was making enough headway that he was beginning to leave me. When I realized that, I made a frantic grab for the saddle horn but missed it. As the rest of the horse went by me, my desperate fingers grabbed something which turned out to be his floating tail. It turned out to be the right thing to do; within a moment or two, he got his feet on the bottom again and made a frantic scramble for a gravel bar, which was almost on the far side of the creek. There is not the slightest doubt in my mind that he saved my life because, without his strength, I would never have been able to get out of that water on the high side of the whitewater chute and the chances of a surviving a tumble through it looked mighty thin. I had a lot of good thoughts for Brownie that afternoon.

Luckily for me, it was one of the few warm sunny days of

Choate's pack horse White Sox near the head of Grant Creek Unfriendly during the summer of 1957 when Choate goofed off and went prospecting for dreams.

the summer. So after wringing out my clothes and saddle blanket, I went over to check out another worthless mineral tracing. As the camp was over on the opposite side of that creek, I also spent the day knowing that somehow I had to get back over there. I couldn't see much point in looking for a better crossing because I realized that the water level was high everywhere. Everything I owned was over there so it had to be done.

But as I rode down the side of the canyon late that evening, the sight of all that boiling water down there gave me the willies. When we got to the edge, it took a few moments to build up enough courage to try it again. If my courage was faltering, the same couldn't be said for Brownie because he hit the water without any hesitation at all. That really surprised me because it's very difficult to get a horse to repeat a bad experience. There was no possible way to stay dry, so as soon as we were into the deep water, I slid off the horse's back and this time deliberately grabbed his tail and he had us across onto the right side within a minute or two. Who is it that always takes care of his own?

The entire summer was spent in the company of the two horses and the wildlife of the area. When I could, my camps were deliberately positioned so I could live as close to the wild animals as possible. Most mornings when I crawled out of the small tent, the first thing I'd see would be the moose and deer that had moved in with the horses overnight. The horses had long since become used to their presence and I believe that they came to appreciate their company as much as I did. At that time of year bull moose are not aggressive; even the largest of them seem to be almost as docile as range cattle. The bulls' own curiosity about us seemed to bring us all that much closer together.

In those years there were still many of those big bulls back in that area, that had not acquired a healthy enough fear of man, because there were very few men travelling back there. An entire summer would probably see only a few cowboys and sheepherders and the odd prospector. The fall would attract the outfitters and their guided hunters, but considering the size of the high country, there were not really that many of them.

Bears were the only animals that the horses did not welcome into camp. Even though the grizzlies were often close at hand during that entire summer, we never once had one bother the camp or the horses. By that time in my life, I had already had a few bear experiences and had acquired a lot of respect for them. They were the one animal that I deliberately tried to avoid camping near. It's one thing to meet them on the trail or while out roaming the hillsides, but it's quite another experience knowing that they are moving around only a few yards from the grub boxes and tent.

After I had made my way into the Snow Mountains, I located many small meadows where the grizzlies frequently fed as could be evidenced by the patches of earth that had been dug open in their quest for roots and plant bulbs. Some of these meadows showed signs of having been ploughed this way for years. Whenever I saw or actually met these bears, I always gave them full right of way, especially if they acted like they expected me to. More often than not, when they saw me they would immediately run for cover, but a few sat or reared up to watch me, just as I was watching them. When that happened, I always detoured a good distance around them or else waited far enough away, until they lost interest, dropped down onto all fours, and snuck off.

One of the things I've learned about bears is that they don't like to be watched or made to feel that they have backed down from a confrontation. So give them every opportunity to sneak off believing that they haven't been seen. A resentful bear can quickly become an aggressive bear. And you better believe it.

Anytime I was travelling in these obvious bear feeding places, I kept a bell on the pack horse. Sometimes I had no choice but to camp in those areas, because it was the only meadow I knew of where there was feed for the horses. In these cases I belled both horses. The idea was to avoid surprise encounters because under those circumstances, any bear, no matter the species or the age, is absolutely unpredictable. To tell the honest truth, that is the best way to describe any bear under any circumstances. The one thing I did not want to do was to have to shoot a bear simply because it was defending its territory. After travelling in this country, I came to realize that it was much more their home than mine.

For those of us who live in the bush and have built our lives around our horses, the sound of their bells is as important and comforting as a clock or door lock is to the dudes who have chosen the urban life. As long as we can actually hear those bells, it's usually the signal that all is well and everybody is present. There are exceptions, of course. A really frantic clanging means the horses are alarmed about something and perhaps even beginning to move out. On the other hand, dead silence is not the most comforting sound either because no horseman is going to go back to sleep until he hears at least a tinkle, or as I often do, get up and wander out to where I hope the horses still are. That silence can mean that the horses are sleeping, which is to be hoped for, but it can also mean that we slept through their escape. No matter how well horses are picketed, they are strong enough to break away, especially if they become badly spooked.

When I am camping in known bear country, I now make it a habit to get up and go visit the horses at night, which tends to calm them. I also believe that my fresh scent out among the horses is likely to keep the bears at a more respectful distance. When doing this at night, I always take my saddle gun, just in case I have a close encounter with one of those bears. A few times, the shadow of one of the horses standing or laying quietly in the bushes has resulted in a breathing change for a moment or two, but that also puts a little spice into what can become a monotonous repetition of life. When there are really a lot of bear signs around, it's wise to make that walk at least three times every night.

There have been a few times when I realized that we had camped in the wrong place. Then I leave the camp with my sleeping bag and rifle out and bed right in the open among the horses. The first time I ever did that, they acted quite curious and a bit alarmed to have me right there, but after a few hours, they settled down to where we were one happy family. I am quite certain that both dogs and horses realize that wild animals are more respectful of man than they are of other four-footed peers. There have been many occasions when both of these types of buddies have deliberately run right up to us for protection from real or imagined dangers.

In over thirty years of travelling with horses in the bush, I have only lost all of my transportation once and that was when two grizzlies decided to take a shortcut through the meadow where the horses were picketed and hobbled. There was no threat of attack; nervous horses were the problem. It was late evening and I watched it all happen, but there was not a damn thing I could do about it. I saw the bears coming down off the hill and was not all that alarmed about their presence, as I thought as soon as they got to the edge of the creek and meadow, they would veer off and go around the horses. I had a rifle, but was not hunting and besides, it made no sense to just up and shoot, before or after the horses spooked. The horses saw the bears coming too, so all of their heads were up watching. Those two bears nonchalantly hopped across the creek and ambled right up among the horses; that's when I found out how well those picket stakes were anchored.

There were three horses on picket and two with hobbles but their decision to leave was spontaneous. Those three picket stakes popped out of the ground like champagne corks and within thirty seconds there was not a horse in sight. All they left behind were two large grizzlies who were so surprised that they stopped in the centre of the meadow and watched those horses hightail it up the trail. Within another minute or two, I had the whole area all to myself and I mean I was alone.

There was no sense going after the horses then, because it was almost dark and since those two bears were mating and not acting nervous about me at all, I did not relish the thought of meeting them on a dark trail.

The next day I found the horses with no trouble but it was a twenty-five mile walk in one direction and then twenty-five miles return riding bareback. It was an experience but in some ways there was nothing to really learn, as there

Beautiful Tosh Creek at the foot of the Snow Mountains.

was nothing I could have done about it. Shooting the bears, or even shooting close to them, would have created exactly the same havoc, so it became one of those memories that became pleasanter to remember with the passage of time. Even though I still enjoy the presence of bears around me, that night and the following day did put a bit of a strain on our platonic relationship.

Lousy weather or not, what a wonderful summer it was. There can be no question about it being one of the high points of my life. Riding, wandering, exploring, daydreaming the time away, no debts, no commitments, the best and most agreeable company in the world. There are people who talk about getting to heaven on their knees, but I discovered in 1957 that you can find your way there on horseback and one of the gates into it is right at timberline of the Snow Mountains.

CHAPTER 14

WELL, EVEN THOUGH I HAD found my paradise, there was no way I could stay forever, so along about the end of August, I had to come back down to a lower plain. To begin with, I decided to ride down to Tex's camp on Gaspard Lake and find out what the rest of the world was up to. He and his crew were there, getting ready for the fall hunting season, so while we were visiting one evening, he invited me to stay and work for him for the remainder of the fall. It made good sense to do it, as by then, I had cooled off a bit from the earlier ordeal with the Gang Ranch and after four months in the bush, it was time to associate with people again. It would also help to make up the money difference that I still needed for my trip north. I had already kept my guide licence up and the wages were up by now too. As head guide I would be paid $300 per month, so it still looked like I would be heading north after all, although a year late. There were not many hunters booked for that fall and Tex had already hired three other assistants, so this time it was going to be easy work.

Shortly after the first of October, Tex returned from town one day and he had my summer's mail. Be damned if there was not a letter from the lawyer with my last winter's wages in it. Less fifteen percent. So now I was free to go, but it was too late in the year to start. Even though I felt pretty stakey, I also had made a commitment to Tex, to see that hunting season through to the end.

It turned out to be a pleasant and interesting fall, as the summer rain had finally let up and it made our hunting easier and more successful too. We took some really big bulls, several impressive mule deer, and a couple of bears. The previous fall, Tex had booked over eighty hunters and had clobbered a lot of game and as Steve Johnson suggested, they had overdone a good thing. However, in this fall of 1957, there were less than half that many hunters, so we hoped it would balance things out.

As our hunting season began to wind down, Tex decided that he wanted to quit the outfitting business and move back to the States, so he informed us that the operation was once again for sale. One of the things that helped him to decide to leave was the rumour in the district that Studdert had passed down the word that the Gang Ranch was still not going to tolerate this camp being here. This really upset Tex because he had really gone out of his way to try and mend the fences between the two outfits, but his overtures were still being rejected by the ranch owners. Tex got along with the Gang Ranch crews OK, but that was only when Studdert wasn't around.

When Tex first arrived here, he had a plan to try and make a deal with the Gang to lease their big Tyee House and turn it into a high-class lodge. There was no question that the building was well suited for that purpose, as it had originally been built as a private English-style hunting lodge and could accommodate a lot of people. Tex was also a first-class carpenter and cabinet maker, so there was no end of the plans that he dreamed of doing with those old buildings. He had it figured, that if he could form some sort of partnership with the Gang, it would be to their mutual advantage by making both operations work together, rather than bitching at each other, as had been going on since the hunting camp had started up. Tex Braatz had as warm and open style of southern friendliness as I have ever met and he was also an experienced promoter, but he could never crack Studdert's insistence that the Gang empire would never be shared.

After all of this had become so obvious that it could no longer be denied, Tex decided he did not want to have to live in the shadow of such adversary, so he said to hell with the entire operation. At the end of '57, he and Slick packed all of their personal gear into the Jeep station wagon and moved back to Oregon.

When the season was finally over, I left too, but only back to Clinton to visit my folks again. As soon as I arrived there and began catching up on the past seven month's gossip, it did not take long to discover that a few things had happened that were going to throw a monkey wrench into a lot of old ideas. Bill Fenton, the game warden of many years, had recently quit the Game Department and his position was now filled by the new warden, Jess McCabe. When I found this out, it didn't take long to conjure up an excuse to go in and meet McCabe.

During one such meeting with him, he asked me what I intended to do with my guide licence, now that Tex was gone. He explained that the operator's licence that I had been issued had been made out completely into my name and that the Gang outfitter had nothing to do with it, unless I wanted to volunteer my services to them, for whatever reason I wanted to. Tex had never given up his U.S. citizenship, so he had never qualified to have such a licence in his own name. The Gang Outfitter Hunting Camp had just become a camp without a licence to operate and that was very interesting.

After going back to my folks' place and talking the new situation over with them, we came to the conclusion that I had stumbled into a windfall that should somehow be exploited. None of us had any money to speak of and by that time I did know that operating a remote hunting camp can be an expensive undertaking. If I decided to try it, there was going to have to be a lot of financial juggling, which was something none of us knew anything about. However, the decision was made to give it a try, so in the late fall of '57, I declared myself as a self-employed businessman.

Other than locating operating capital, the first thing to decide on was a name for the new operation, because we had decided to finance it by advertising the business and then paying expenses out of advance deposits. But to get the money rolling in, the venture needed a name. Considering where the guiding operation was going to be located, it did not take us long to decide to use the nickname that some of the other riders had already laid onto me, so it became Chilco-Choate Hunting Camp. From then on, my name gradually changed from Ted to Chilco.

The next thing on the agenda was transportation as I still did not own a vehicle, or for that matter a driver's licence. But now that the plunge had been made, there was no getting around having to make the next one, so with the advice of a brother-in-law, I made a down payment on a new Mercedes-Benz Unimog, which is a one-ton 4-wheel-drive diesel tractor truck. It was actually a 1955 model, but had been sitting in a Vancouver show room for too long, so they gave me a very good deal on it and as it turned out, it was to become the best equipment investment I have ever made. With the exception of a few welding jobs and replacing some small parts in the fuel pump, it has been almost trouble free. My Dad came to Vancouver with me and drove the machine home.

A driver's licence was quite easy to get in the small towns in those days. When I pulled up at the local R.C.M.P. station in Clinton to take my driver's test, the young Mountie who came out in his nice clean uniform took one look at my

Mercedes convertible and then turned to me and exclaimed, "What the hell is that?"

I explained to him in great detail what it was and what it was going to be used for, as Unimogs were still quite rare in Canada. I also had to apologize to him for having to take my driver's test in it, as my Dad still did not trust me well enough to loan me his car for the job. The Mountie walked around the Unimog a couple of times, kicking the tires and taking note of all the dust on the seats that I probably should have cleaned off, all of the time shaking his head and making comments like, "What will the fuckin' Krauts come up with next?" He was still quite curious about the machine, so I also mentioned what it cost.

He then gave me an incredulous look and blurted out, "For Christ sake, Choate, for that kind of money you could have bought two Canadian trucks that won't scare people off the road like this contraption will. Why this goddamn thing looks worse than a fuckin' Volkswagen." Volkswagens were beginning to show up in the Cariboo by then and were not yet very popular.

After he had wound down a bit, I asked him if he was ready to jump in and give me my road test, but he took another look at the dirty seats and declined. He stepped back away from it, still shaking his head and said, "If you drove that fuckin' thing up here from Vancouver, then I'll assume that you know how to drive it, so I'll pass up the invitation for the ride." With that, he did go back into the office and signed my licence application, which put me out onto the road legally. I can still remember the glow I had that day, because from that moment on, I had become a Mr. Modern.

Now that I had my licence and transportation, the next major decision was to decide where to set up my base of operations. I had already contacted Tex in the U.S. to enquire about the possibility of buying his camp, which was by then completely vacant, but we could not agree on a price. The valley where his camp was located was the only obvious area to use as a base, because to all intents and purposes, the road ended at or close to Gaspard Lake, which is also the geographical center of the licenced guiding area. With that in mind, as soon as the road would permit, I drove out to Gaspard Lake and staked a Crown land lease on the lake shore, about two miles from Tex's camp. McCabe had already told me that he was not going to issue another guide licence in this area, as he figured there were too many in this part of B.C. already. That information made Tex's camp look pretty useless, except perhaps as a fishing camp or a summer home.

At the same time, I also staked two small cabins sites in the mountains to be used as satellite hunting camps. The most important lease was for a horse pasture. After having spent two seasons working for Shorty and Tex, I now knew that a horse pasture was more important to a hunting operation than any cabin or lodge would ever be. The amount of time that we had spent looking for strayed horses was unbelievable — at least two days out of every week.

As this was naturally going to be a horse outfit, then I was going to need more than the two horses I already had, but money was becoming noticeably short. So instead of trying to buy more, I made a deal with Steve Johnson of Canoe Creek to come over and work for me in the fall and, at the same time, he would also rent me twelve of his family's horses. We agreed that his new wages would be $300 per month, which was twice as much as Tex had been paying him and also more than twice what he could earn riding as a cowboy. The horses were going to be rented at thirty dollars a head for the season, which nowadays sounds very cheap, but at that time, those same horses could have been purchased outright for seventy-five dollars each. As it turned out, both deals were a very good

The cabin that Choate built at Gaspard Lake during his first year as a self-employed outfitter. It was later cut up for firewood.

investment, because not only was Steve always a top hand, but we also became good friends.

The spring and summer of '58 were the longest and hardest working days I have ever put in. I single-handedly built three cabins and started a fourth. Steve came over and helped me finish the last one, just to be sure it would be ready before the first hunters arrived. During that same summer, I widened some of the main pack trails as it was something that nobody had done since very early in the century. Those closing-in trails had resulted in many pack wrecks and I was fed up with the problem, as it's very time consuming and usually happens when we are in a hurry to get somewhere.

The Unimog was turning out to be everything I hoped it would, as it could manoeuvre through the muddiest road conditions. The roads above the Gang Ranch headquarters area were still so bad that very few other people even tried driving them until after fall freeze up. But with chains on all four wheels and the big winch on the front, the Unimog ground its way through all kinds of weather. Even at that though, sometimes the road became so bad that, even with the chained-up Unimog, it would still take me six hours to drive the twenty-eight miles between the Gang Ranch and Gaspard Lake. Most people today do not have the slightest understanding of what bad roads really are.

My diary says that on the 19th day of May, at my home place at Gaspard, a Gang Ranch truck passed by heading up into higher meadows. The passable road does not go far past the lake, so when the truck didn't return after a few hours, I had a hunch it might be stuck in a mud hole, as I had also noted that their truck did not have a winch. At that time, the Gang and I had sort of buried our hatchet over the wages deal and we were being what I would call "cool but civil" towards each other. So it seemed like it might be a neighbourly thing to do to drive up that road with the Unimog and see if there was any trouble. I did not have to drive far before I saw the ranch truck bogged down right to the frame in the center of the area I had recently staked for a horse pasture. There were two older men with the truck, both strangers to me, but after winching them out onto dry ground, I finally met Floyd Skelton, the other co-owner of the Gang Ranch. The other fellow was a very large man named Melvin Sidwell. They were both from Idaho.

Looking back on that day now, it becomes rather clear that our muddy meeting was also to become the beginning of many changes for the rangelands of B.C. and for some people, it was also to become the time marker for the beginning of the end of their way of life. After the trouble that Studdert had gotten the ranch into the year before by neglecting the cattle, there had been some sort of shakeup between the Gang

Ranch partnership so Studdert and Skelton had traded places. From now on, Skelton was going to be the front end of that partnership and this new fellow, Sidwell, along with his two sons and their families, was going to be moving onto the Gang Ranch to take over the management. Jim Bishop had been pushed back into the cowcamp and was cowboss again.

After pulling them out of the mud hole, we all drove back down to my new homesite beside the lake and we proceeded to have a country meeting as we leaned across the hood of the ranch truck. They were as interested as hell over the news that I was moving into the area to start up a new hunting camp and it was very easy for me to get the feeling that Skelton was not one bit pleased with the idea. Several times in the course of our conversation, he mentioned that he couldn't understand how I could possibly have a legal right to move into the middle of their range area. There was not the slightest doubt that these two Yanks firmly believed that the open range their cattle used was the same as private land to them.

That day we were quite civil towards each other, but at the same time we all felt the tension and knew that we were also jockeying for position. After they drove away, I spent a long time sitting at the front of my new home, mulling over many apprehensive thoughts.

CHAPTER 15

A COUPLE OF WEEKS BEFORE Skelton and Sidwell showed up, there had been other visitors as well. Late one afternoon as I was working on the cabin at Gaspard Lake, three riders rode up driving a small herd of cows and a lot of calves. It only took me a moment and a quick glance over the herd to realize that something was not right. When I recognized one of the riders, my gut tightened. He was a French Canadian fellow whom I had met before and was one of those people whose reputation usually precedes his arrival into an area. The three of them rode over to me and the Frenchman introduced his two buddies by their first names and we began making the customary small talk about the weather, the grass and other such things. The two strangers were Chilcotin Indians who didn't speak very good English, but that was common back in the '50s. For reasons which will become obvious, I'm not going to name these riders, since one of them is still alive, and this information might create some problems. The story is mostly about the Frenchman so I will refer to him as Frenchie even though l can't remember ever calling him that.

After a bit more conversation, I realized they were making noises about camping somewhere close, so it seemed like a neighbourly thing if I invited them to stay with me for the night. Unfortunately, they accepted the offer.

I had never liked Frenchie and still didn't. He was one of those loud bragging types who liked to be known as the toughest, meanest S.O.B. that had ever left Quebec. One of the stories that Frenchie liked to tell about himself, was that he left Quebec because it got too hot for him after he had killed two taxi drivers while robbing them. If you knew Frenchie, that story was easy to believe. Those of us around here who knew Frenchie also knew that Quebec must have become an instantly better place when he left it.

The cows and calves had obviously been driven quite a ways that day because when the boys let them go a hundred or so yards past the cabin, the cows immediately went to feeding and most of the calves bedded down.

From the very first sight of this herd, I was curious. It was hard to not stare at them and I guess it became noticeable to Frenchie, so he decided to enlighten me. Every one of the cows bore a very clear Gang Ranch brand, but Frenchie didn't beat about the bush. He told me the obvious — that none of these fellows was then working for the Gang Ranch. He and his partners were back on the Gang collecting unpaid wages. He admitted that this herd of cows were all Gang Ranch stock and not only that, every calf in the herd was also still unbranded or what we call a "slick."

But there had to be more to the story because there was a considerably higher number of calves in this herd than there were mother cows and I knew damn well that there were not that many twins in the entire Chilcotin. These calves were a fair size, but still, in May it was way earlier than they would normally be weaned. Some of the calves might have been three months old, but no older and the whole scene just didn't make much sense.

Over supper and the evening visit afterwards, Frenchie

revealed their new business in great detail. He and his crew were on their way to the Chilcotin Valley by a rather roundabout route, because they wanted to meet as few people as possible. They had collected the cows and calves down in the lower country near the Home Ranch Valley and it had taken the riders many days of cruising the Gang while trying to locate the cows that still had these unbranded calves with them. When they found the ones they wanted, they would then drive them into a small meadow, as far away from the main trail as they could find, and then they would shoot all the mother cows, thus making orphans out of the calves. The men would then ride away, leaving the calves right there.

Three or four days later the riders would return to the meadow and round up as many of the orphans as they could. A three-day orphan is easy to spot so they usually found most of them. Frenchie would then mix these motherless calves in with a few wet cows and their calves, and start chasing them all towards the border of the Gang Ranch range area where they would mingle with the cattle from other ranches. From there, they would drive the herd further away, well off of Gang Ranch range, corral them, sort all the slicks out to one side and then turn the branded cows and calves back towards where they had come from.

Since one of these riders owned some cattle of his own and so had a registered brand, they used his iron to mark all of these new calves. When branded, theft then became impossible to prove.

Up to that time, the only certain way theft of a calf had ever been legally proven, was when a suspected stolen calf would return to its natural mother. It is extremely rare for a cow to nurse a strange calf so these cases had held up in court. This matchmaking has to be set up quite soon after separation, inside of a week and when it does happen, the emotions of the reunited family are as obvious as they would be for humans.

After a week or so, I suspect they would become progressively indifferent to each other. But if a natural matching is shown to happen and the brand on the cow and the one on the calf don't match up, then it can make for some embarrassing questions.

Frenchie had it figured that the key to getting away with this operation was being able to prove that they did have a right to be in that area branding calves and, if they got challenged over a mix-up, then they could always plead that it was an honest mistake. To the detriment of the rest of the neighbours, Frenchie's lifestyle and livelihood hinged on that very legal cattle brand.

Stealing a calf or cow once in a while is quite easy, but if you're stealing large numbers for money, here rustling becomes a very risky venture. Frenchie was able to minimize the dangers, however. There was another entrepreneur over in the Chilcotin Valley who owned a large ranch and he was paying these fellows twenty-five dollars for each calf that they could give him a bill of sale for. That year on the open market, those calves were worth about fifty dollars, so for taking very little risk, the rancher was doubling his money.

"We keep him happy, he keeps us happy, so everybody is happy," Frenchie laughed. I didn't ask if the Gang Ranch shared in the merriment too.

I shouldn't have invited Frenchie to spend the night. Just as with his rustling, he believed it was better to take than to give. After that first visit, he stayed with me whenever he felt like it. Even though I had no love for the Gang Ranch, I knew that there was considerable risk in having him and his partners around. If he were caught, I would be tarred with the same brush. But it was more than that. He was always armed with at least one pistol, a knife on his belt, one in his boot, and he also sported a 9 mm Broom Handle Mauser machine pistol that was usually slung over his saddle horn. His

Indian partners both carried regular saddle guns and belt knives. Frenchie was always haranguing us with his wild stories about his past and how in the future if the cops ever cornered him over something serious, he wanted to go out in a great blaze of Western glory.

He loved to intimidate people with these stories and if the opportunity presented itself, he would back them up by showing off his ability with weapons. He was always practising and I have never seen anybody else who could throw a knife the way he could. Overhand, underhand, wrist flick, you name it and Frenchie could do it with accuracy.

His shooting was not all that great, but with a pistol, he was fast. One summer evening in front of my cabin, he was giving us a demonstration with his guns and when he invited me to try, I bested him with his own .38 pistol. That may not have been a wise thing for me to do, because by then I knew that he lived by some sort of code of "one-upmanship" and he took such things dead seriously too. It seems strange that a grown person would sulk about a thing like that, but he did and for several days at that.

I don't know if it's a virtue or a flaw, but I have been afraid of very few people in my life. But whenever Frenchie was around, I made it a point to be cautious. With his unpredictable temperament, it was like living with a pet rattlesnake in the house, so a person had to be a bit careful about what he said or did when he was around.

There came a day when Frenchie and I arrived at a very sudden mutual understanding about a few things. I had just returned home from a ride and noticed that Frenchie's horse was tied up to a tree, but there was no sign of him. I assumed that he was either out back in the throne room, or asleep in the cabin which would not be unusual, so I never thought much about it. After unsaddling my horse and hobbling him, I carried the saddle to the porch, pulled the rifle from its scabbard, and walked into the cabin with it. The door was open and as I stepped across the doorsill — THUNK! A goddamn knife was quivering in the doorframe, less than a foot from my shoulder.

For some reason, instead of jumping back outside, I went straight into the cabin, but as I did so, the rifle came up at full cock. In that one forward step, the explaining end of the Winchester stopped about a foot from Frenchie's nose with the trigger pulled maybe half way. We both froze in that position until I recovered a bit and realized that the loaded rifle was still pointed at Frenchie's head. He had not moved a muscle or said a word until I lowered the gun barrel and said to him, "You stupid son-of-a-bitch!"

We both understood how close he had come to becoming a good Frenchman because he had an extremely surprised look on his face as he blurted out, "Jesus Christ, Choate; if I knew you had the rifle, I would never have tossed the knife." It was not clear to me what he meant by that but for a long time afterwards, we were very quiet and polite to each other.

The only good thing about Frenchie's visits was his willingness to talk and I was able to learn something about the darker side of life. Even though he was some sort of psychopathic liar, many of his stories must have been based on a fair amount of truth because he could spin them together with such ease, and I doubted he had the brains to fabricate them all. I would be willing to suggest that most of his stories were "mostly" quite true.

He was a classic small time crook and under the wrong circumstances he could also be a very dangerous one. From time to time, however, he did take on honest work, but mostly he just wandered all over western Canada looking for larcenous opportunities. I believe the only time he might have undertaken honourable labour was in order to case an area, such as he had done when he was working for the Gang Ranch. At that time he had actually come to look over the possibilities of catching some of the slick one to four-year-old colts that the Gang always had running on the open range in those days.

Frenchie always carried a small "running iron" with him made from a piece of round iron bar that had been bent into the shape of a quarter moon. When he sat around camp at night, he would practice on a piece of wood, at altering every brand he had seen in the area.

"Changing the brand on a young growing calf is easy because the alterations will soon grow and blend in with the old brand, but on an older cow, it takes a lot longer for the two burns to meld together," he taught us.

Another trick he had figured out was how to keep up a fresh meat supply when he was travelling on the trail. This has always been a problem because during the summer months, meat can only be expected to keep about three to five days, but this guy was innovative.

"What I do, when my meat is getting low, is to chase a steer or yearling cow up into the bush and then shoot it in the throat with a 30:30, so the bullet goes right through," he said. "Then I skin back a piece of hide on the rump, cut out ten or twenty pounds of the best meat, and leave the rest of it for the coyotes and ravens. Within the next two or three days they will have covered all of my knife cuts and tracks. Don't ever shoot a cow in the head or cut any of the bones, because that will tell the rancher exactly what's going on," he warned us.

After several of Frenchie's visits, I finally got around to asking him how long he intended to work this area, because I was getting nervous about the type of attention he would attract to me, if the Gang Ranch or, more particularly, the R.C.M.P. became suspicious. His answer reassured me.

"Last year when the Gang had almost no cowboys on the range, I figure we killed maybe 300 cows, because we sold

255 calves, but this year the Gang got too many cowboys around here and so far we got only sixty-two calves, so I think we quit soon."

If those figures were close to being true, and I believe they were, then Frenchie and his crew had received a high rate of interest on their investment in the Gang Ranch Compulsory Bank. It made me wonder how many others had done the same thing.

For once Frenchie told the entire truth because that visit was the last time I ever saw him. Several years later the moccasin telegraph brought us word that he had been killed in an Alberta prison. About the same time that he left, one of his partners was killed in a drunken knife fight here in the Chilcotin.

Some things and thoughts do mellow with time, but even now, after more than thirty years, I still find it hard to believe that this world lost very much when Frenchie left it.

I still cross trails with the other fellow, usually in the town of Williams Lake. This last rider is now getting up in years and though he still doesn't speak very good English, it's certainly understandable. In the past, any time we have met, I have always opened our conversation with asking him how long his rope is. I always received the same answer, "I got the long slick rope." This has always been good for a laugh and a few drinks and stories about earlier and better days. The last time I met him, which was quite recently, I asked him the same old question, but this time he just shook his head and said, "My rope too old, got too many knots in it now."

People like Frenchie and his crew weren't the only ones with long ropes. Some of the Gang Ranch cowboys, while they were working for the company, kept a private watch for good-looking slick colts. When they located one, they would either make up some excuse to quit the job and then go back and catch it, or if they stayed on, they would send a message to friends who lived or camped nearby. Bishop was always interested in who camped close to the horse range and when he located such a camp and discovered who the campers were, he would go to considerable effort to find out if they had any buddies working in his cowcamp.

In much more recent times, I watched a different type of operation going on, right in the center of a logging road, not far from the Gang Ranch headquarters. One evening as I was driving home from Williams Lake, I came up on a small flat deck truck equipped with stock racks parked with its lights on, blocking the road. As I pulled up behind it, I could just make out three men and a small herd of cows, milling around in front of the truck. My first thought was that they had hit a cow and were trying to drag it off the road. I could see that there was enough room for me to slowly drive around them, and as I came along side the three men, I noticed that one of them had a lariat in his hand and the other two younger men were trying to haze a large slick calf towards him.

When I realized for certain what was going on, it was obvious that my presence was not wanted, so I waved, grinned, and kept on going. At that time, we were not getting along very well with the Gang Ranch or the entire cattle industry for that matter, so it did not twitch my conscience one iota if they stole every cow off the open range. As I drove on down the road that night, I can still remember laughing to myself over how easy it is if a person is bold enough to try.

These cases of cattle rustling are the only times I have ever witnessed cattle being stolen. Over the years, the cowboys have often reported locating dead cattle on the range, that have been shot, but this does not always indicate theft. When we listen to the scuttlebutt from around the range lands, there are also stories of disgruntled hired help who sometimes up and pot some of their employers' livestock to settle various types of grievances. Shooting cattle and burning haystacks and buildings have long been a way of settling accounts in the Chilcotin.

I know for certain that Frenchie and his partners were never caught, even though they were running what must have been a large operation, because if they took approximately 300 calves off this range, it seems hard to believe that they were not doing it elsewhere as well. The fellows with the truck were never caught either as we would have heard about it on the moccasin telegraph. Convictions of cattle theft cases are rare and when they do happen, they make the local headlines.

It's hard to tell what prompts people to steal or shoot cattle, but most of the cases I have heard about stemmed from shifty ranching practices that came back to roost on the rancher. My guess has become, that as long as ranchers persist with this chiselling and cheating of their hired help, then it's going to remain as an ongoing problem for them. There is also another world developing out here nowadays and it's possible that the ranchers may have the same problem when they clash with environmentalists or other land users.

We are living in changing and interesting times.

CHAPTER 16

THE REST OF THE EARLY SUMMER of '58 was mostly uneventful. The diary reminds me that we were getting along fairly well with the Gang Ranch and especially the cowboys; I used the Unimog on several occasions to haul supplies up to their cabin in Hungry Valley. The managers of the ranch still didn't trust the cowcamp to have a truck assigned to them and it meant that they were still dependent on those horse-drawn, iron-wheeled wagons being pulled by the horse teams. The lack of a truck in the cowcamp probably did not upset Bishop all that much because he never knew how to drive one anyway, but I do know he used to become quite frustrated about the time it required to move his camps and supplies. It took the cowboys four days to make a return wagon trip to the ranch from Hungry Valley, but if the weather was reasonable at all, I could do it with the Unimog in half a day.

Bishop and his cowboys had definitely turned warmer, but by the end of the summer there was a noticeably cool breeze coming from the management down at the headquarters. By that time, the Land Inspector in Clinton had advised me that the Gang Ranch was challenging all four of my lease applications. Past history had already told me that when the Gang Ranch wanted something from the government, it almost always got its way. The Land Inspector was a friendly fellow and often offered good advice, which I certainly needed. On this occasion he said he would recommend three of my lease applications, but even at that, he was not optimistic about my chances of getting them. They would still have to be approved by the local Cattlemen's Association, of which the Gang Ranch was a very active member.[13]

This information did not sound very encouraging so there was another pow-wow with my parents, where we discussed what I should do in case the applications were turned down. We knew the final decision could be stalled off for over a year, but the time would eventually arrive when it would have to be dealt with. The only conclusion we could reach was that since I was already committed for that season, the problem would have to wait. In the meantime we'd just play it by ear. I also asked the advice of several older rancher friends who lived around the Clinton area, but all they could offer was that I had made a mistake by tangling with the Gang in the first place. That was not really very helpful or encouraging, but it did tend to strike home that I was going to be going it alone over this issue.

This was to be the first hunting season that I was on my own and I was discovering still another fact of life that we had not allowed for about running a business. Even though I already had many hunter contacts in the U.S., I soon discovered that very few of those hunters were prepared to send cash deposits for a future hunt to an inexperienced twenty-three-year-old kid.

After contacting well over a hundred such people, all I was able to get out of most of them were verbal assurances that they would certainly book a vacation with me, but perhaps

---

13 These local associations had always been, and still are, very influential in this part of B.C.

not for another year or so. Only fourteen of them were willing to gamble their 1958 vacation with me and that was at a time when a combination moose and deer hunt was selling for $225. All the fun I thought was associated with running a camp was rapidly becoming a gut-binding situation.

The one thing that did hold up for that fall was the weather; it turned out to be the most beautiful Indian summer I had ever experienced, and it certainly helped to increase our hunting success, which I prayed would help boost next year's business. Nature may have been accommodating but there were still those manmade hurdles that seemed to be hiding around every corner. Just as the hunting season dates were announced, I received a message to come to Clinton and contact the Game Warden — a message an outfitter does not ignore. This time Jess was a bit apologetic, because he had received word from his superiors in Victoria that he was to issue another guide licence to a fellow by the name of Mark Hugo, who was taking over Tex's camp. McCabe said that he had not recommended the licence and still would not. He still stood by his earlier assessment that there were too many outfitters in this part of B.C., but Victoria overrode his on ground observations and nobody down there would tell him why.

I already knew a little bit about Hugo. He had recently sold his "Mons Lake Lodge" to a friend of mine, Ron Nelson, who lived over at Big Creek. Hugo had about eighteen years experience at running the Mons Lake Lodge, so he was not going to be greenhorn competition. So, I was not going to have the guiding area all to myself after all. Suddenly the road to becoming an independent outfitter was becoming rockier at every turn. As a matter of fact, it was beginning to look downright depressing. But I had no intention of giving up on the business yet.

One October afternoon, while I was guiding a hunter from

our cabin in Hungry Valley, we met another rider coming up a trail that we were heading down on. It was a clear bright day. The wind was rattling the trees a bit, but it was still a splendid time to be out riding. The hunter and I had given up that day and were heading back towards the cabin, so we stopped to chew the fat with the stranger. It turned out that he was an American hunter from Hugo's camp. Knowing that it was illegal for a guide to turn a non-resident hunter loose, I asked him where his guide was.

"Oh, Mark is down in the swamp somewhere, trying to chase a moose up to me," he said.

I already suspected something like that but I didn't bother explaining my question, so we exchanged a few more pleasantries about the weather and hunting conditions. As we started to part company, we nudged our horses past each other, so we could pass on the narrow trail and, as the stranger and I were alongside of each other, there was an almost deafening bang from a gunshot that sent all three of our horses straight up into the air. The shot was so close that I felt the blast from it. The horses made a few jumps each, but we soon had them under control again.

My first thought was that this stranger must have been carrying a cartridge in the chamber of his rifle and it had somehow gone off. I was just about to chew him out for careless gun handling, when I noticed that his horse was staggering all over the trail with a fountain of blood spurting out of its rear end. It dawned on me that the shot had not come from the strangers rifle, but rather from the nearby bush. Some survival instinct made me wheel my horse around to face down the trail again while still trying to figure out what the hell was going on. That's when I saw a man crouched behind a tree, only a few yards away. I realized that this guy was reloading his rifle which looked like it was pointed directly at me.

The puzzle fell into place instantly and I grabbed my rifle from the scabbard and bailed off my horse, jacking a cartridge into the breach as I did so. (I was young and fast in those days.) I can still remember my intense frustration because of the time it was taking me to get down onto the ground to sight the rifle. He had his rifle almost back up to his shoulder, so it was going to be only a split second determining which one of us was going to be able to fire the next shot.

Fate was with me that day, because I landed on my knees with the cross hairs of my scope lined dead center on the other fellow's neck. As I started pulling the trigger, I hollered one last time, "DROP IT!" He threw his rifle out onto the trail and it was all over. That was how I finally met my new neighbour, Mark Hugo.

I can't remember all of the conversation we had immediately after that, but his own hunting client who had been riding the horse that had been bungholed seemed to be a bit more dazed than the rest of us and I do remember him stammering out, "bu-bu-by God, Mark, that was damn close".

It sure as hell was close and as we all stood there for the first few moments, each one trying to figure out how and why it had happened, a few things did begin to fall into place. My own client, Woodie, and I were by this time standing off to the side, watching Hugo pull the saddle off his dead horse. My hunter and I compared theories about the incident and we both agreed that if the stranger had not moved his horse ahead when he did, that bullet would have hit me square in the gut. Woodie turned to me and said, "I think that son-of-a-bitch just tried to kill you." I had already come to the same conclusion.

Hugo must have heard Woodie say this because he stopped unsaddling his dead horse and stood up, and stared straight at me. However he didn't say a word, probably because I still had a very loaded rifle pointing in his direction. I was almost angry enough and it was sure as hell tempting, but I guess Hugo and I were both lucky that there were too many witnesses.

As Woodie and I rode away from the other two, I regretted not having taken Hugo's rifle along with me, because until we were well out of sight, there was a very sticky and prickly feeling around my hat line. Until we were a long way down that trail, I kept looking back over my shoulder and every time I did so, I noticed that Woodie was doing it also.

Later on that evening, after we had returned to our cabin and had related our experience to Steve and his hunter, we had visitors come to see us. Be damned if Hugo, his hunter, and his cook arrived to invite us to share a bottle of whisky that they had brought along. It seemed hard to believe that Hugo could have so much gall, but he sure as hell did. In the course of the conversation that evening, Hugo admitted that he had come over to try talking us out of reporting the incident to the authorities, but I had already decided to do so. I was still suspicious that it was not an accident, which might mean that we would be destined to meet again at a later date, on a quieter trail. I told Hugo all this to his face and he replied that if I did report it, then all he was going to do was claim he thought he was shooting a moose. He figured that since it was his own horse that had been shot and the hunter who was riding it was not going to lay charges, then it had nothing to do with me.

Woodie and I did report it, so the Game Warden and an R.C.M.P. corporal came out to inspect the scene of the accident. They easily located where Hugo had dismounted, tied his horse up, taken the rifle from the scabbard, and had then crawled ahead to the tree where he fired from. When the investigators paced off the distance from where the shot was fired to where the horse was hit, they decided that twenty-five yards was the probable range. We were never able to figure out how a guide with eighteen years experience could possibly mistake, through a telescopic sight, a horse and rider for a bull moose.

After much time had passed, the authorities decided to lay a charge under the Wildlife Act; Hugo pleaded guilty of "attempting to kill game while guiding a hunter." In those days it was not legal for a guide to shoot a game animal when having a client in the field. Hugo was fined $100 and his outfitter's licence was never again renewed for this area. Later on, I also received an official letter from the top brass in Victoria assuring me that they would never again be issuing another operator's licence in this area. I have kept this letter.

The bones from that "moosie" horse still remain alongside the Lost Valley trail and every time I ride by there, the sight of them never fails to remind me of that long ago encounter.

After the end of the 1958 season, I contacted Tex again and this time we did get together and worked out a deal so I could buy his camp and all of the equipment that I could locate. By that time, the camp had been more or less vacant for over a year, so there was tons of equipment that had been pilfered away and spread all over the country. Out of the twenty-five horses that were supposed to be here, Steve and I could only locate fifteen of them.

The day that Tex and I finalized the transfer, we had a good visit and of course the Hugo incident was still very much on everybody's mind, so we went over it in detail. Tex thought it was the funniest thing he had ever heard of. He knew Hugo and he knew me, so he said that he had received a different story from both of us. While he was comparing our stories, he was laughing so hard, he was crying. Tex Braatz had a Southern sense of humour that was very contagious and before the night and bottle were finished, he had me beginning to wear different glasses too.

The deal with Tex worked out best for both of us. He

was able to liquidate his business for a fair price and I was able to voluntarily drop two of those lease applications that might not have been approved as they would have been too expensive for me, anyway. It also gave me a sense of security knowing that I would not have any more outfitters competing with me. We decided against using the old name so the "Gang Outfitter" was officially finished by the end of the '58 season. The location of Tex's camp was far better than the one I had built the year before, so I cut the new cabin up for firewood and moved all the loose equipment over to the old home base.

So by the beginning of 1959, I was right back to where I had started in '55, except this time I really had returned home. We never have hung an official name onto the property, like some people do to their ranches or lodges; people just refer to it as Choate's Place.

By the end of that '58 season, I may have been over one hurdle, but by midsummer of '59, the old original problem began showing up again in the form of the Gang Ranch "squeeze." Their weapon this time was the Grazing Division of the B.C. Forest Service (BCFS). Having and holding the horses had always been a problem for this camp and none of the previous owners had really tried to solve it. Shorty and Tex both had a grazing permit for twenty-five horses, but when Tex turned the leases and permits over to me, the permit had been reduced to twelve head. I forget the verbatim conversations I had with the BCFS over this, but I do remember getting the impression from them that the Cattleman's Association with its considerable political clout, had influenced the reduction of my grazing permit. I could smell the Gang Ranch's manipulations. We still had friends who belonged to the Association and some of them would leak us information. One friend advised me that the Gang Ranch was warning everybody that Choate and the camp could become a "foot in the door" danger to all of them.

The Unimog standing in front of one of the four cabins that Choate built in 1958. The cabin was later cut up for fire wood

There was no question that my most vulnerable spot was through my horses and my guess was the Grazing Division, trying to give the impression of being fair, didn't cancel the entire permit, but only half of it, thinking that it would slowly starve me out of here anyway. This would have been a very logical assumption because most hunting camps who used horses at that time were working with herds of forty or more.

At an earlier time their scheme would have worked, but the Unimog saved my bacon. The places we drove that thing into were almost unbelievable. People were always taking pictures of the bog holes it was crossing and the stumps it could straddle, so it did take the place of that second string of horses. At the same time, by raising my rates, I had reduced the number of hunters and that made a difference too.

There were still many times when we found ourselves short of horses, as some of them were forced into doing double duty and it did make things harder. But at the same time,

The Unimog being used in place of the 12 horses Choate lost in the shuffle with grazing licences with the BCFS. It continuously amazed us where this versatile machine could go and Choate still figures it was the best equipment investment he ever made. There were a few places it wouldn't go, but not many.

everything did keep working. Up to that time, I don't believe there was another full time hunting camp operating with only twelve horses, so I guess I did open a few eyes when I proved that it could be done.

All through 1959 I noticed that the Gang was becoming noticeably bitchier. They began threatening to lock the only road into the back country. Before they actually got around to trying it, I had the records to the old roads searched out and was able to accumulate enough ammunition to feel confident that I could scotch that scheme if they ever tried it.

One of the Gang's nastier little tricks involved moving a herd of cattle into one of our established camping spots before we arrived in the fall. A couple of the hired hands delighted in doing this and they used those cattle like weapons.

They became a real pain in the ass. If we wanted to continue using that location after the cattle had finished with it, I had to go to the expense of hauling hay in to replace the missing wild grass. Sometimes we even ended up having to pack hay into remote camps on pack horses and at only two bales per horse, it became very time consuming, which also meant more expensive. Oh, they were getting their message across alright, and I was becoming goddamn angry about it too. But this time the ranch had not tangled with some meek homesteader who was going to quietly fade away.

Month after month the contention built up. However I don't think the Gang realized what an advantage I had gained through working for them in the past. I had met Studdert and knew how he thought and what tactics he favoured, and this gave me an uncanny ability to predict what he would do next. I was able to meet them head-on at the passes, rather than letting them get too many jumps ahead of me.

Starting in '59, it seemed like every time I went to town for mail, there would be another registered letter from some branch of the government, complaining about some injustice I was supposed to be inflicting on the poor old Gang Ranch. Most of the letters came from the Grazing Branch and referred to the fact that some of my twelve horses had been seen on such and such a meadow before the yearly turnout period was in effect.

At first I did respond to these complaints by asking them that if my horses were such a bane to the open range, then why were the hundreds of Gang Ranch cows there not ordered out as well.

The answer was usually no answer, but sometimes they flat out informed me that this range was designated for cattle use and I was lucky to be allowed to have ANY horses here. When I asked them how they rationalized the presence of the Gang horses, then they told me that the ranch needed them to work their cattle with. When I asked them why six or eight cowboys needed eighty to one hundred horses up here, that became none of my business.

I was trying to get them to see that what was sauce for the goose was also sauce for the gander, but the FS wouldn't buy it. I carried on as usual, silently daring them to roundup or shoot my horses, and after several years the letters stopped coming.

At first, these letters frightened me a bit, but there got to be so many of them that eventually the sight of any government correspondence merely made me indifferent. One thing about it all, though, it made me stop and really think about how these government departments operate.

I had always supposed that the individuals who work within the Grazing Branch of the BCFS were supposed to be managing the forage resource for the benefit of the majority of the people, but I started to question that. From my on ground observations, it became more probable that these people were really working for the benefit of the local Livestock Associations and it was only incidental that their paycheque came from the public purse. It took many years to force some wedges between their cozy relationship with vested interests, but back in '59 public scrutiny of such things was still unheard of.

The hunting season of 1959 was the largest business operation I have ever attempted, as we took out forty-two hunters who bagged thirty-seven moose, ten deer, and a black bear. We tried for a couple of California bighorns, but got completely skunked. Some of those moose were really big bulls as the largest one had a horn spread of fifty-six inches, which is very large for this part of Canada. Some of the mule deer bucks were quite impressive too.

Not all of our hunters were after horn trophies; some of them came to deliberately take home a barren cow moose, for

Chilco Choate with a successful client in Hungry Valley.

they know the difference in the quality of meat between bulls, wet cows, and these barren ones. For many of us, a fat cow moose is more preferred than the best beef you can buy. At that time, the price of a seven day moose hunt was $350 and the chances of bagging a dry cow was almost 100%, so the meat hunters could estimate the cost of their winter's meat at about a dollar a pound, but at the same time, they had a vacation thrown in. For those of them who became involved in horse wrecks, water spills, mud holes and the like, they received more excitement during their vacations than they originally bargained for. But that's all part of hunting and that's one of the reasons our business refuses to mechanize.

There were lots of moose around here that year and the resident hunters came and took their toll as well, but we also noticed that they took wet cows and calves out of here by the truckload. There is no way to know if any of them even tried to be selective; it looked more like most of them were simply shooting the first moose they saw which, too often, was the wrong kind.

We really began to lose our proven breeding stock that year, or what a farmer would call the "basic herd." It's not fair to place the blame entirely on the hunters, since most of them were urbanites who did not know the difference or even what the difference meant. There were no hunter training courses and the game laws were so liberal then that any yahoo could buy a licence and tag and then go do his Buffalo Bill act.

The moose population was not the only species to suffer. The mule deer herd got clobbered too and for all of the same reasons. Most of our American clients were not very interested in deer hunting and they only shot one if it had an exceptional trophy size set of antlers. But the residents made short work of herds of young deer when they arrived down near the roads on the winter ground. The cowboys told us of meeting a big flat deck truck coming out of Lower Churn Creek that had thirty-one does and fawns on it. They said the hunters were delighted over their "harvest" and acted like they believed they had done the country a favour.

In 1959 there were stories like this were coming in from all over the Chilcotin and for many of us living here, we felt a terrible sense of foreboding.

CHAPTER 17

I SPENT MOST OF THE 1959-1960 WINTER in Clinton with my folks, so I could send replies to business inquiries fast enough so that they would not be lost to competitors. Clinton at that time was much smaller than it is today with the population hovering around the 600 mark, so it did not take long to get to know almost everybody I had not already met. There were very few single girls over the age of seventeen in the area then, but there was a huge influx of young single men who were coming north to work in the new sawmill industry. The few single girls there were had things pretty well their own way, at least as far as manpower was concerned. This situation had never been any particular problem for me, because I was still very wary of women. Most of the ones I had met seemed to have the two things on their minds that I did not want: to have kids and to live in town.

Many of the girls who had been raised on the local farms or ranches could hardly wait to get off them, so the ones who stayed were rare birds. My mother explained to me that this should not be surprising, because life for women in remote areas was not really very much fun after the first child was born. Running water, central heating, and electricity were not yet common on Chilcotin ranches or hunting camps, because these things hinged on having private power plants, which were too expensive for most small outfits to buy and maintain. Our mother had raised three kids in a rural area and had acquired some very strong opinions on that subject.

Needless to say, any time a new girl did arrive in town, she attracted a great deal of attention and that's the way it was when Carol arrived that winter to work as a waitress in the Cariboo Lodge. That type of news travelled with the speed of light and in less than a day the Lodge became a very popular hangout for most of the young men within a thirty mile radius of the town. I had always been interested in girls, especially pretty ones; it was only the risk of the long-term price that might have to be paid that had kept me at a very respectful distance. However, in this particular case, there was another large problem that came with the girl and it was in the form of a very big Mountie who told the rest of us that Carol was his fiancée and the rest of us had better bugger off.

This Mountie was a few years older than me and no question that he had been around more too, so he should have known better than to make such a statement in a cowboy-logger town like Clinton because, from that moment, the entire situation became a very interesting challenge. I guess Carol enjoyed the popularity, because she seemed to be playing it both ways. It did not take the rest of us long to find out that she was not really a waitress, but a psychiatric nurse who had come up on a working holiday to be closer to her boyfriend.

For some reason I became as interested as the others, but having never dated a girl before, it took a while to hatch a plan that might make the attraction reciprocal. I did know enough about female psychology to know that most girls are suckers for fancy cars, so one day while sitting in the Lodge and having Carol refill my coffee cup, I casually dropped the information that I owned a Mercedes convertible. It did not take her very long to rise to the bait, and she agreed to go out on a date with me to see such a vehicle.

Luckily for me, Carol was a good sport about being duped by a Mercedes Unimog and, partly because opposites sometimes attract, we hit it off really well. After the first date, things fell into place pretty fast. It did not take us long to agree on several important issues such as wanting to live in the bush and not being encumbered with kids. About five weeks after we first met, we surprised everyone by getting married. I really did feel sorry for the Mountie. He was a nice person, but this was a case where he discovered his man-catcher training did not work as well on women.

Up to that time Carol had been a purely cosmopolitan person and when we got married, part of her wardrobe consisted of $3,000 worth of party dresses and ball gowns. She may have had a pair of jeans, but she did have a very well-fitting stretch ski outfit, which attracted all the attention she could handle. Opposites did attract in our case because I don't dance or enjoy going to small-talk parties, which must have been the circle that Carol had lived in before meeting me. I do know that several of her nurse friends began kidding her about having married a "case." Of course they exaggerated beyond reason.

Even with Carol's urban background, she really took to life in the bush. When we moved out to the camp at Gaspard Lake, the home she moved into had been a bachelor's "boar's nest" for the last four years. After putting me to work on yard cleaning chores, she spent her first two weeks here scrubbing burned pots and cleaning cabins. Looking back on it now, I was mighty lucky because Carol had much more marriage adjusting to do than I did.

1960 was a very good year, especially for me. It did not take me long to realize that having a wife out in the bush was a far better way of living than the life-style I had been used

One of the rough guest cabins at Gaspard Lake.

to. The camp was still very rough, but a woman's hand in such a place becomes very noticeable and that summer we had several parties rent the hunting cabins from us, something that had been rare in the past. Carol suggested that putting linoleum on the floors and scrubbing the cabin walls once in a while, would make the place more habitable to the type of people we wanted for clients. "We aren't trying to rent this place to your old cowboy and prospector friends, you know," she said. "Your days of sleeping in saddle blankets and using a dog to clean the pots are over. And furthermore, you are having a bath at least once a week, whether you think you need it or not."

For the sake of our marriage, I bowed to these unreasonable demands.

That summer we did take a part time job expediting for an oil exploration outfit from Calgary called CanPet Explorations. These people turned out to be a different type of prospector than I had ever met before; they could best be described as gentlemen. Up to that time, the only ones I had ever known or heard of seemed to be trying to stay at least one step ahead of their reputations, for most of them were notorious for their penchant for going broke and leaving a mound of unpaid bills behind them.

However, CanPet proved to be the opposite and it allowed us to meet and work with some really nice people. The crew were strictly geologists, who with their little hammers, were checking over the out-crops of seashells that crown many of the mountains around this area. Helicopters were scarce in this part of B.C., so we were able to do a good business of packing their supplies, moving camps, and renting them horses.

The chief of the party, Phil Clarke, insisted that he had to keep in touch with his office by radio telephone on a daily basis. His telephone was one of the older types, full of fragile tubes and whatever else is inside those things that makes them work, so we had to be careful how we moved it around.

As long as I could use the Unimog for moving their camps, the radio phone was no problem. But later in the summer we finally worked our way back into the higher hills, where even the Unimog could no longer go. From that point on, the only way to travel in this part of the Chilcotin was by saddle and pack horse, which is not a particularly gentle method of moving equipment. I don't believe that Clarke had ever worked with pack horses before, because he started getting real worried about whether his phone was going to arrive at the next campsite in working condition. (On the other hand, maybe he *had* worked with horses and that was exactly why he was getting nervous.) For several days before we were scheduled to move, he kept asking me what I thought the chances were of moving the phone safely and it got to the point where he was beginning to make a doubter out of me too. None of us really knew how much of a thump this thing could withstand and there was nobody in the party who knew anything about fixing even a minor problem if the damn thing quit.

The chief had us all in such a stew about that goddamn phone, that in order to shut him up until we really had to deal with it, I made him a proposition that I never dreamed he would accept. I offered to pack the damn thing into the next camp on my back and I would guarantee its working arrival for $225. This was at a time when we could hire the best help for $10 a day, and so to me, it was an outlandish figure that no sensible person would even consider. Holy Christ, I should have asked for $500 because Phil grabbed the offer almost before I finished proposing it.

When moving time arrived, Steve and I started the twelve-mile pack; he rode a horse and led six pack horses and I walked along behind with a sixty pound radio phone on my back. There was a sign on it that said, "This Side Up," whatever that was supposed to mean, because there was no way it could be back packed if a person took those words literally. It was packed on its side, the only sensible way that it could be done.

It was a hot summer day and I must have sweated a gallon out of my system, but other than that, we arrived at the next camp with no problems. The entire crew was waiting impatiently for us as they had been making wagers as to whether I really would get there with a working phone.

After depositing the phone into the center of their compound, I helped Steve unpack the horses while the prospectors tinkered with the generator. When one of the men fired up the generator I began praying to every mountain and cloud in sight. That day nothing could have sounded sweeter than the sound of the operator's voice that came over the airwaves, repeating, "Vancouver, Vancouver, Vancouver." Phil Clarke must have been as astounded and pleased as I was, because he immediately reached into his pocket and handed me $225 in traveller's cheques.

Business with CanPet made 1960 a profitable year for us; we worked for them, off and on, all summer until it was time for us to start hunting again. However, if it was good for us financially, it turned into a disaster in another way. On September 2nd after we had left the CanPet crew in the mountains near the head of Big Creek, the bush plane they had chartered to take them back to civilization crashed into Lorna lake, killing half of the crew and the pilot. There were no witnesses to the crash. When we heard about it several days later, it sure left a mighty empty feeling in us, for they had all become our personal friends.[14]

It turned out to be a good hunting year for us too, but it was the last big hunt we ever tried. We took out thirty-seven hunters, who bagged thirty-one moose, eleven deer, and a black bear.

When the season was over, we sat down and talked about what we had seen and especially what we were not seeing, and we began to realize that these hunting trips for quantity could not be sustained for much longer. In the five years that I had been here, the scarcity of moose in particular was becoming more and more noticeable, so we decided to try organizing the business more towards quality experiences rather than emphasizing the number of animals one could shoot.

That decision showed how green we still were because we were ignoring a very important ingredient that I should have understood by then. Regardless of how hunters talk about fair chase hunts, sportsmanship, wildlife conservation, and all those other high-flown theories, most of them still want to be

---

14 Phil Clarke survived. There had been two flights and he went out on the first one.

194

successful. Foiled hunters become peeved and, since this type of business is carried forward mostly by word of mouth, those unsuccessful hunters can break an outfitter.

Don't get me wrong. There are lots of unsuccessful hunters who understand that it's all a gamble and can roll with the punches. I am merely pointing out what can happen from a few of the other kind. Some of the outfitters get around this problem by arming the assistant guides, which can sure as hell keep the success percentage up, but that was a branch of the business we decided to avoid. There is a point of ethics here and there is also a point of law because helping a friend or client to fill his tag is illegal and it always has been. The only time we encourage an assistant to carry a rifle is when we are deliberately hunting for grizzlies and then the reasons are obvious. I suppose the reason I have bothered to mention this problem is because we were very much affected by the "other" type of outfitter. It's a tough business as there are only so many clients and the competition for them becomes fierce.

On top of this, the weather had turned noticeably drier and new roads were being built in the lower country which, in turn, allowed a flood of resident hunters into areas that had been sparsely hunted in the past. I do not believe anybody had the slightest clue as to how many antlerless moose and deer were killed around here during the 50s and 60s. What was worse, the so-called authorities who should have been caring were simply in the business of selling licences. There was a stretch of several years then, when a hunter was allowed to take three deer per season and two of those could be antlerless. When we now look back to that time and begin to realise what the probable kill really was, there can be almost no dispute that there was a fifteen-year slaughter in here. There is absolutely no other word to describe the reality. Why was it allowed to happen?

People who live out here in the hinterlands find it

especially difficult to really understand what makes the bureaucrats and politicians in the provincial capital tick. Believe it or not, we once had a Social Credit cabinet minister in charge of wildlife who was quoted in the press as saying, "Wildlife is desirable, but unnecessary." This fellow had previously been the Minister of Mines and he served those masters very well. I always felt that he may have been placed in charge of wildlife to be in a better position to control people like us.

So it was against attitudes like this that the outfitters and hunters had to learn to survive on planned diminishing resources. It has not been easy to do and for people like myself, it created a hatred towards those decision makers that will probably never die. For the life of me, I can't understand how they can live with their consciences after coming up with some of the policies they did. It's difficult not to become paranoid and feel that there is a conspiracy among the highly placed bureaucrats to bankrupt our wildlife. With their reams of written and verbal gobbledygook, they try to make the whole system seem so confusing (or "complex" as they love to call it), that it becomes very difficult for the rest of us to point an accusing finger at individuals. But somehow we must, because, partner, that is the only way we will ever get the collar on those bastards.

In my personal opinion, the "whys" and "hows" of resource decisions are originally the ideas of individual people, so the rest of us should not let them get away with camouflaging bad ideas behind stuffed uniforms and offices of power. The plastic world that they are offering us in place of the natural world has a mighty hollow ring to it.

CHAPTER 18

For us, the early '60s were still very much touch and go. Inexperience, underfinancing, fewer and warier game herds, and that always present squeeze from the Gang Ranch all conspired to keep our lives in a see-saw situation. Even though Bill Studdert was no longer directly involved with the running of the ranch, we still felt his attitude radiating through the new resident manager, Melvin Sidwell and his sons, Blain and Irvin. There was never any doubt in our minds that this manager and all of his family resented us and objected to our being here. They may have felt this way because of besting the ranch by collecting my wages, which in turn severely curtailed their "Compulsory Bank."

They also connected me, through the pictures I took, with the ranch's conviction for neglecting livestock. Management now had to be very careful because a second conviction could possibly result in a court order forbidding them to ever own livestock again.

Another reason for their resentment was over those lease applications of mine, of which three had been approved. These were the first land applications the government had approved in this area since about the end of World War I. These acquisitions, located right in the center of what for over a hundred years had been considered Gang Ranch Country, must have shook them to the core. Other ranchers throughout the Cariboo kept telling us that the impossible had happened. I was astounded myself, as I figured the applications would get the usual nix from Victoria. The government must have wanted to start a land boom; the hundred-year doldrums were over.

All of this happening so close together must have set alarm bells jangling, because by then we knew that we were approaching each other on what was a one-track road.

Sidwell had to hold the old land and cattle empire together if he were to succeed as manager. I knew Studdert well enough to know that the ensuing days and months were going to be a desperate gamble for us. I was well aware that when dealing with ranchers like Studdert, there could never be a lasting agreement about anything, especially if it might mean that the Gang had to compromise. We also knew we had to be extremely cautious over any dealings with them, because the Gang had a reputation for coming out on top of any agreement they made. Because of this past history, we decided that the best way to live here would be to have as little to do with the ranch as possible and to absolutely avoid letting ourselves become dependant on it for anything. It had to be done that way but it was not always easy to do because the geography kept getting in the way.

During this period our working relationship with the ranch management was another one of those on again, off again situations. We were both feeling each other out for weak spots and jockeying for what we hoped would become positions of strength in future negotiations. There were times when we were polite to each other and even did each other small favours. I continued using my Unimog to assist the cowboys when they were in a time pinch, since the ranch still had not given them a truck to use. The ranch had acquired some new rolling stock, but their trucks were the conventional kind that often could not negotiate these roads after a long rain storm. In return, the cowboys would sometimes corral our horses when I was short-handed and a few times we were allowed to use the ranch telephone, which saved us a 160 mile drive to Clinton and back.

However, there were other times when we wouldn't be on speaking terms with the management for months at a time, usually brought on by conflicts over the use of the open range. As we were both totally dependent on the wild forage, we often clashed over attempts to set rules on how much either of us could use. They were used to having it all and refused to recognize that it might not remain that way in the future.

As soon as the Sidwells arrived here, they began increasing the cattle herd, as it had fallen to about 2,000 head. Within a very short time it was up to 3,000 and still climbing and the increase became quite noticeable when the cattle were left too long on meadows where the camp had always picketed our horses. Our total livestock was still frozen at twelve horses.

Of course when things like this happened, we complained to the ranch but got little from them except to be told that perhaps we should camp elsewhere. That did not come across as very neighbourly advice, so we took our problem to the Grazing Division of the BCFS where we received just about the same advice from them.

In the 1960s there was never any question about who got first choice at the wild forage; it was cattle first, second, and often last too. According to the Grazing Act and every livestock association in B.C., not even wildlife was considered to have a legal share of the wild feed. If the ranchers and government resource managers decided to leave some grass behind the cows, then the rest of us could use it, but if the rancher wanted it all, then that's the way it was. We were up against a system that was used to making its own rules concerning land use so you can guess about how willing any of them were to relinquish any of their power and authority which they wielded in the style of divine right. I feel that the wild forage had become theirs by a theft that was so huge and involved so many people, that the sheer size of the Act had to be covered up politically, so laws were made to legalize it after the fact. Wildlife and Indian horses were here first but were "reduced" to make more room for cows.

We also had and still have disagreements over water use. Gaspard Creek is a mid-elevation creek which drains an area of about 250 square miles. Gaspard Lake lies half-way up the creek. Late in the last century the government gave the Gang Ranch a water licence which enabled them to dam, store, and drain this entire watershed to irrigate the main ranch. The old records report that Gaspard Lake was originally 144 acres in size, but after the ranch built a dam on the lower end, it's now closer to 1,000 acres.

The old Indian families who used to live around here, recount that their people used to travel considerable distances to come and catch the rainbow trout that were here before the dam was built. Now, some prize in the government licencing bureau either never noticed or deliberately ignored the welfare of this natural fishery, as it was never protected or even mentioned in the water licence. The "Big Dam" as it's now called locally, was built in such a way that the entire water flow into the lower creek could be shut off. When this occurs, there is then a massive fish kill directly below the dam and we have pictures that show dead rainbows by the thousands. Whether this is done deliberately or accidentally does not really matter because, either way, it's still perfectly legal. However, even though things like this continue to go on, a fisherman had better not be caught catching more than an angler's limit, or he will feel the full bite of the law.

The dam didn't have to be closed to affect the fish. If the draw down was done too rapidly, then a great many trout

One of the several summer fish kills at Gaspard Creek that have been witnessed by Chilco Choate and many other travellers. A single turn on the headgate wheel will kill rainbows by the tens of thousands.

were left stranded in the shallows in the upper end. Then to compound that problem, now that the lake is often a 1,000 acres in size, the size of the fish population has risen proportionally. We drew this conclusion from the fact that in years when the lake is drawn down to its former size, there are so many fish in there that we end up with winter fish kills that number in the tens of thousands. When the ice goes out of this lake in the spring, it's depressing beyond words to have to watch these beautiful rainbows being squandered this way. (The size of these trout average about two pounds and the odd one will weigh up to five.)[15]

---

15 I have a copy of this water licence, which is only a few lines in length. About all it says is that the Gang Ranch may store a certain amount of water for a certain number of months. Then they may drain that water during other months.

It was sometime during the early '60s when Carol and I began questioning the legality and morality of a resource management system that allowed things like this to happen. It took many arguments and letters before we learned the bitter truth: namely that, in the name of agriculture, anything can be made legal.

We did get one piece of good advice from a bureaucrat in the Water Rights Branch, when he quietly suggested that the only way such reckless practice would ever change would be through some sort of public pressure, because an outfit like the Gang Ranch would never willingly give up a word that was legally secured into this water licence. Obviously he was referring to a lobby group that was large enough to convince the politicians that the priorities should be changed. If such an organization existed at that time, we never knew about it, but the idea made enough sense that we began to inquire further afield.

In this area the winter of 1962-63 was almost a repeat of 1948. Carol had already moved into Clinton as we had decided that fast replies to our mail was essential since we still had not built up a total repeat clientele. There are always a certain amount of winter chores that need doing around the camp, so we determined that I would spend most of the winter in the bush and drive into town with the Unimog every couple weeks or so.

There was only a basic grub supply left over from the previous hunting season, but if I was going to town every so often, I could re-supply myself throughout the winter. However, in early January a heavy wet snowfall built up to about four feet which took the entire district by surprise. The Unimog with four chains is capable of scratching its way through maybe two feet of snow, but this amount made its use, and my plans of restocking the grub supply, completely out of the question.

The Unimog parked in the yard at Gaspard Lake during the big snow of 1962.

The night before the snow began, another compounder to the food problem arrived at the cook house in the form of Jim Russell, who came staggering in wearing a pair of bedroom slippers, even though there was already close to eight inches of snow on the ground and the temperature was around 0° F.

He had been working at a job feeding cattle for the Gang down near the headquarters at Bear Springs, but that morning he had a heated argument with one of the Sidwells. Jim said he got so goddamn angry that he lit out up the road without even putting on his boots or grabbing a coat. He must have been in an awful snit because he said he was a long way up the road before he realized that he had made a foolish and dangerous decision. From where he left to our place at Gaspard is at least twenty miles. When Jim began taking stock of his situation, he figured he was already half way here so he decided to keep coming in this direction. I don't know if he was sober when he left the Bear Springs cabin, but he sure as hell was by the time he arrived at this end. He was certainly fortunate that he made this trip before the snowfall.

As it turned out, Russell was looking for a new job and a place to spend the winter, but I had nothing for him to do nor money to pay him, so he volunteered to cut some wood in trade for his winter grub and some warm clothes, so that's how he did spend the rest of that winter. Now for sure there was not enough grub in the camp for two of us, so I decided to snowshoe to the Gang Ranch and catch the mail stage back to Clinton. I told Jim I would send more food out by plane. He was also completely out of snuff and he said that was an absolute must or he would go nuts before spring. He had wintered in the bush alone many times before, so he understood what his needs and priorities were.

The mail stage came into Gang Ranch every Wednesday afternoon and left Thursday mornings, so I decided to play it safe and start out of here on a Monday because it was going to be a hard trip with this unusual wet and heavy snow. I started out early one Monday morning carrying a light pack with some cooked meat, dehydrated soups, a small pot, a .22 rifle, and a plastic ground sheet which I intended to use under the snow in place of a sleeping bag. My snowshoes were only four footers and would support my own weight, but they would be too small if I carried anything more than the bare essentials. With winter clothes on I weighed around the 200 mark. Kim, our big Collie, was coming too; there just wasn't enough food in camp for him to winter on. Anyway, Kim was always good company on the trail and I was going to use him as a bed warmer in that plastic sheet under the snow.

The day we started out, the weather was beautiful except for that damn wet snow that was still clinging to everything. Many trees were so loaded that they bent over the road and the snow was so deep that not a single stump or log was visible. It did not take long for me to realize that I was going to need all three of these days for the trip. With each step, I would sink down over a foot and then the heavy snow would fall onto the top of the snowshoes, making them like lead diver's boots to lift.

I was young and strong and the possibility of not being able to make it was a thought that never crossed my mind. Many times before, I had broken trail through twelve miles of snow a day and as this trip was going to be twenty-eight miles in three days, I knew it was going to be tiring, but I believed it was really going to be just another challenge and a bit of a lark as well.

By the end of that first day I had gone only eight miles and as I was preparing to make camp, I made a somewhat alarming discovery. I had not brought an axe. At first it didn't seem that important. In this lodgepole pine country, it's always easy to find a dry stump, log, or branches to build a fire; however this snow was so wet, that all wood was too soaked to burn. After wasting a box or two of matches, I finally gave up on it and decided that because the weather was still hovering around the freezing mark, a fire was not really necessary.

Kim and I shared a piece of meat and I located a nice place for a snow bed. I used a snowshoe to dig a trench in the snow to lay the plastic sheet in; the idea was to then lay down on it, pull the rest of the sheet around me, and then pile a foot or so of snow over top of that. I had never used this method of snow bedding, but there was a book at the camp wherein the author had explained in great detail how it was to be done and he swore that once the initial cold wore off, my body heat would keep the bed as warm as anything else would. It was my idea to use a dog for additional heat. But as soon as I pulled the sheet over him, he absolutely refused to stay and co-operate. No amount of coaxing or threatening would get him back into that cozy hole, so I finally said to hell with him; he could damn well sleep alone, which he immediately did.

I did everything the book said to do but three hours later I woke up knowing that the author had lied like hell. The son-of-a-bitch!! By the time I scrambled up out of that hole I realized that I was not only goddamn near frozen, but I was also soaking wet. Ohhh that bastard!! It was dark by then, but I knew I had to get moving before I got any colder, so I packed up my gear and started out. That goddamn dog was acting so comfy in his snow bed that I had to call him three times before he would even get up out of it.

I did locate some pitch trees and I was able to whittle off enough shavings to get a feeble fire going. The pitch wood burned adequately, but with only a knife to cut it, there wasn't enough to dry out larger pieces so they would burn. These fires were so small that there was almost no heat to them at all. They became merely an excuse to rest while getting some psychological warmth and strength from watching the flames for a while. Sometimes I dozed while standing up or leaning against a tree, but with only my body heat, I was not really resting. I had enough food; the problem was that the lack of sleep and warmth were beginning to get to me.

Each time I re-shouldered the pack to go again, there was another very obvious mistake I had made and it was that goddamn .22 rifle. By that time in the trip I could not remember why I had chosen to bring a gun, because there was nothing that could harm me and I didn't need it for getting food. I couldn't con myself. I had made some stupid blunders. I should have been more careful because fate does not often offer second chances.

About noon of the next day, I arrived at Augustine Rosette's old cabin, but it had been empty ever since he had sold out to Tex. Inside I located an old tin heater, but there was no stove pipe for it. After setting it up in the doorway, I pried some dry boards off the walls and finally got a good fire going. Getting warm again, even if only one side at a time, was an indescribable luxury. Sleep was still difficult, because the plastic sheet was still useless as a blanket. However, it did serve quite well as a windproof wrap while I cat-napped sitting between the heater and a wall. Having to keep the door open to let the smoke out meant that there was no possible way to warm the cabin itself.

Along about evening I woke up, used the last of the wood to boil a pot of Lipton soup, and then hit the trail again even though it was beginning to get dark. The weather and temperature were still holding in my favour, so I decided I had better take advantage of it while it lasted. There was still fifteen miles to go and by then I knew it was going to be nip and tuck for timing if I wanted to catch the stage. It was a long, staggering march. Noon the following day brought me into the first hay fields above the Gang Ranch in a place known as Bear Springs.

There was a cabin there sitting right beside the road. I immediately noticed two very important things: the ranch had ploughed the road down towards the headquarters, and two men were unhitching a team of horses alongside the cabin. I waved to them and they invited me to come in as they were knocking off for lunch. That was an invitation they did not have to repeat.

These two men, Joe Aubin and his partner, had recently taken on the job that Jim Russell had quit and in the course of the conversation at lunch, they invited me to stay the night with them. I accepted because the stage would not leave the ranch before 8:00 A.M. the next morning and I could easily walk the five miles to the ranch in the morning.

I arrived at the Gang Ranch store and post office a little before 8:00 A.M. but learned from the storekeeper that, although the stage had not arrived last evening, she expected it sometime that day. The weather had turned colder that morning and I was still just plain weary, so after buying some chocolate bars, I sat down on the "bummers roost" (a bench beside the wood heater, that all rural stores had in those days) and prepared to wait for the stage. It was not long after that when one of the ranch foremen walked in and spotted me sitting there.

"What the hell are you doing in here?" he snarled.

I explained how I got there and that I was waiting for the stage.

"There ain't going to be any stage coming in over that road today," he said, kicking the bench I was on, "so you better start right in walking again, because you sure as hell aren't staying here."

It sounded like this was going to be one of those times when we weren't going to be getting along very well. There must have been a recent reason, but I didn't recall what it might have been.

For a moment or so, I wavered. I knew the store and land were located on their private property, but there had to be some sort of public access to the government post office that they were paid to operate. But rather than argue the point, I decided to leave. Out onto the road again, I was looking at a sixteen-mile walk to the Canoe Creek Ranch where I had friends, but this time the walk would be easier over a ploughed road. Two days earlier a D-6 bulldozer had come the sixty-five miles from Clinton, so there would be no need to use the snowshoes. There was also the possibility of meeting the stage which would mean my problems would be over.

The road I faced wound along the benchland of the Fraser River and there was not so much as a single tree between the two ranches. Even at this lower elevation, there was still three feet of that wet snow, so there would be no shelter from the wind or any chance of building a fire. All of the fence posts were soaked and I still missed not having that very essential axe. As I walked out of the ranch yard that day, I contemplated sneaking over to one of their hay stacks and burrowing into it. Such a nest would be warm enough to survive in. However, all of the stacks that I could see were still within sight of the ranch buildings, so I gave up on that idea. Considering the mood that the ranch seemed to be in that day, there was always the possibility that someone would be sent to follow my tracks, to be sure that I really did leave, so it was the open road.

After the first two miles down to the Fraser bridge I rediscovered just how weary I really was, because as soon as I began to climb the hill on the east side of the river, I started getting dizzy spells and found myself walking into the snow-banks that the dozer had piled up alongside the road. Resting frequently helped a bit, but the cold wind off the Fraser River made the stops very short and painful because I would begin to shiver and shake. After about the fourth mile, I went to sleep while walking and woke up after tripping and falling over a chunk of frozen snow. This happened several times until I was weaving all over the road. I finally could not walk a step further, no matter what, so I lay down on the lee side of a snowbank and passed out.

What wonderful sleep! I don't know how long I slept that first time or what it was that woke me up. Perhaps it was the cold. I remember all too vividly those first few minutes after awaking and trying to regain my bearings. I attempted getting to my feet but a pain knocked me flat out onto the ground again. When I say a pain, I mean a REAL pain, an absolute stabbing sensation that jerked the muscles right into my heart. My fingers, knees, and back were also affected. I didn't actually pass out from it, but I wished that I could.

After wriggling around on the road for a time, I finally did get up into a sitting position and onto a block of snow. It took quite a while trying to get up enough nerve to start working the joints loose. They hurt so much that it had to be done one at a time. Finally I was able to struggle to my feet again and got things functioning well enough that, even with the pain, I continued my trek.

I remembered a conversation I once had with an old trapper who had told me of a similar experience happening to him. He described the same kind of pain and suggested that it was caused from ice crystal in frozen joints. It was the signal that the end of the trail could be very near. He said if he ever got caught that way again, he hoped he would die, rather than wake up half-way through. That experience had caused him to come to the conclusion that there wasn't much difference between dying today or some other day. As I walked along those Fraser River banks that night, I understood exactly what he was referring to.

Those past few minutes had put a good scare into me and I knew I was in serious trouble. The prospect of not making it was becoming very real. After staggering around for a while, I finally did get started in the direction of Canoe Creek, still another ten miles away. I wasn't really walking; it was more like a slow, wandering shuffle. The few times that I emerged from my daze, I was standing still, but my senses told me that I was walking. That's a strange feeling.

In one of my lucid moments I decided that the next time I had to rest and sleep again, it would be done standing up. I was afraid that either I might not be able to get up again, or worse, I wouldn't want to. If that stage did not come soon, then Kim might be finishing this walk alone.

I found the best way of sleeping while standing up was to stick the heels of the snowshoes into the snowbank on the edge of the road and then position the toes of them under each arm, then lean forward onto them just enough to take part of my weight but not so much that it would push them over. When I did fall completely asleep, I would fall over and wake up. After about three sessions of that, my strength would build up enough to allow me to move on. I probably made a mile or so the first time, but after while the distances shrank to a half or third of a mile.

The one overwhelming thought that kept me going and probably saved my life was my rage at the Gang Ranch. They were going to wish they had not given me the bum's rush out of the post office. My anger certainly kept me very warm on the inside, and probably helped keep me a few degrees warmer on the outside too.

It was close to midnight when I arrived at a large hay field belonging to Jack Koster's Canoe Creek Ranch. This field was about three miles from the main ranch. Over on the far side of the field, I could barely make out a small, board shack. I remembered that the irrigators used it during the summer growing season. The road over to it was completely snowed in, but as it was only a quarter of a mile off the main road, there would be no problem snowshoeing over to it. The alternative was still the steep road up to the ranch. By that time I was so tired and groggy, it was becoming difficult to think clearly, but I did stand there for a while and tried weighing out the "possibles and probables."

It came down to the reality that three miles at that point might just as well have been three hundred miles. The night was becoming darker and the wind was coming up as the temperature was going down, so that shack was the only answer. I knew it was a summer operation and there was no way to know if the haying crew had left any wood in it, but if they hadn't then I had decided to burn the shack. I would have one last warming and, if it went up bright enough, the fire might attract attention up at the ranch and bring somebody down. I knew the Koster family as friends and I can remember thinking to myself, if I have to burn their cabin and do survive, then next spring I'll build them a new one.

To make sure that the stage, if and when it came, didn't pass by me, I rolled some big blocks of snow onto the road, so the driver would have to stop and remove them. Then, with a snowshoe, I made some arrow marks in the snow pointing towards the shack, because I knew if there was wood in there, I would be going into a sleep so deep that I would never hear the truck. When I reached the shack, it took a few minutes to clear the snow drift away from the door. When I finally got it open and struck a match to see inside, the first thing to catch my eye was a stack of split dry wood piled along an inside wall.

Unbelievable! I had made it after all! My God, how do you describe such a feeling? The few minutes it took me to get a fire going and the joy of knowing that I was actually going to see my wife and family again was completely intoxicating. I sat on the edge of the wooden bunk and began laughing until I rolled over and went to sleep.

I do not believe that I slept for very long, because I woke up to a very strange sensation, which turned out to be Kim licking my face. It was very dark in the cabin and as I lay there trying to wake up and make my senses work, there was a realization that something was different. The "something" turned out to be a set of headlights shining in the window. There was the stage truck parked in the road. I was by then warmed up and rested a bit, so it didn't take me long to snowshoe back over to it. The owner/driver of the stage was Sid Elliott, a family friend, and he had a passenger with him who was heading over to the Gang to go to work. They had seen my markers in the snow and smoke from the chimney, so they knew something was wrong and were getting ready to wade over to the shack and check it out.

I explained my predicament to Sid. The road was too narrow to turn the big truck around in to take me up to Canoe Creek, so he suggested I come with them back over to the

Kim resting on the trail during the return home from the ordeal of snowshoeing out in 1963.

Gang where he had a private room in their bunk house. If the ranch would not let me stay there, he said we would drop the mail, and pack up that night, and drive back to Canoe Creek or even go all the way back to Clinton. The danger was over by then, so rather than draw other people into this problem, I decided to go back over to the shack and spend the rest of the night. Sid could pick me up on the way back the next day. So that's the way we did it.

Back in Clinton, it did not take very long for this story to spread through the town. Part of the aftermath of that ordeal resulted in a very polite Gang Ranch manager for several months. But that foreman of his remained a surly son-of-a-bitch and he and I have rarely had a pleasant word for each other since then.

Time has turned this into just another interesting experience, but I still remember what the old trapper said and I concur. It's not the sort of thing anyone wants to go through twice. And, in spite of my anger and vows of revenge during this ordeal, it's not even the sort of thing I would wish onto an unfriendly neighbour.

CHAPTER 19

Our life here was not always plagued by unfriendly neighbours; there have been good times as well. One day in 1963, a cowboy brought us the news that the Sidwells had left the country. They had originated in Idaho and the word was that they had now returned there. From this end of the range, there was a sigh of relief as it seemed inconceivable that the owners would be able to locate another family like them in the same century. Their management position on the Gang Ranch was then replaced by a family from Montana and this is how we met and got to know the Robisons. Wayne became the resident manager and his son-in-law, Don Lower, became farm-boss, responsible for hay production and rolling stock.

Marvin Guthrie, who had already been here for a year or so, moved up a notch and became cowboss. He and his family were originally from Wyoming and had come up to B.C. to try a different facet of ranching. Marvin's wife Pat became the school teacher in the small one-room school house that the government had recently built at the ranch. Jim Bishop had long since left the Gang and there had been a whole series of short term cowbosses while the Sidwells had been here.

For us, this was going to become one of the good times, as Wayne turned out to be a different breed of cat. He was a big man who was pure rancher, but we also heard that he had done a long stint in the army as a master sergeant. If this was true, then he was a natural for it, because he had a voice which he could bring up from the depths of his huge belly and he understood how to use it. On several occasions I watched him make some of the younger hands tremble like wet noodles when he cussed them out and cowboys are not known as being easy to reduce that way. Unlike previous managers, Robison didn't do a lot of work himself, but he understood people and could delegate authority to the right ones at the right time and place. During the years he managed the Gang, he had the longest staying and loyalest crew since the days of MacIntyre.

There were several interesting people who worked under Wayne Robison and most of them were top hands at whatever they did. One of the best allround hands the Gang Ranch ever had was Roy Williams, who originated from Montana. The ranch hardly ever used Roy as a cowboy, because he was so versatile that he became their top fix-it and handyman. Whether it was driving tractors, fixing sticky equipment, skinning the cat, fixing irrigation systems, or helping Guthrie at branding time, Roy could figure out how to get the job done easier than anyone else ever had. He had a knack for getting his crews to work with a will, rather than trying to turn a job into some sort of unionized goldbricking. With that big friendly grin and a disposition to go with it, it's for certain that he will always be favourably remembered by everyone who knew him.

Marvin Guthrie was another cowboy who understood livestock as well as anyone ever could, as horses and cows were his life and they always had been. While he operated the Gang Ranch cowcamp, he maintained a permanent crew of five to six men, who seldom left while he was here. This core crew would be supplemented with four to six short term cowboys during branding time and the fall roundup. It had been a long time since the Gang had been able to induce that many top hands to stay in the cowcamp continuously for a long period of time, but it surely pays off on an operation that is spread out as far and wide as this one.

That last little item right there is one of the major operating problems that the Gang Ranch has always had, as it is spread out over too large an area. After living here for over thirty years, I know that it takes at least three full years before any cowboy can truthfully say he knows the Gang Ranch country. Even after that amount of time, he still won't know all of the meadows and trails, but he should know most of them. I figure that it was about seven years before I was no longer stumbling into new meadows and pot holes that might be quiet retreats for livestock and wild animals to hide in.

There have been times that the Gang paid dearly for not having an experienced crew during their fall roundups, because on many occasions we have discovered small bunches of cattle that the cowboys never found. In an area like the Gang Ranch country, where late fall temperatures will fall to 50F below on top of a foot or more of snow, the results for those cattle are always disastrous. Most ranchers will not even discuss this subject with outsiders, so it's hard to guess how they rationalize it among themselves. The government subsidies and bailouts must help, but it's doubtful if they cover the real loss, and back in the '60s they wouldn't have. There can be a positive point in this situation if we adopt the callous attitudes of the ranchers, only in reverse and that would be to shrug our shoulders and say, "The wild meat eaters have to eat something." What are my feelings about this? Well, at least when the wild carnivores are eating beef, they aren't so likely to be killing moose or deer.

By the 1960s the Gang was not always able to hire as many experienced cowboys as they needed, because the wages offered were usually less than what could be earned elsewhere. Not only that but the past reputation of the place was beginning to take its toll, so the cowboss was always having to train green hands. Some of these novices, because they had the strength and enthusiasm of youth, were soon able to do the work as if they had been born into the life. We noticed that the men Guthrie chose for his permanent crew were the type that he could most count on to stay on the job when the going might become a bit rough. Many so-called "cowboys" are only out for a fair weather lark and then drift off.[16]

Even though we got along well with Wayne Robison and his crew, we still had disagreements over resource uses. As the cattle herd continuously increased, it became impossible not to notice the disappearance of the grass behind them. By the mid to late '60s when the cattle were kept too long in the high meadows, they were leaving little in the way of forage behind them for any animals other than moose, which are browsers of brush. We became almost certain that the increased number of cattle was beginning to displace the feeding places and migration routes of mule deer and bighorn sheep who were grass eaters.[17]

We rarely argued with the Gang about the overuse of the grass at that time, because we did not yet fully understand the ecology of wild grass and other forages. There is no way to know how well the Gang understood forage management either but they did have access to advice from the BCFS

16 These drifters have picked up all sorts of descriptive names such as saddlebums, saddle tramps, and Hank Snows ("I'm Moving On"). One time, when the entire Gang Ranch crew quit all at once, the cowboss bade them goodbye by referring to them as a "fuckin' road crew."

17 Deer are browsers, too, but their browse is so fine and tender that it is also used by cattle, especially if they are left in an area after the high quality feed is gone.

agronomists, who were supposed to be managing the resources on Crown land for the benefit of all people in B.C. However, the problem eventually became so obvious that anyone living here could see that something was out of balance.

It was during those years that we directly challenged the FS agronomists for answers as to what the hell was going on and that was when they more clearly confirmed our earlier suspicions about where their loyalties lay. I had a conversation with an agronomist from Kamloops and asked him why he was allowing the cattle to over-use the range. After a bit of verbal sparring, he finally shrugged his shoulders and told me that if the Gang Ranch wanted to destroy the range, he guessed it was their business because it belonged to them. This man was talking about Crown land!

During the late '60s we were forced to come to the conclusion that the wild forage was being managed entirely for the benefit of the open range cattle industry and the obvious collusion between it and the FS allowed them to pretty well set their own levels of use. This meant that in many cases range management was almost non-existent.

One thing that Wayne Robison and I really did tangle over was bears, especially grizzly bears. Since the domestic sheep (and the herders' poison) had been taken out of these hills in around 1959, the grizzlies were starting to make a noticeable comeback in the high country. Cattle and grizzlies are poor mixers, especially after the bears have had a few free meals from the cattle carcasses left over from poor fall roundups and the poison weeds that cattle will sometimes eat. In the case of the Gang Ranch country, the bears have had this type of table set for them for more than a hundred years and they have now acquired a definite taste for beef. This can hardly be surprising, but the problem between bears and cows becomes very acute when the weeds or winters do not produce enough beef to satisfy the bears' appetites, so some years they tend to hasten the process a bit. They don't kill many cattle in a year, but they do kill some and the ranchers, especially the Gang Ranch, have never been charitable towards them for that reason.

Initially we did not often question the cowboys' actions when they killed a bear that we knew was killing a cow, but some of the hands took to shooting bears on sight. We eventually found out that the ranch management was even encouraging these killings, so that was when I decided that enough was enough and it was time to have a discussion with Wayne over the issue.

The day I arrived at the Gang Ranch office, Wayne was in there alone, sitting behind his desk smoking a big cigar. His booted feet were propped up on the desk, in the grand manager's style and that day I could tell at a glance that Wayne Robison had been born for this job.

As I entered the office, he waved to a chair and the coffee pot and said, "Glad to see you. Pour a coffee and sit down and bullshit a while." He was not glad for long.

After pouring myself a coffee, plopping down in the chair, and discussing the weather for a few moments, I got right down to the reason for the visit. I have always been short on tact so I started right into this bear slaughter problem. Wayne never said a word as I began laying it on, but I could tell that I was making an impression on him: every time I emphasized another point, his face went a shade darker. Most of my argument that day centered around the theory that ranchers have no right to kill bears in remote areas, especially when they very knowingly drove their cattle right up to the bear dens. If the ranchers insisted on grazing their cattle in the high country, then the ranchers should be prepared to absorb the loss of a few cattle to pay for it. Then I went maybe a little too far.

"How about all the cattle that die from neglect, right here on your winter feed yards?" I challenged.

For the old master sergeant, that was the last straw. Down came his feet and he hit the deck with both fists at the same time, as he bellowed straight into my face.

"Well Jesus Christ! You come down to this ranch in the winter and warm your ass beside our stoves. Then you sit here today and drink our coffee that was paid for with cows and you still have gall enough to complain about us killing those goddamn vermin that you call valuable animals! What the hell kind of man are you anyway?"

After trading a few more niceties similar to that, we both cooled down a bit and finally Wayne suggested that I take on the job of controlling their nuisance bears myself and he even offered to pay me for doing so, either in wages or bounty for scalps. I declined because I didn't think that anyone had the right to declare those bears a nuisance as long as they stayed up in the wilderness valleys.

We never did come to an agreement on this subject, but after that meeting we did hear through the telegraph that the cowboys had been told to be more reasonable and be certain that they shot only "cattle killer" bears from then on. The bear killings seemed to slow down for the rest of Wayne Robison's time here.

As I mentioned earlier, this part of the '60s were good times for us and it was not only because we didn't have to watch over our shoulders any more, but it was also a good time for the business as well. 1964 was the year we were able to buy a new Volkswagen pickup to use during the dry months. The roads were beginning to dry up so there were fewer times that we had to use the Mercedes convertible for the 20° below rides or drive our old 1931 Model A Ford, which ran mostly on prayers. This was also the year when we bought one of the first snowmobiles seen in this part of the country and it was an education too.

In those days it was called an Autobaggen and it was made in the U.S.A. by Polaris. It had a few good design points, but basically it was an undependable machine. It took us into many places, but it rarely brought us home again. Several times I ended up walking many miles back home and then having to catch a horse to put a driving harness onto so I could pull the Autobaggen home again. Sometimes I arrived back riding the horse as he also pulled the machine and other times I gambled at staying on the Autobaggen and driving the horse with a set of lines. After cursing and struggling with that machine for three winters, we finally traded it in on a twin track Skidoo, which served us very well for many years after.

Another piece of equipment that we acquired about then was a gas-driven washing machine. Up to that time, Carol had been doing the laundry in wash tubs down beside the creek. I figure that women today have little to complain about if they have not spent a year or so washing clothes on a scrub board and rinsing them in a creek of very cold water. When we were younger, doing the wash this way during the summers was sort of fun, but during the fall it became harder to find any humour in it. Women who had to raise kids under these conditions had a mighty tough life and we continuously congratulated ourselves for having chosen not to try it. That washing machine made Carol's life here a great deal more bearable.

Two machines that made my life a great deal easier were an IEL chainsaw and a two-horsepower gas-driven water pump. It seems odd that I would even mention having a chainsaw then, since they had been in use for quite a while, but it was not until that time that they were honestly reliable. Even at that, there were lots of cross-cut saws still in use as well, but for me I was finished with them. Over also were the hours of packing water up the hill from the creek.

What the chainsaw really allowed us to do was to cut and store enough wood in a short time. If I want to, I can now go out and cut and haul a year's supply of wood in a week, but wood cutting has become my winter's work project, so I'm really not interested in doing it all at once. In the days of the cross-cut saw, I had to cut wood continuously all year round, a time-consuming labour. It's a strange thing though — now that I have saved all that time, I can't really say what I do with it.

The new twin track snowmobile really opened up our winters as it allowed us to rove around much more freely than we had ever been able to do before. Up to then we could travel only on snowshoes or saddle horse. The snowshoes were very slow and riding a saddle horse during a Chilcotin winter is not much fun. There is absolutely nothing that can draw a man's yo-yo up behind his belly button like a frozen saddle.

Another thing the snowmobile did for me that winter of '64, was to satisfy one of my longtime curiosities and begin a controversy that still goes on to this day. On the fourth day of March in 1964, I started from home on the snowmobile heading for Gang Ranch to pick up the mail. While on that trip, I drove right up beside the first elk I had ever seen here.

For the past few years, we had been seeing some strange looking tracks on a big timbered mountain near home and we knew they were not made by cattle or moose, and we suspected that there might be a small herd of very wild elk living up there. Many times Steve and I had tried to catch up to those track makers but they had always outsmarted us. Up to that day, I had never met anyone who claimed to have seen one here either, but that March day finally confirmed that a few Chilcotin elk really did exist. Those elk consisted of only three animals: a bull who had recently shed his horns, and two adult cows.

When I arrived down at the Gang that day, I was bubbling

about what I had seen. That gave Wayne Robison, who had been quite an elk hunter in his day, the excuse to regale everybody in the store with tales of hunting the wily Montana elk. After listening to him that afternoon, he had me chomping at the bit for the opportunity to be able to do it right here in the Gang Ranch country.

We all knew that three elk hardly constituted a breeding herd, and even if there were more around, it was obvious that there were not many of them here. We immediately contacted the F&WB people to inquire about the possibility of having more of them brought in artificially. When the word of this sighting spread, it became very infectious, and we soon discovered that there were many people in B.C. who wanted to see this elk herd re-established too. As time went on, that elk sighting was to have a profound effect on our relationship with the Gang Ranch and most other ranchers as well.

By the spring of 1967 we had learned to enjoy and appreciate the comfort of having friendly neighbours, but it was only a warm interlude. One day word came up the road that Wayne and his family were leaving and so ended the Robison Years at the Gang Ranch.

CHAPTER 20

I think it's safe to say that good times are nearly always followed by bad times. At least that was the way we viewed our fate when in 1967 we heard the ominous news on the telegraph that the Sidwells had returned to manage the Gang Ranch again. This time they were not only back here as managers, but they were now going to be operating the Gang on a share system. From now on they would own a percentage of the livestock and all the equipment, and be responsible for the day-to-day operations of the ranch. The u.s. agricultural community call this system share-cropping.

On the surface this appears to be a good, efficient way to run a ranch or farm, but down south they have at least 150 years of records that prove that it is seldom the case. Farm land is often purchased purely as a real estate investment and can be a fairly safe money and tax shelter, depending on what the absentees had to pay for it. Hence share-cropping is often built around a land base that is owned by absentee owners. They, in turn, must locate someone to operate the ranch for them, preferably someone who understands ranching but might not be all that bright when it comes to financial matters. Not all of these type of deals are based on a fifty-fifty split; it's strictly whatever can be negotiated. So the owners try to increase their profits at the expense of the share-cropper. Usually the land owner ends up on the big end of the stick, but if he is not all that knowledgeable about ranching and makes the mistake of going into a partnership with a share-cropper who is smarter than he is, then that can have interesting spin-offs too.

This is why you will rarely hear stories about these type of partnerships where both parties remain friends for very long. If ever there was a game called "screw your buddy," then this is it. In the case of the ranching industry, however, there can be more losers than the two partners, especially if it's the share-cropper who discovers that he has become involved in a bad deal.

Once he is hooked, the only way he can improve his position is to over-use the ranch and whatever Crown land has been allotted to this operation. Anybody with ranching experience knows that a ranch that has a past history of being able to run 500 cattle on a sustained basis, can also be boosted up to perhaps twice that many for a short period of time.

There are two ways of wrecking a cattle ranch. One is by over-irrigating the hay fields which leaches and salinates the soil through evaporation. The second way is to put too many cattle on the open range. This, over time, reduces the following year's grass recovery and often paves the way for destructive weeds to take over.

Another consequence of over-using cattle ranches in B.C. is a change in land use designation. When a ranch has been reduced to the point where economic agricultural recovery is either unlikely or impossible, the rancher applies to the provincial government to have the ranch land re-classified so it can be subdivided and sold as hobby farms, or that nauseating phrase, ranchettes. This is about the only way cattle ranchers in B.C. ever become millionaires, because those ranchettes have become gold-plated investments. Is there anybody out there that hasn't ever had the sneaking feeling that the land developers and some of the politicians must have quiet little meetings when it comes to re-classifying agricultural land? In the long term, there is almost no way that a land owner can really lose, as long as he bought at the right price. Otherwise, the in between years of paying taxes can eat up future profits.

The real loser becomes the public and the wildlife. The Crown range lands of B.C. contain some our most productive wildlife habitat and also is so beautiful that it has very high social value for the rest of us. As time goes on, we will learn more about these last two, especially if we end up losing much more than we already have. There is nothing else that makes people more appreciative of something, until it is lost and especially if it ends up being lost forever.

But now that share-croppers had a personal stake in the Gang Ranch, they returned here with a vengeance. Not very long after their arrival, Marvin Guthrie, who was still cowboss, rode into our yard one day and quietly tied up his horse. He was acting very subdued and after some small talk, he suggested that we needed to discuss a few things, so he, Carol and I went into the cook house for coffee. Marvin started the conversation.

"We all have a problem and I want you to hear it from me first. A couple of weeks ago we took a herd of yearlings up to Relay Creek and as we passed through Lost Valley, we used your cabin, just like we've been doing for the past few years. By the time we got to Lost Valley, the trip had taken longer then I expected, so it looked like we might run short of grub before we got the cattle positioned around Relay and Paradise Valley.

Well, I decided to borrow some grub from your cabin, just like we've done before, because as you know, when we did that, Wayne always replaced it or made some other arrangements with you folks."

The head of Relay Creek in some of the high country above Lost Valley.

Carol and I agreed that this was true and we also mentioned that there was nothing wrong with continuing the practice, even though Wayne was gone.

Marvin shook his head as he said, "It looks like it's not going to be quite that simple. When we took that grub we made a list of it, because there was a lot of it, about two pack horse loads to be exact."

We could understand why he had made the list, because this was much more than they normally borrowed.

Marvin was still quietly shaking his head as he continued, "You folks aren't going to believe the rest of this, but I've just come from the ranch, where I handed that list to the manager. He looked it over and asked me what it was supposed to mean, so I explained it to him. Do you know what he did then?" Marvin asked us.

Under the circumstances, we were almost afraid to ask, but we did and Marvin replied, "That old son-of-a-bitch

Lower Lost Valley. This is proposed wilderness area.

handed me back the list and said, 'I never authorized you to take that grub,' and then he turned around and walked away."

The three of us sat there and had a sort of left-handed laugh about this turn of events, because it was almost unheard of that any neighbour would do this under any circumstances, but that's the way it was.

Guthrie told us that from then on, they would not be using our cabins and he even suggested that perhaps we should put locks on them in case some of his crew decided to keep right on borrowing things. There was good reason to suspect that they might, as we fed our clients a different grade of grub than the cowboys received from the ranch. In those days the Gang fed quite well down at the headquarters, but the quality and quantity that was sent out to the cowcamp often left much to be desired. Things like spreading cheese, jams, honey, paper towels and even toilet paper could be rare items in a Gang

Ranch cowcamp. So that was the beginning of locked cabins in this part of the Chilcotin.

That grub was worth about $300 which to us was almost as much as we received for a two-week hunting trip. Marvin offered to pay for it out of his own pocket, but Carol and I decided that we would rather try and get it out of the Gang Ranch ourselves, perhaps by embarrassing them into reconsidering their decision. Well, it never worked, so that was also the beginning of our investing money into the Gang Ranch operation. I had to sort of laugh about this, because it was shaping up to look like we were about to open up another account at the good old Gang Ranch Compulsory Bank. We were quite certain that this little episode was only a prelude for things to come and we were right.

My diary tells me that 1968 was the year when things really reached the boiling point around here. Jim Russell came back to winter with us that winter. In February he and I skidooed down into lower country, where we had a satellite hunting cabin. Russell was planning to use it as a prospecting base the following summer, but during the spring he intended to cut his wood supply. When we arrived at the cabin site that day, there was a small problem that changed his plans. The cabin was no longer there. In its place we discovered a pile of ashes and some twisted metal that used to be the stove and bunk beds.

It was obvious that the cabin had burned quite recently as there was no snow on top of the ashes, and we immediately began searching for tracks or other clues. The first tracks we located had been made by a twin track Skidoo, similar to the one we were using. They were not common around here; the only other one that we knew of belonged to the Gang Ranch, so Jim and I gave each other a few "I thought so," nods.

As we searched around a little longer we found a set of horse tracks as well. It was impossible to prove ownership to the horse tracks but we did note that both them, the skidoo and the fire, all seemed to have been made about the same time. Unfortunately we could not be certain which preceded which. There had been no new snow in the past month, so everything must have happened during that spread of time. I asked myself, who would be most apt to be up here on horseback in January? I damn well knew where that horse had come from but, in the eyes of the law, there is a wide difference between knowing and proving.

A few days later I went into the Clinton police station and reported the fire and the circumstances. But because I could not be precise on the timing, plus the fact that the cabin was not insured, they decided that it was not worth their time to come out to do an on ground investigation. The corporal agreed to ask my suspects a few questions the next time he made a patrol out to that area.

It was obvious that if there was to be a real investigation, I would have to do it myself and that's exactly what I did. The information we finally received came by way of a cowboy who said he heard it directly from the person who was claiming to have lit the match. As the story went, the arsonist had been on horseback and he had bragged that he had torched several other small shacks built by local resident hunters down along lower Churn Creek and another larger cabin owned by prospectors.

When I took this information back to the R.C.M.P., I was told that even though this fellow had admitted doing it, the information came out of a drunken cowboy party, which would never hold up in court.

"This fellow is an old bullshiter," the cop advised, "and all he has to say in court is that he was drunk and just telling his friends a bullshit story and no judge in the land would convict him."

He knew I was not totally convinced so he added a final

touch by suggesting, "If we run him in on that kind of evidence, we can be sure that his employers will get him a damn good lawyer, because if we did get him to talk, they might somehow become implicated and they can't afford to have that happen."

The real squeeze was on and we knew that we had to make some important decisions and make them damn soon. From having lived and worked on the Gang, I knew there was no such thing as reasoning with that outfit. The only way we might make them back off, was to squeeze them more than they squeezed us. Gus Piltz had been gone since '59, but many of his survival stories were beginning to re-surface in my mind.

The method we chose was public pressure. By that time we had already made contact with many other people and a few organizations who were as disgusted as we were over the way the Gang Ranch was squandering the rainbow trout in Gaspard Lake. Another area of vulnerability was their glaringly obvious over-use of Crown range land. To our way of thinking, these two situations seemed to be the ranch's Achilles' heel, so we decided to exploit it to the nth degree. Very quickly, we knew that we had guessed right, because in no time at all we were inundated by other supporters rallying to the call. The major reason that there was suddenly so much public support was because these were affluent times in B.C. By then more people had both the time and equipment to travel into these remote areas. The Gang Ranch and the government resource managers, who were supposed to be managing these Crown jewels in the best interest of the public, were finding it much more difficult to ignore or cover up the blunders. There were simply too many witnesses.

By this time too, we were becoming very suspicious that these so-called mistakes might not really be that way at all, but more likely to be very calculated gambles. It's not all that difficult to begin thinking this way when you look at all the many rancher comforts built into the Range Act and other Forestry Service (FS) decisions that make no sense to the public.

For instance, look at the drift fencing system that is used to control cattle on Crown rangeland. These drift fences are applied for by ranchers, approved by the FS, and are largely paid for out of the FS range improvement programs.

When I first arrived here, only three of these fences crossed public roads. But by the early '70s there were ten of them, not one of them equipped with a cattle-guard.[18] All ten of these fences had been built with gates across roads, which meant that a driver had to get out to open the gate, drive through, and then re-close the gate. Multiply that by ten times over a thirty-mile road and you can understand why so many people saw them as nuisances. Is it any wonder then, that these gates were often left open? Not only that, but in some places they were located on steep hills, which means a lot when the road is wet and slippery.

In any event, the ranchers and their allies expected all gates, regardless, to be re-closed. What they demanded from the travelling public and what they began to get were two different things. With so many more people travelling into these remote areas, it was the wrong time in history to start a fence building campaign unless they made it extremely easy for the public to pass through. Once more, the Gang was out of touch with reality.

The damn fools never once built a fence or pasture off to the side of these roads; it was always right directly across them. A growing number of angry travellers rebelled and this naturally made the ranchers equally angry.

------

18 A cattle guard eliminates the need for a gate. It is a perforated deck built into the road and allows vehicles to cross without stopping but stops cattle since they refuse to walk over the deck.

I wouldn't be the least surprised to find out that the ranchers and the FS deliberately incited this situation in the hopes that feelings would run so high that the politicians would then close the range lands to outside travellers. Don't think for a minute that this is a farfetched idea, because at that time some ranchers did begin to threaten to lock some of these Crown land gates with or without government approval, and a few of them actually did so.

So with all this ammunition, we began our counter-squeeze. The word soon spread that Choate was deliberately trying to encourage more people to travel into the Gang Ranch country, which was perfectly true. After that, any time a gate was left open we were directly or indirectly blamed for it. Of course by this time we did not care what anybody thought and that word got around too.

Many of the new wave of travellers into here were not hunters. We began meeting summer fishing parties or people just out driving around in their newly acquired 4-by-4's who were having a weekend of back country exploring. During the 1950s and early '60s we rarely saw a strange boat on Gaspard Lake, but by 1970 it had become a common occurrence. These new travellers could now witness for themselves such things as the fish kills in the Gaspard water system. When they did see this carnage, many of them then arrived on our doorstep trying to find out what the hell was going on. We encouraged as many of them as possible to take pictures, write letters to politicians, or do whatever else they thought they could that might help put an end to the needless destruction.

Everybody that we ever talked to about the fish problem agreed with our earlier contention that the water licence which allowed it to happen must somehow be rescinded and rewritten. All we wanted was a four-inch cleat on the bottom of the gate so that the water could never be completely shut off for any reason and a higher water level maintained. However,

The outflow pipe from the Big Dam at Gaspard Lake. During the heat of summer when the flow has been reduced to this level, the warm water becomes deadly to the rainbow trout living below the dam. However, the same amount of water during the colder months would be sufficient.

even with all the support we received, the Water Rights Branch still resisted the idea. They claimed that the original water licence could not be rewritten. I have come to believe this is mostly because the idea of adjusting things to a more natural level was too simple a solution.

The Gang Ranch was not prepared to voluntarily make the necessary adjustments, so when many of the public began challenging the way they were using and abusing their resources, both the ranch and the bureaucrats in the Water Rights Branch began to get noticeably hot under the collar. We were told time and again by these people, that no agricultural water licence had ever been readjusted to favour wildlife and then they would lean back expecting us to accept the situation as written in stone that goes into perpetuity. It seemed incredible to us that these people really believed that we should meekly accept their stuffed shirt authority as being final, when our very eyes said that they were wrong.

The situation was very similar to the problems within the Grazing Branch. The bureaucrats there had never before had to justify their decisions to the general public. They met the challenge by maintaining that there was no problem. That worked for awhile, but when the heat increased, they cast around for an individual scape-goat. Around here, those goats have turned out to be former administrators who have already been transferred elsewhere or have retired. Apparently, there is no way that these people can be forced back here to explain their reasoning. This person isn't fired or forced to resign; instead, they usually take the flak and then transfer to the other end of the province where I guess they begin screwing up and covering up all over again.

CHAPTER 21

W HEN SOME CONCERNED CITIZENS around here found themselves being stalled off by all levels of government, they started taking the law into their own hands. Here at Gaspard Lake some people started re-adjusting the valve in the Big Dam to suit their own convictions. The Gang then put a chain and lock on the valve, but then the locks were cut. The Gang then put on bigger locks and tougher chains, until someone decided to cut the entire shaft that works the head gate and on it went.

By 1968, all this interference that the ranch was receiving led to an even more belligerent attitude than they had projected in the past. One time when Carol and I were driving home from Clinton, we were waved down as we passed through the ranch yard by Irvin and Blaine Sidwell, the manager's two sons. By the time of this meeting, Irvin had acquired the position of Acting Manager anytime his father was not around, so that day Irvin did most of the talking. They wanted to talk about a recent investigation the Water Rights Branch had done at Gaspard Lake. We had already heard about it and had come to the conclusion that it was nothing more than another whitewash since no adjustment in the licence had been recommended.

What Irvin wanted from us, now that the government investigation was over, was to get off their backs and accept the verdict as it was. He went on to explain that, because of the dry years, there was a shortage of water and if they couldn't use what they needed to irrigate the hay fields, then they would have to reduce the herd.

Well, that made sense, at least from the ranch's point of view, but when I asked him how they proposed to protect the fish at the same time he exploded.

"Goddamn the fish! We got a water licence up there so the water belongs to us. What the hell do you think comes first in this country, fish or the twenty jobs on the Gang Ranch?"

We flat out refused to accept it and that's when Irvin really blew his plug. He's a big fat man who appeared to have a blood pressure problem to go with it, because when he started hollering, he began to go red in the face until he was almost purple. He must have stopped breathing for a moment because he started stumbling around and grabbed the mirror on the truck and I believe if his brother had not grabbed him, he would have keeled right over. Carol and I laughed at his predicament and that did not help cool the situation either, so I put the truck in gear and drove away.

Later on in that same year when I was driving home in the Volkswagen one night, just as I arrived at the foot of a hill near the Big Dam a set of head lights from a truck parked beside the road snapped on and then the truck lurched right into the center of the road in front of me, almost forcing the VW over the bank.

It turned out to be Irvin and his new cowboss. Someone had been leaving the gates open again and they were angry. They both jumped out of their truck and came running over to mine, trying to get the doors open, but they were locked. Irvin banged on my window as he wanted to talk or fight.

There was two of them so I wasn't interested in getting out of the truck, as even if Irvin had been alone, I was not about to volunteer to tangle with him because even though he was a big fat boy, he was also an extremely strong one, so I stayed put.

I made the mistake of opening the window to talk and then when Irvin decided he did not like some of the things I said, he reached through the window and grabbed me, trying to pull me out through it. That was the moment when I realized that I was totally unarmed, which was unusual, as all outdoorsy people carry a knife of some sort. He was lucky about that, because if I had mine he would have lost his arm. We were in a Mexican standoff. Then another truck with some resident hunters in it came around the corner and parked behind the Gang Ranch vehicle. They never got out of their truck, but Irvin cooled down a little, because he let go of me and just stood there cursing, hollering, and waving his fists. I couldn't see his face clearly, but guessed he was seeing purple again.

When the cowboss moved their truck off the road so the hunters could get by, I followed them. I have no way to know how far Irvin intended to go that night, but those hunters, showing up when they did, may have saved my life. Right then I vowed to never leave home without an equalizer again.

The contention had built up far enough that the next time I went to Clinton, I went into the police station to inquire about getting a permit to carry a pistol.

The corporal was just leaving but when I told him why I was there, he went back behind the counter and sat on the edge of his desk. I gave him my arguments and he listened to me deadpan. When I finished, he didn't move for a few moments. Then he stood up, came to the counter, and slammed his hat on it. His face came uncomfortably close to mine and when he started to speak, it was with the voice of a man obviously trying to control himself.

"Ted, what the hell's the matter with you people out there? Isn't a million acres enough for you to avoid each other? Do you think that you're living in Wyoming or Texas or something? You know goddamn well that I can't give you a pistol permit under these circumstances. If I give you a pistol permit to protect yourself from them, then they will demand to have one to protect themselves from you. It'll become a case of higher escalation and we're not going to become part of it."

"Now if you really believe that you need a gun for protection, then what you can do is carry a double barrel shotgun in your truck with a rack of shells handy. In a pinch, you can load and fire that gun with one hand, but you better not let us catch you carrying that thing in the truck loaded, or you'll get a ticket and lose the gun," he cautioned.

"And furthermore, you pay attention to what I'm telling you next. If any of you goddamn fools end up shooting one another, then you had better understand that very few Canadian juries have ever accepted a plea of self defence and I can assure you that the penitentiary is not a pleasant place to spend the rest of your life."

I understood what he was saying alright, but also knowing that the alternative could mean being beaten to death or shot on the trail, I decided to go the shotgun route anyway. The way these confrontations were building up I well knew that there were always more of them than there were of me, so there could be no illusions about the survival probabilities from either type of showdown, should it actually come to that. I never again left home without an equalizer and I made sure the opposition knew it.

The entries in my diary continue to remind me that all during 1968 relationships between the Gang and us got worse as the year progressed. Twice during that summer, someone chased our horses off onto another range. The first time it

240

happened the horses came home on their own, but the next time it took several days of riding and half a day in a chartered plane before they were located. We were very suspicious about who was running them off and I spent several days and a few nights, laying in ambush, trying to catch them in the act, but with no luck. Finally one of our friends, Ronnie Nichol, who was still working at the cowcamp, came over and told us who was doing these deeds and our suspicions were completely confirmed. There was nothing we could do about it, as nobody had actually stolen anything, so we just chalked it up to experience.

Our intelligence system saved us. The biggest and stupidest mistake they ever made — and still do — was in not realizing that some of their hired hands did not agree with their methods. As soon as those hands left the ranch, they began talking about them. Some of them didn't necessarily wait until they left either and we became quite dependant on this type of information. But at the same time, we had to try to be very careful not to overreact until some of the stories could be checked by other sources. I always worried that one day they might deliberately feed us some false information, hoping that we might fall into some sort of trap over it. So far, I have been lucky at being able to sort the truth out of piles of bullshit.

In the fall of '68 I took a resident guide and two hunters out to the cabin at Hungry Valley. When we arrived I found that I was missing another two pack horses of grub. This time it was not borrowed, but flat out stolen. This time we had fresh tracks to work with.

The entire scenario was easy to read. Two people with two horses had tied up right in front of our cabin, broke in, took a set of our pack boxes and loaded them with mostly canned goods.

In that valley, the Gang Ranch and we have our cabins

about a quarter mile apart. I was goddamn angry, so I grabbed a rifle and followed those tracks right to the door of the Gang Ranch cabin. The door was closed but I knew someone was inside and not only that, right there beside the door stood one of my pack boxes. So this was it. I finally had them red handed and this time I was going to settle accounts right then and there. It doesn't make any sense trying to be polite at times like that, so I kicked the door in and had the rifle levelled. The two people in the cabin who found themselves looking down the wrong end of that rifle were not who I was expecting. Instead I found a young Indian couple who had recently hired onto the Gang. I lowered the rifle and calmed them down. When I asked them about the theft, they quickly told me that they had nothing to do with the reason I was there.

Their story implicated the same two riders whom we had been told had chased our horses off. They had arrived at the Hungry Valley cabin expecting to meet a Gang Ranch supply truck. It wasn't there, so rather than wait around for it, they decided to raid Choate's cabin instead. According to the young couple, the two riders had brought the stolen grub and equipment over to the range cabin, sorted it out, reloaded it into their own pack boxes, and then left for the Gang Ranch cabin up in Graveyard Valley. The only thing they left behind were my empty pack boxes.

After a few more minutes of conversation I had cooled down somewhat, so after taking down their names and getting a promise from them to tell all this to the Mountie when he came, we then took my boxes back to our cabin. After I got the resident guide and the two hunters organized well enough to leave them for a day or so, I headed back to Clinton to replace the grub and report to the R.C.M.P. This time I figured that there was so much evidence, the police would finally have to nail this pair to a cross. I was mentally visualizing the

Mounties going up to the Graveyard cabin in a helicopter, locating the evidence (which included some hardware items that could be easily identified), and then bringing the bastards out of there in handcuffs. What a dream!

After listening to the story and this time taking notes on it, the corporal said he did not think this case warranted the expense of a helicopter, so he was going to pursue it from a different angle.

"I don't doubt what you've told me is true, but one of the suspects appears to be a juvenile and there is no court that is going to jail him for stealing food," he advised.

"I'll go out to the ranch and talk to his father and we'll see what comes of that. The next time you're in town, come back in and we should have some answers for you," he said.

I was in no position to argue, so that's what I did.

The next time in Clinton I beat a fast trail up to the cop shop and this time the corporal finally had some answers. He brought out a file and started going through it. Yes, the kid had admitted to the theft so charges could be laid. However, the father had suggested to the Mountie that rather than go through the court, which might not really benefit Choate very much, how about if the ranch replaces the grub, and Choate drops the charges?

The Mountie then went on to explain what the probable outcome of a theft charge against a juvenile and an illiterate old man would be.

"The courts are becoming very lenient on these kind of cases and if we do go ahead and arrest them, I'm almost certain that you will never see either of these two go to jail over it. The most I would expect a judge to do over this is put the kid on a year's probation and suspend the sentence on the old man," the Mountie suggested.

"Of course it's entirely up to you," he continued. "You do have a good case and perhaps a principle that you want brought out into the open, but if we do go ahead with criminal charges, then you will never see a dollar's worth of groceries."

Considering that we were out another $300 worth of grub, I thought that perhaps if we allowed the kid to avoid a criminal record, the whole affair might be conciliatory enough to cool down a lot of other things a bit too. I told the Mountie to send word to the Gang that we would accept their offer.

A few days later when I was not at home, Blaine Sidwell (not the father) drove into our place and apologized to Carol for the incident and asked her to send a list of the missing grub to the ranch and it would be replaced immediately. We sent one in the next mail. After a couple of weeks with no reply to our letter, I stopped Irvin on the road one day and asked him about it. I shouldn't have been surprised by his answer.

While they were waiting for my reply regarding the possibility of laying charges against the kid, they had contacted a lawyer. The lawyer recommended that the ranch should not replace the stolen property, or else they would be establishing a precedent of accepting responsibility for their hired help. As Irvin so diplomatically put it that day, "You can think or do what you like, but we are not replacing that grub."

This turn of events made me as angry as ever, so next time in Clinton it was back up to the cop shop again. When I related the recent outcome of the case to the same Mountie he became almost as angry as I was, but he said there was nothing more he could do because I had already signed a quit claim to the case. As I stood up to leave, he shook his head in disbelief again and said, "Well, I guess that's the price of experience for you."

As it all ended up, the Mountie was right, but the cost of our legal experiences was getting higher and what was worse, we were getting absolutely no satisfaction for our money.

CHAPTER 22

THERE WAS NO QUESTION in our minds about the possibility that the squeeze was really on and every time I had to drive the road through the Gang Ranch into Clinton, I had the feeling that it was a dangerous corridor for me. Irvin Sidwell, who appeared to be running the Gang most of the time, began replacing some of the old crew and we began to notice increasing hostility from some of the new hands. Add to this Irvin's four boys, who by 1969 had grown into big strong teenagers, and I had more people to have to watch out for. While I mostly travelled alone, the more belligerent men on the Gang seldom did, so anytime we met on the road or on trails there were always more of them than there were of me.

Beginning about 1969 we began to experience fist shaking, cursing, proffered fingers, and other expressions of malice from these people and in my own mind the seeds of apprehension were becoming well rooted. I couldn't help but feel that it was only a matter of time until a violent eruption occurred. Although I always had an equalizer within reach, I was living with a sense of impending danger day and night with no end in sight. Then, even the warm comfort from a cold gun stock begins to wear thin. I've never considered myself as timid, but

I'm not suicidal either. We were all armed and something could happen without warning at any moment. Mix in anger, pride, and stubbornness, plus a dash of stupidity and you have a volatile combination that can become impossible to predict or control. In this case both sides possessed all of these traits, so none of it boded well.

Living in the bush with no close neighbours gave us a great deal of time to think and we examined our situation over and over. The might of the Gang Ranch was almost legendary and there were times when this continual confrontation caused us to nearly despair. With the financial and political resources that we knew they had at their disposal, there came times when we had to start asking ourselves: What if the Gang never gave in or even became neutral, but just kept the pressure on us forever? We knew that such a situation was very possible but, other than gun-barrel justice, how could we end this stalemate?

If there was going to be a violent confrontation, I felt it would most likely happen on one of the roads where we had clashed on previous occasions. The Gang had always come on the strongest when we met close to the ranch headquarters, but since that was the only viable road into here, there was no way to completely avoid those encounters. But there were ways to reduce the pressure, at least during the winter months. We began receiving our mail over at the Big Creek post office, which is twenty-five roadless miles around a mountain in the opposite direction of the Gang Ranch.

We had another reason for deciding to do this. The Guthries had left the Gang Ranch and Marvin was working for another large spread in the Chilcotin Valley called the Chilco Ranch. His wife Pat had become the schoolteacher at the one room school at Big Creek and had her own trailer a mile from the post office. This allowed us to warm our butts beside her stove again, but this time without having to take any ballyhoo from a Gang Ranch manager. During those winter months we left our truck at Big Creek too, so this gave us the option of getting supplies from Williams Lake instead of Clinton. Food supplies at Clinton were never a problem but mechanical parts that we were becoming more dependent on were. Since Williams Lake was much larger, we could usually buy whatever we needed right on the spot rather than have to order them and then wait for their arrival on the freight trucks or buses.

Another benefit we gained by travelling this route was that we became acquainted with some of our westerly neighbours. Most of these people were small ranchers, including a few outfitters like ourselves. Despite my battle with the Gang, the ranchers were still friendly although some of them were certainly more than curious about our hassles. None of them had any particular love for the Gang but by that time it had also become common knowledge that I was challenging things like cattle numbers and grazing systems in my area and some of the Big Creek people did comment that they hoped none of the flak would spill over onto their ranges. We had no plans that any of it should, but at the same time I knew that we were breaking new ground and we honestly did not have the slightest idea of where or how any of it might end.

One of the more interesting men I met at Big Creek that winter was an old, semi-retired trapper by the name of Helgi Johanssen, who was working as a part-time handyman on the Church Ranch where the post office was located. In much earlier times Helgi had lived and trapped all through the upper Big Creek and Snow Mountains.[19] He could remember witnessing the very first cattle being taken into upper Big Creek as early as 1905.

Helgi, who is gone now, still had clear memories of those

------

19 I believe this was between 1910 and 1940.

247

years and many vivid recollections of animal encounters, severe weather situations, and just plain survival conditions. He had known most of the original mountain cowboys who had worked for the Gang. He had been encouraged to stay in their cowcamps with them because he had become the resident "wolfer" for this area.

Helgi had been a very proficient wolf trapper and was perhaps the one person most responsible for bringing the local wolf population under control. He had many wolf stories to tell about the Gang Ranch country and I was most curious to hear all I could because, by 1969, they were making themselves noticed again.

During the late '30s and early '40s the government had taken over the wolf problem and with poison had very nearly exterminated them. There were two reasons for eliminating the wolves at that time. First, the general consensus was that all wildlife, not seen as beneficial to man, was considered to be vermin. Secondly, at that time most people who lived here were still quite dependent on harvesting wild meat. Even the ranchers who were raising beef relied on game since it took all the cattle they could rear and sell just to make ends meet.

Helgi had been right in the center of it all and had seen the results of the plan. He had very little tolerance for wolves and in 1969 he still considered the poisoning well done. The benefits were almost instantly obvious, he said, because the moose and especially the deer population exploded. The caribou and elk in the area were already pretty well finished, so it was too late to save them. The major beneficiaries, of course, were the ranchers as up to then the wolves had been preying quite heavily on their calves and colts. They were also quite capable of killing fully grown livestock, and often did.

But it was Helgi's descriptions of where the early wolves had lived and ranged that interested me the most. He could still remember exactly which thickets and rocky knolls the early wolves preferred. I was surprised because, even after a twenty year pause in their activities, the new wolves were choosing the same areas. There is such a thing as a "wolfy" place and, as Helgi advised me then, "As soon as you can learn to think like a wolf, they become quite easy to figure out. From then on, you won't have any trouble catching them."[20]

Like many who had spent most of their lives alone in the bush, he enjoyed talking to those with similar interests and I was very fortunate to have met him. I sincerely hope that someone has or will write down more of his observations before we are all gone. His knowledge and memories are invaluable and it's astounding how quickly memories and unwritten histories fade.

While on the subject of wolves, a few years later I had an interesting wolf experience with some amusing repercussions. A small pack of wolves had been hanging around close to home and lately their tracks told me that they had become bold enough to make periodic sashays through our yard. At that time I was staying alone with only my dog for company and the thought that these wolves might have shady plans for Shep was disturbing because he was a good buddy of mine.

I had set out a line of snares for them but with no success. So Shep and I made an evening habit of walking the edges of the meadows hoping to be able to set a gun sight on them.

On one of those evenings, when we returned home after another unsuccessful search, we found tracks all through the yard telling us that those wolves had come to visit us and had

---

20 In later years public pressure increased to protect wolves. It was largely urban based because in the interior rural areas, they were still considered vermin. Let's not kid ourselves; saving wolves might be O.K. for people not living here, but we knew better.

spent a lot of time snooping into everything that was of interest to a wolf. They had been here in broad daylight which was unusual but their tracks were very clear and interesting to read. They must have had a hilarious time chasing Carol's cats under all the buildings where they still were refusing to leave. The visitors had also thoroughly investigated the moose carcass that was hanging too high up a tree for them. Perhaps that was why they had proceeded to piss and scratch up the whole yard. All those piles of yellow snow seemed to upset Shep even more than it did me.

There was about a foot of snow in the valley and since there was more than an hour of daylight left, I decided to track them on the slight chance that they still might be in one of the nearby meadows. Trailing a pack of wolves on foot is usually a waste of time but I had nothing better to do. On this occasion we had gone barely a mile through the timber where their tracks headed for a brushy meadow. When we arrived there, be damned if there weren't four wolves right at the edge of it, all sitting on their haunches waiting for us. The range was only 100 yards, so in the space of five seconds I emptied the four rounds from my rifle. When the noise and excitement were over, there were three dead wolves in front of us. Shep chased the fourth wolf out of sight before he returned and helped me examine the results of our hunt. I could tell that he was just as pleased as I was because he made a deliberate show of going around and pissing on every one of them. He came over to me and seemed to be wondering why I wasn't doing the same.

We were not very far from home so I decided to go and get the Skidoo and a sled to haul the carcasses back rather than trying to skin them out on the meadow. When we arrived back at the house we found a group of strangers on snowmobiles in the yard. When I told them about the wolves, they fired up their snowmobiles and we all roared up to the meadow and brought them home draped across our vehicles rather than bothering with the sled.

After we had laid them out under a tree, it began to dawn on me that my next day was going to be a chore. Wolves are not that easy to skin and, furthermore, they stink like hell during the actual skinning.

These visitors hailed from Vancouver and, even though they were all hunters, they had not thought to bring their guns with them on this occasion. All the same, these dudes were very impressed and envious. Because of the excitement and our mutual interests, a camaraderie quickly developed. I invited them to spend the night and they accepted.

There were lots of hunting yarns swapped that night. Periodically we would go out to look at the wolves for they did have beautiful pelages. We were able to steer the conversation onto the topic of what the probable value of fur would bring me. With the bullet holes in them it was decided that they might bring $100 each. It was an enjoyable evening and after we had toasted the hunt with two bottles of their rum, I decided to let my new friends "steal" all three of those wolves from me for a total of $200, thankfully freeing me of the task of having to skin them.

I was very proud of myself because it was the largest single wolf kill that I had ever heard of in this area so it didn't take much encouragement to get me to keep telling the story. I knew that the wildlife biologists working out of Williams Lake would be interested, so I went over to their office to give them the full benefit of the hunt.

After listening to my story, they weren't as enthused about it as I thought they would be. Then one of the game wardens who had been listening from across the room casually walked over to me and smilingly asked me, "Do you know how many wolves you are allowed to kill in a year?"

Oh God! I had forgotten all about wolves having recently

had a kill quota set for them. Well, there were too many witnesses by then to back out, so I brazenly piped out, "I think it's three."

Actually I didn't have a clue what the new law allowed as I never expected to find myself in a situation where that law would ever be a problem.

The warden was still smiling as he nodded and replied, "That's right and you'd better remember for the rest of this winter that you already have yours."

That was too close a call; if there had been more cartridges in that rifle, I surely would have laid out all four of those animals.

When green grass finally returned and we had to go back to using the road through the Gang again, we were able to go quite a while without having any critical flare-ups with them, but the subtle squeeze was always there. Hardly a week went by without something happening: pasture gates left open, fences cut, the small horse pasture packed full of cattle, horses run off, and an endless number of cute things like these. We never found out if these little tricks were done on management's orders or whether the new hired hands were simply creating some western-style fun and games.

The cowboys learned to use the cattle like weapons. They would innocently drop a few salt blocks right beside our pasture fence. One time I watched one of them actually roll a couple of the blocks under the fence so the cattle would have to tear the fence out to get at them. They may have thought that they were doing the ranch a favour, but it didn't always work out that way.

Once when we were moving a party of hunters out into a satellite camp, I arrived there in the Unimog first while Steve was taking a longer way around with the hunters, trying to locate a moose on the way over. As soon as I got to the campsite I knew that this was going to be a good hunt as the small meadow that we used for picketing the horses had not yet been discovered by the cattle and the grass was at its peak.

I had just finished setting up the camp when I heard something out on the meadow and so I walked out to the edge to investigate. It turned out to be a cowboy on horseback leading a pack horse loaded with salt blocks. He began dropping them in among the picket stakes that I had just driven in. His intent was obvious so there was no sense in saying anything to him as this was part of the old game. I decided that as soon as the cowboy rode away, those blocks were going to be tossed into a nearby bog hole.

However, as he rode out of sight, three other cowboys arrived from the same direction driving a herd of about 500 cattle and hazing them out into this meadow. That number of cattle would eat the grass completely out within twenty-four hours which meant we would have to move the camp again the next day. But there was a slight chance that the cattle might not want to stay there. With our camp set up so close, they might just drift right by us and look for feed somewhere else. The cowboys must have come to the same conclusion, because instead of merely dropping the cattle and riding back to their own camp, they positioned themselves around the meadow to make damn sure the cattle did stay there. I don't know how long the boys intended to ride herd that way but by then I was goddamn angry and I decided to speed up the drifting process.

Out in the center of that meadow a large rock protruded above the grass. It was about 200 yards from our camp so it was exactly the right size and distance to be a convenient "siting in" rock for a rifle. The cowboys and the cattle were still well off to one side so there was no danger from ricochets. I fired off five shots and determined that my 30:06 was still hitting right on the mark. Cowboys or not, by the time my fifth bullet whanged into that rock there was not a single cow on that meadow, or for that matter, within sight. The cowboys shouted curses at me from across the meadow but they never offered to come over and discuss the matter at closer range. Instead they followed their cows back down the trail from where they had so recently come. This was one of the few incidents that was quickly and simply resolved but there were too many others that were not.

CHAPTER 23

AFTER ANOTHER WINTER was behind us, the early summer of 1970 brought me the sad news that my long-time friend and trail partner was dead. Steve Johnson had been killed in a truck accident in front of his Canoe Creek home. Over the past fourteen years Steve and I had shared a lot of campfires and in many ways we had become as close as brothers. We had both been born to hunt and ride and had done much of it together. His time with me here had been as a hired hand but our relationship was much more than that. There were many times that when we got fed up with the dudes, we would ride up into the alpine country with only two saddle horses and a pack horse and camp up there for a week or two. There was no commercial reason to go up there but we just wanted to go exploring in the type of country we loved the best. We never did revert back to the stone age but there were times when it had a pretty strong appeal, too. Trips like these gave us such warm and glorious feelings that when we came back down, we felt rejuvenated enough to tolerate the humdrum life we needed in order to be able to purchase the necessities of life. Steve had married and had started raising a family at Canoe Creek, so we had begun to drift apart. Now, except for the photographs and the memories, it was all over.

On the right is Steve Johnson who was one of Choate's best friends. This was the country and life he loved the best. Sometimes when they were not hunting, Choate and Johnson would pack up a horse with a few days' grub and head back up into this country to just lay around and soak the land and feelings into their souls. To be able to do this made the dudes and life at lower elevations a lot more bearable.

That was also the year when we began to expand the business into trail riding and snowmobile tours. By that time the new twin track Skidoo had proven its potential and we had almost complete confidence in it. Any time we left the home valley we still carried snowshoes, but the chance of needing them had become quite remote. Except for the noise, I soon discovered that the machine opened up a whole new winter world.

It also gave us the opportunity to make much more accurate game counts than we had ever been able to do on foot or horseback and in the winter of '70-'71 I discovered that the moose and deer numbers were on the rise from their 1964 to 1966 low. They were still lower than they had been in 1955, but now that the F&WB had finally begun backing away from the long antlerless seasons, the animal numbers were responding correspondingly.

Actually I only tried those snowmobile tours for about three winters. They never did become very popular and perhaps that was a good thing since the Skidoos of this era had excessive engine noise, especially compared to the earlier Autobaggen with its four cycle engine. The latter's engine gave off such a different sound that it never seemed to bother or frighten animals as much. But with the newer Skidoo I noticed that the animals were beginning to shy away from the trails we travelled frequently. Even the horses and dogs didn't like the sound from the two cycle engine.

Those commercial snowmobile tours also taught me a little more about human psychology. I found that too many people are affected by snowmobiles in much the same way that others are by big motorcycles. It absolutely astounded me that so many people, who should have known better, wanted to chase wild animals with them. It was not so much a case of them wanting to kill the animals; they just "wanted to see how close we can get to them." When this is done to pregnant moose and deer, a long and terrifying chase often results in miscarriages and death from exhaustion. I sometimes had a difficult time convincing these people that they should not do this and it made me wonder what they would have done if I had not been there as a witness. Although smaller animals such as coyotes, wolves, and foxes are not as seriously distressed as the larger ones, even they have become much more wary about where they travel. They don't spend nearly as much time out

257

in the center of large openings any more. So deep down, I was secretly glad those tours fizzled out on their own and we didn't have to make the choice ourselves.

The other business we began expanding was the summer trail rides up into the high country. By the early '70s we knew that our hunting enterprise was much too narrowly targeted for us to be able to depend on it for a long term livelihood. Since we already had the horses and the beautiful mountains so close to home, this was the most natural direction for us to go. We were extremely vulnerable to game numbers which we knew could fluctuate not only from normal causes, but also from governmental blunders. As well, there was a growing anti-hunting movement which could no longer be ignored.

The summer trail riding was targeted towards the non-hunting fraternity and by now almost every outfitter in B.C. has tried these vacation packages, with varying degrees of success. It all depends on the geography where the trips will be conducted. After being in the business now for many years, I can make several observations. Several of the purely hunting operations are located in very rugged terrain that represents an endurance test not only to get into them, but also to travel within the area. While these are challenges that hunters will endure and even appreciate, very few family-type vacationers will.

As well, the cost of operating in remote areas is a great deal higher than it is for those located close to easy access. This last item has turned out to be an important one as it reflects right back to the cost of the vacation package. Hunters are prepared to pay whatever it costs to get the game and the experiences, but sightseers have proved to be very cost-conscious. The trail ride business seems to come in fits or flurries: one year we might have a half a dozen trips and then only one or two or even none the next year. Only the hunting business remains quite constant and I can't explain why the difference in the two activities.

With the early '70s came the suspicion that this area was into a drought. The ranchers who were dependent on irrigation water were the first to really notice it. Even though we do not put up any hay on our place, it began to affect us too because the Gang Ranch was still trying to build up its cattle numbers. This meant that they had to develop new hay fields which, in turn, required more water from the Gaspard water system. So it intensified the old conflict between livestock and fish. But the problem went further than that because the drought also meant that the wild grass in the natural meadows was not receiving the moisture it needed to grow anywhere near the quantity or quality it had when I first arrived here. And all of this on top of an increasing cattle herd. Somebody was nuts.

Another part of our business diversification plan was to try increasing our cabin rentals to summer fishing parties. We had always felt that one of the reasons our fishing business had remained quite slow was because of the terrible access road conditions and for the past several years we had been kicking around the idea of building a small dirt airfield to accommodate the fly-in fishermen that were going right past our place to one of the many fishing camps to the west of us. We didn't own enough land to build such a strip so it required another lease application to the Provincial Lands Branch. We made the request for a 3,000 foot strip through some scrub timber, but of course the application was then taken to the local Cattleman's Association for their approval. What that boiled down to was getting the Gang Ranch's blessing. We would have had a better chance if we had asked the sultan for the room key to his harem.

Because of the Gang's rejection, it took us three years

before it was finally approved, and even at that, my dad had to make an appeal through a friend who knew a cabinet minister.

Shortly after we had received government permission, the manager of the Gang, Mel Sidwell, drove into the yard. He was really worried and perhaps with good reason. If we encouraged more fishermen into the area, it was almost bound to put more public pressure on their already unpopular water licence.

He must have been really concerned because that day he became very conciliatory over other issues. If we would agree to drop the airstrip application, then the Gang would never again complain about our horses being on the open range. He even went so far as to offer us the use of some of the ranch's pastures.

His proposals were certainly very tempting, but I still kept getting that gut feeling that they were only offering these things because they felt I was successfully blackmailing them. If so, then it was likely that they would renege later on.

When I hesitated, he mentioned the possibility of us getting together to lock the road off near the ranch headquarters. We could then share the key between us and therefore be able to control all other travellers into the Gang Ranch country.

I would be a liar if I said I was unmoved by these proposals but every time temptation rose up, the doubts about trust swept it away. I simply could not keep myself from thinking: Oh yeah, control the general public today, and who tomorrow?

When I declined his offers, he jammed his cigar in his mouth, climbed into his truck, and angrily slammed the door.

"Alright, you son-of-a-bitch, if that's the way you want it, then we'll just figure out another way of discouraging those goddamn tourists from coming in here!"

A few days later, we noticed that the level of Gaspard Lake was dropping at an alarming rate. A three-mile ride down to the Big Dam told us why: someone had turned the valve wide open and, since the ditch system was only capable of handling about two thirds of that amount, the rest was being flushed straight into the Fraser River. The valve was locked so there was nothing we could do about it and it was left that way until half the lake was drained. After that, the ranch had no problems proving their need to use all of the remaining water.

Perhaps the manager could rationalize that move but we often wondered if the owners could because, as it turned out, that action had a very sharp double edge to it. It really was the beginning of a long drought and the Gaspard has never fully recovered since. If you figured out the subsequent hay loss to the ranch and showed it to any other outfit, they would shudder in disbelief.

We did end up building the airstrip but the increase in fishing business never did materialize. After maintaining it for a few years we finally gave up on it and let the lease revert back to the Crown. It's now classed as a very rough emergency runway to be used at your own risk. It's still used by a few people, one of the more consistent users being the Gang Ranch.

One of the bandaid cures the Gang attempted in 1970 after the lake went down was to drain an area known locally as the Big Swamp, a 1,000 acre meadow area that had filled with water and had remained that way up to this point. By 1970 it had become what would best be described as a very shallow lake and it was now an absolute haven for thousands of muskrats and nesting waterfowl.[21]

---

21 The first time I laid eyes on the Big Swamp was just after freeze-up in 1955 and there were over 200 muskrat lodges built there, the most I had ever seen in an area of that size.

There are no feeder creeks to keep the swamp topped up, but there were several springs that were large enough to stay open most winters. It was difficult to tell how much water there really was, but in a drought year it was water, the Gang Ranch was classed as agriculture, they wanted it, and you can guess at the outcome.

We never have found out which resource branch of the government recommended that the application to drain the swamp be approved, but no doubt it was endorsed by more than one of the highly educated "experts." The Gang contracted a D-8 Cat to go in and dig a huge ditch from the swamp into a feeder creek that drains into the Gaspard Lake at a rumoured cost of $10,000, a lot of money in those days. Eventually more than ninety percent of the swamp was drained and naturally, because of the lack of incoming water, it has never refilled since. Within a year or so, the Gang went back and put a dam in their new ditch in an effort to restore the water, but the drained swamp refused to hold water. The drainage also left a foot of silt at the head of Gaspard Lake.

Although part of the old meadow is beginning to revert into a marginal grazing area, this fiasco provided the Gang with only four days of water.

The question here should be, how is it possible that all those government experts were so goddamn stupid as to not realize that the swamp was so shallow and, with no creeks coming in or out, it could not possibly have become a commercial water supply? If there had been surplus water there, it would have already built up and formed a natural overflow into the creek, but there was no such thing. The springs and the annual runoff were just barely able to maintain the delicate level that the past twenty years had established. And these are the same experts who know what's good for us so don't ask questions or rock the boat, thank you very much.

1971 began as a sad year as word came along the telegraph that informed me that my old friend, tutor, and employer had died. Jack Maindley had long since sold his ranch and retired to Victoria, but he and I still corresponded quite often. He had always remained interested in what I was up to, although he didn't share all my opinions, especially my more recent attitudes I held towards the cattle industry. I can still remember one of our last conversations when we were discussing that topic and he obviously didn't agree with something I had said.

He laughed and said, "You bloomin' young fool, you can't stop those sort of things from happening."

Old Jack was a grand old rancher. He had always been a tolerant person and it's too bad there aren't more like him today to put the finishing touches onto some of the wild youth who are being squandered because of a lack of stable guidance. When I think back to my three years with him, I realize that he knew how to keep just enough rein on me, so that I never felt locked in but never got into any serious trouble, either. He understood how to do that and, at the same time, get enough work out of me to run the ranch. When you think about that for a moment, it was quite an accomplishment. I have always hoped that Old Jack felt he received as much value for his efforts as I received for mine.

The year was not cheerful for another reason as well. By then Carol had been here eleven years and she decided that she had had enough. I forget all of the reasons for her decision, but it was mostly economic and partly because of our continual confrontations with our big neighbour that we never seemed to win but that I still refused to walk away from. A feeling of being perpetually squeezed is depressing and it takes its toll in the end. Once when we were discussing the possibility of her leaving, she said she was going back to town to become civilized again. She invited me to come along if I wanted to.

In the end she did leave and went back to nursing and, even though we visited back and forth for sometime afterwards, the fire slowly went out of us.

CHAPTER 24

W HEN JIM HATTER MOVED into the higher echelons of Victoria and Lawson Sugden moved elsewhere, this area received a resident wildlife biologist by the name of Harold Mitchell. Mitchell became very well known throughout the Cariboo-Chilcotin country and almost every rancher, outfitter, logger, and prospector has their own favourite stories about him. He must have been posted here around 1963, but I never met him until 1970. In time he and I became personal friends which must have stemmed from the "birds of a feather" syndrome because in many ways our theories and methods for benefitting wilderness and wildlife complemented each other. Of course there might be a few ranchers and forest wreckers around here that would dispute some of that. Harold was not the easiest person to get to know or like, especially for people who did not share his opinions about wildlife management.

I first met Mitchell when he came to an outfitters' meeting being held in the town of Alexis Creek. This was only a meeting of the local outfitters, but the F&WB always sent a representative and that day it was Mitchell's turn to be their rep. He was probably under orders to go because it was at a time when the antlerless hunting seasons were still very hot topics in these small towns and the local wildlife biologists were constantly under fire over them. During this particular meeting, when Mitchell stood up and gave the F&WB report, he never once mentioned antlerless seasons. But the way these meetings are conducted, the F&WB must floor questions about all forms of wildlife management. That day nobody in the audience wanted to talk about bighorn sheep or habitat. All they wanted to know was, why the hell were we still killing so many cow moose? Mitchell had heard and answered these same questions many times in the past and he was fed up with explaining his views on the subject. By then we all knew he was not the sort of person who was easily moved to change his mind about something and that day was no exception. Well, we were just as bull-headed as he was, but after a while the questions were becoming repetitious and that was when he raised both hands and said, "Look, if cow moose season is all you people want to talk about, then I don't have any more to say to you."

Nobody offered any other questions so he walked over to a bench at the side of the hall, lay down on it, closed his eyes, and went to sleep. The rest of us continued on with our meeting and when it was over I noticed that he never offered to join us for our yearly farewell beer at the hotel.

The F&WB is not without its own share of closeted skeletons and in this part of the B.C. interior it has been in the form of the long, antlerless hunting seasons. As I mentioned earlier, the first of those seasons was imposed on the moose in 1954 and almost the entire concept was the brain child of B.C.'s first wildlife biologist, Dr. James Hatter, who later on got elevated all the way up the ladder until he headed the F&WB. As far as we were ever able to find out, he based the need for killing these animals on his own observations of game counts plus the fact that the system had worked in Europe, especially Sweden.

Dr. Hatter and a few of his assistants came up with the theory that the Cariboo-Chilcotin moose range was overpopulated, even though, after 1948, there were very few local residents who agreed with them. There was a consensus that the ratio of bulls to cows was way out of whack, but that was all. However, once the season opened, the government sold licences and tags to all comers and the annual moose kill skyrocketed. I figure that it took only about three hunting seasons to rebalance the bull-cow ratio but the government continued that antlerless season for about fifteen years and some of those seasons were left open for up to sixty days.

By 1964 everyone who lived around here knew or suspected that the moose herd was in deep trouble and it had nothing to do with overpopulation, but just the opposite. It had become a case where, in order to keep the kill numbers up, we were killing off our basic herd, so the juvenile recovery was nowhere near what Dr. Hatter's text books said it was supposed to be.[22] Something in the planning process went wrong and again it was the simple and obvious things that went right over top of these experts.

To begin with, Dr. Hatter's moose counts after the winter of 1948 could not possibly have reflected the true numbers that were here by then. Hatter did not have the technical

---

22 We now have meadows where few moose have fed in for years and so have become overgrown from this lack of browsing. In the Gang Ranch country between 1965 and 1974 (where cattle herds were allowed to increase beyond the grass resource to feed them), the cows actually did begin extensive browsing on brush.

However, after 1974, and also in areas where cattle have not overgrazed, the browsing bush came back in leaps and bounds. I have pictures that show where some meadows have become so brushed up that it has taken over the grass cover. This sounds like it should be good news for the moose, but there are no longer enough moose to utilize more than a small fraction of the new feed.

ability to make accurate moose counts over large areas. Remember, before 1954, there were no snowmobiles, and helicopters around here were still very rare. All they had to work with were a few trucks, short distance foot patrols, and occasionally an airplane. Perhaps to someone who has not tried it, the use of a fixed wing plane might sound like an effective machine to use for game counting, but I can assure you that in the timbered areas of the Cariboo-Chilcotin they aren't. To sum all of these words up, Hatter's moose count must have been haywire and damn rusty haywire at that.

Another area of moose management he slipped up on was his attempt to copy the intensive management systems used in Europe. The difference in conditions between there and this part of Canada are almost incomparable and he should have realized it. Firstly, there are not enough wolves in Sweden to affect any other animal populations such as there are here. Secondly, poaching is almost unheard of in Sweden, but in parts of this country it's estimated to equal the licenced harvest. Thirdly, Sweden does not have to contend with the native food harvest which was always here and still is. Back in the early '50s when Hatter did his studies, there was also a very heavy moose harvest being taken by the ranchers and other new white settlers that were beginning to pour into here. Hatter must have known about these extra harvests that were over and above the licensed kill, but for some reason he seems to have ignored it or grossly underestimated it.[23]

Even though Dr. James Hatter is now known throughout the academic world as an expert on Canadian moose, I still consider him to have been the worst thing that ever happened

---

23 I know a great deal about the local white game harvest. When I lived over near Alexis Creek, we were very much a part of it and we were by no means isolated cases. I could give you kill figures that would curl your hair but, for obvious reasons, I'm not going to.

to moose management in B.C. To come up with that theory I offer my argument in the simplest terms, such as, if Hatter's management is to be considered to have been right, then why has this moose population declined?

A few years later, Mitchell and I did have a one on one conversation on that antlerless moose topic and he gave me an explanation for his previous stand. He told me that when he took over the job in the early '60s, the antlerless moose season was already well established and as a junior biologist he inherited the entire package. When he arrived here, he said, there still appeared to be lots of moose around, so he had no particular reason to dispute Hatter's earlier estimates. Besides, even if he had wanted to do so, he had no way to prove the earlier figure might be wrong, so therefore he was in no position to challenge the senior bio. Mitchell said he actually did figure that Hatter's figures were close. It was not until the '70s, when he had access to more helicopter time, that he began having some doubts and before he was finished here, he had begun reducing the antlerless seasons, but for some specific localities, it was getting mighty late.

In the 1970s the drought became worse year by year, and so the overuse of the land by putting more cattle in the high country became much more noticeable. A group of people from the little town of Goldbridge, about fifty air miles from Gaspard Lake, were so concerned that they proposed making a park or wilderness area out of about half of the Gang Ranch's summer grazing area. They went so far as to suggest a name for it: the Charlie Cunningham Wilderness Park.

As soon as Mitchell and I heard about this proposal, we jumped onto their bandwagon. Harold was able to provide professional expertise and I used my noisy typewriter to fan up support.

However, again we learned of how slowly governments can move. The final decision has never been made and in the

269

Choate with clients and friends in the Sheep Camp cook tent.

end this area will probably be designated as single use, which means we will either wreck it or reserve it completely.

After Carol left, there was another interesting change in the business and my life as well. After having had a woman's touch around here for eleven years, I was acutely aware that most of our clients appreciated that fact and I did too. I might have been softening from age because when the opportunity to revert back to the bachelor days of "boar's nest" living actually arrived, it no longer had the appeal that it had fifteen years earlier. Carol had never come out to cook in the satellite camps or on the trail, but just having her touch at the home place was always something worth coming back to, so it didn't take me long after her absence to decide that there was going to be a female camp tender here, even if I had to hire one, which was exactly what I did.

Over the period of the next several years there was a continuous procession of these women and you can safely bet

270

your poke that I received a great deal of ear-burning comments from most of my male friends about it. Of course those fellows viewed the situation in the wrong perspectives and I know that they were just jealous as hell of what the possibilities could lead to. The fact that every one of those women was very good looking, right up to almost beautiful, didn't help cool their leering thoughts. Two of them were models who came up to the bush just to get away from the city for the summer. Some years there were two of them here at the same time as one was hired as trail cook and the other remained at home as housekeeper and caretaker.

There were some other positive aspects to this situation and it's not what you think, either. All of these girls were young, bright company and when the word about them being here started circulating, it must have burned the moccasins off of the old telegraph system. All of a sudden Choate's place at Gaspard Lake became the turnaround point for more young game wardens, forest rangers, and cowboys than I could shake a stick at. It seemed like every time we looked out the window, there was another truck coming through the gate.

This was also at the same time when I was becoming much more involved in the politics of environment, wilderness, and wildlife, so many of those government employees brought us loads of information that I would never have known about if there had not been those warm feminine smiles and cups of hot coffee. Most of those women were as deep into environmental issues as I was, so they needed no instructing from me, as to what sort of information we needed from these people.

The cowboys became mighty helpful too because most of them were younger then I was and around a place like this, there is always a forgetful horse or two around that needs re-educating, so it allowed those boys a chance to show the young women how good they were at taking the kinks out of them. These Chilcotin hills learned that smile-power can move mountains.

I don't know if I was the first outfitter around these parts to deliberately hire women but it's quite possible that I was. These were the "hippy" years but even so, only a few of those girls really were like that. Most of them arrived here because of the new women's liberation that had finally allowed them to come out and partake of some of the outdoor "fun" jobs that we men had always been able to corner and keep for ourselves. Personally, I have never been afraid or jealous of feminism, so when these young women arrived here, I just let them fit into whatever part of the operation they wanted to try. All of them were horse crazy, so several of them became wranglers as well.[24]

I have many interesting and humorous memories of those girls. One of them that arrived here was a very pretty twenty-year-old red-head. It did not take the rest of us long to realize that she tended to be a bit different from the general run of people who circulate around a hunting camp, because she turned out not only to be a vegetarian but also a Greenpeacer. By that time Greenpeace had become a very bad word among the ranching and outfitting industries, so she had wandered right into a lion's den, but in spite of this, she decided she was staying. For a while, it seemed hard to believe

---

24 The one job I never gave them was as a hunting guide. There is no reason why a woman cannot become just as proficient a hunter as a man. But when it comes to guiding others, then the problem of packing the game out of the bush comes up. I still cannot figure out how a 120-pound woman is going to lift 150 pounds of moose quarter up on to the back of a packhorse. I do know how they get around those heavy loads. Considering that there would always be a hunter around, perhaps it's another of those things that can be done by smile-power. Either that or they must be very big.

that she was serious, but considering that she was willing and able to do the work, our summer became an interesting social challenge.

I am a meat eater and usually have it with every meal and sometimes it's my entire meal, so we often found ourselves setting up two different menus for the same table. The cook had no problems with cooking meat for the clients; it was only that she didn't eat all of her own cooking and that does become noticeable. It became much more so when she and I were alone at camp, because under those conditions she was not expected to do all of the cooking, even though she did do most of it. She was not on a monthly salary, but rather on a contract rate for the duration of a trip, so in the interim, she could do as she pleased. Under these conditions most of the meals became more to her liking than they were to mine. But as long as she was volunteering her services, it didn't seem like a wise idea to complain about the food unless I was prepared to take over the preparations myself, which I wasn't. She was into the natural food kick as well and when she discovered that the blankets of wild mushrooms that grow here are good to eat, you can guess what our table became. I like mushrooms too and still do, but for me, they go best with a steak. However most of that summer we had them in every conceivable way except with steaks.

We sparred over food all summer and by the end of that season she ended up going into town where she bought herself a hunting licence which she used to pot a young moose to take back to the city for her winter meat supply. I had already taught her to shoot a 30:30 in case she ever needed to use one for protection and she had become a pretty fair shooter. I don't believe she belonged to Greenpeace any more either.

By the time these young cooks began working here, I had already started getting into the summer trail riding business in a bigger way than we had ever tried before and that opened

273

my eyes a little wider too. Our sightseeing clients turned out to be mostly non-hunters and on top of that, most of them were women between twenty and forty. We even had some parties that were made up entirely of women, mostly professionals such as nurses, secretaries, teachers, and stewardesses. There were parties that involved men too, but I noticed that when the party began writing for information, almost always the writer was a woman.

I expanded the summer business by lengthening the season, not by the party size, as we still rode out with groups of two to four adults, making the total party not more than six. I usually took along my big dog. Dogs love to travel with the horses and they are great trail companions, especially at meal times. A good dog earns his steak bones by patrolling the camp and horse herd at night and many times a midnight growl from Shep or Snoodle brought me wide awake and out into the meadow with the horses just in case a bear was prowling too close. I don't know what the growls did for the clients but I noticed that anytime I got up to do a foot patrol, it always caused the flashlights to come on in their tents, but rarely a volunteer of help. It must have been the cool night air that kept those tents zipped so tight, since a person can get quite chilled while wandering around in the dark that way. However, we were always lucky, because of all the mountain rides I took those people on, we were never once bothered by an aggressive bear.

These summer rides also meant that I was actually up in the hills far more often than I used to be. That meant that we were living closer to the cattle operation than we had in the past, because without the commercial rides, there was no particular reason to head for the hills that often. As the dry years progressed this brought us into direct competition for the scarcer amounts of grass and it often became a problem for us to locate enough of it to feed our ten or twelve head

*High up on Elbow Mountain with Mt. Dorrie to the left and
overlooking the headwaters of Big Creek. Lorna Lake is just out of sight
to the left.*

of horses. A few times I misjudged the advance of the cattle
and we found ourselves having to camp right in among large
herds. When this happened, the horses ended up with short
rations. Occasionally it became so bad that they had no night
feed at all, because the poorly managed cattle had eaten the
meadows completely bare.

When this would happen, campfire conversation was not
very cheerful. It wasn't easy trying to explain to several young
women why their new found loves were not going to be able
to eat until the following night. At times like that they weren't
very interested in hearing stories about cowboys, forest rangers,
and wilderness ranching.

However, there was a positive aspect to these situations — by the time we returned home, another group of allies had been created eager to help in the crusade for the grass ecology and the proposed wilderness park.

Those summer rides also further exposed the ranchers' vendetta against bears. Any time one of my trail riding groups located a dead bear in the mountains that had obviously been killed out of season by bullets or poison, it brought forth the same gut binding reaction that the lack of wild horse feed had done. It is always depressing to find these dead bears, especially if there are no dead cattle near them, which means that they have been needlessly killed by someone with a barnyard mentality.

One time we came across one of these summer-killed grizzlies and in this particular case it had been skinned. Since we knew someone was in possession of that hide, we reported it to the F&WB. It again involved the Gang Ranch, as one of their cowboys admitted to killing it and he turning the hide over to the management at the ranch. The aftermath of that case exposed either a strange collusion between ranchers and a branch of the government that should know better, or just some very stupid people within the ranks of a government ministry.

The illegal bearskin was located in a deep freeze at the Gang Ranch headquarters and the local investigation revealed that some "brass hat" in the higher echelons of the F&WB had recently issued the Gang some sort of special permit to kill bears that were molesting their cattle. I never saw this letter but Jess McCabe explained to me that there was no provision written into it that would require the ranch to prove molesting or attack. Apparently the permit was left wide open so that the word of the ranch personnel would be accepted as fact.

In the past this system had not been all that uncommon, but in the late '60s there were more people who were beginning to challenge the practice. Not only that but even those previous permits had always had a written provision in them that stated that the kills must be reported and no meat or hides could be retained by the shooter. In this particular case everything was done wrong; the pelt had been kept and the kill had not been reported until we did, so it put a strange taint to the whole affair.

Much later after the final investigation, I was told that the F&WB had decided not to lay charges, as the brass hat had not written the permit up properly and he could not even remember if he had verbally instructed the ranch not to keep the bear. Another angle to this case that made it stink higher than ever was because that was the beginning of a time when grizzly skins and claws were skyrocketing in value on the black market.

This particular case had begun when a ranch cowboy had taken it onto himself to report it to us, because he felt that the killing was completely unnecessary since it was well known among the cowboys that the bear was not a marauder, but had been killed purely for its cash value.

This type of wanton bear killing went on within the Gang Ranch for several years, well into the '70s and we suspect that it was renewed for a while during the early '80s, so it became a very contentious issue between ranchers and the new wilderness travellers that were beginning to demand truthful answers and better accounting from both government and the resource industries.

Because of the growing public demand for better resource management, the old guard in the provincial government came under increasing pressure. But time and again we discovered how hard old values and practices die. We continually encountered powerful bureaucrats who viewed all new ideas as merely passing fancies.

In my opinion the most powerful government influencers are not the politicians, but the deputy ministers. They don't have to worry about elections so they just keep worming their way deeper and deeper into the system, to the point where they hope that nothing will work without their personal fingers being involved in it.

You may wonder why I have mixed so many of these dry political ideas in a story about trail riding, but it was exactly that activity where we began meeting the types of people who understood how to pry out the answers to questions that had never been satisfactorily aired before. Let me tell you an absolute fact, brother. If you send me a young woman who loves animals and especially horses, I'll take her to the hills for a week and by the time she returns from there, if she wasn't before, she will by then, be a new wilderness activist. If writing letters about wilderness or wildlife is needed, then she is the one who is most apt to do it, rather than her male partner.

And furthermore, I have noticed that a woodsy woman will almost always raise a woodsy family, where the father alone often does not, as most children seem to be more influenced by the mother than their father.

The clients and the hired help I had on these mountain rides still bring back amusing memories. The food we used on these occasions was a lot different from the grub we provided for our hunting parties. For instance, one of the trail cooks insisted that we must have a bottle of wine with every campfire dinner. To me it seemed like an expensive excess and it meant that much more heavy garbage to pack back out, but we have to keep the cooks mollified so I relented and made up a special pack box that held up to eight wine bottles.

But I had to admit that the cook had been right in her

Chilco Choate and a client getting ready to celebrate another successful sheep hunt (circa 1984 or '85).

priorities because most of our riders were very duly impressed, especially by some of the selections, because I also let the cook decide what types of wine to use. She used her own palate as the judge and she had expensive tastes because that juice was several notches above table wines. At first I found it a bit strange sipping on a fine wine as we sat around smoky campfires eating off tin plates. It was all very different and interesting and those impressive barbecuing steaks were a lot better than hunting camp mulligans too.

I had to retrain myself in handling the evening story telling times. Up to that point I had been telling hunting stories to hunters and I knew what subjects impressed those people. But I learned very quickly, while out on those summer rides, to downplay what I did for a living in the fall. There is nothing else in this world that will cool horsey young trail riders, than by telling them how we blow away bighorn sheep at 400 yards.[25]

Everybody enjoys having a little spice in their lives and I have found that the best campfire stories are about events that have happened in the same locality. The ones that seem to go over best are about bear and Sasquatch encounters. In my own case, there have been many bear experiences that were not hunting related but so far, only one about a Sasquatch sighting. Of course stories about the latest confrontations with the Gang Ranch are always quite popular too. Horse and dog stories are an ongoing trail experience every day, as that is what almost every ride becomes centred around. Everybody in the procession keeps their eye on the dog, to see what he flushes from the bushes along the trails and every evening campfire brings out the comparisons of those encounters because the trail party is often spread out over a quarter mile of trail so not everybody sees the same things. It's a rare ride that does not produce a pack wreck of some kind as a ride without a wreck has become to be considered as an uneventful trip.

Wild animal encounters are always to be hoped for, but as this area is not a park, those types of experiences are not at all consistent. On some trips we see dozens of large animals, but then on other rides people begin to wonder if there are any around at all, so it's mostly a matter of luck. In an area like the Gang Ranch country, the nearly ninety-day hunting season on most game type animals keeps them very timid state all year round. That's a good thing, because if they tamed

---

25 Many of those people give me icy stares when they see me slipping a saddle rifle into my scabbard, which I still feel is a trail necessity in case of a bear attack or the possibility of a seriously injured horse or rider. So far I have never had to use it for any of those reasons, but such situations have happened elsewhere. It's a case that so far I've been damned lucky.

down too much during the off season, they would be slaughtered at the opening of the next one. There are exceptions to their shyness and that is what we look for during the summer rides.

One of the funniest animal experiences that I can remember happened while out on a ride into Graveyard Valley with a party of young nurses. In that valley there are colonies of hoary marmots with a population in the thousands, so we often camp there as they are always excellent performers for the cameras. There is usually an ongoing life-death ecology when the golden eagles come skimming a mountain ridge so they can swoop onto the marmots that are careless enough to play in the very high basins and swales that have little or no cover from sudden attacks. Then there are the coyotes and sometimes a fisher or wolverine that comes to try for a fat dinner; each of these predators using its own unique system for catching the same prize. In that particular valley there is always some such thing going on, so even if the large animals are not cooperating, we can count on seeing lots of action from these small creatures. We come away from there realizing that the marmots have a mighty tough life.

On this particular occasion we had set up camp right out in the open, quite close to the Indian graves and, as it was still quite early in the summer, we had set up our small ground tents just a few yards back from a central campfire and cooking area. There were three riders on this trip, plus the cook, so the four of them were sharing a nine-by-twelve-foot floor tent. Considering the number of marmots that are there and have always been there, there is virtually a marmot hole or tunnel under every square yard of that valley, so it is nearly impossible to set up a tent that does not have some old or new workings under it. Well, we never set up over new diggings but we often have to do so over old ones, and in this case I did, just like we had done a hundred times before.

My own tent was set up directly across the fire from theirs so we were probably about ten yards apart. On the following morning I was the first one up, so had perked the fire and was sitting on a pack box, soaking up as much of the surroundings as a mind can absorb. The sun was about half visible and the marmots were beginning to stir around the edges of their burrows and whistling to each other. So everything was exactly normal for this time of day. The girls were on holiday, so rarely arose until the sun came up high enough to warm their tent and melt the frost off the camp, so for me, this was one of the best times of the day, because I could sit in that one spot and see all of the horses were acting as calm as the morning and Shep was out among them, peeing up his territory markers and checking to see if anyone had dared to pee over them during the night.

All of a sudden there was the goddamndest shriek that came out of the girls' tent that you can imagine. It took me by such surprise that I spilled my coffee and before I could recover, that alarm was followed by screams and the most ungodly language and ear-burning phrases that I had ever heard. I had been sitting only twenty feet from their tent and the entire camp was far from the nearest trees, so I knew we had not been raided by a bear. My next conclusion was that the girls were having a real free-for-all fight. I had always suspected that the cook was capable of such antics but had not had time nor reasons to judge the others that way. Well, it wasn't really any business of mine, or at least I hoped it wasn't, so I just sat there, wondering what the hell was going on. The way that tent was jumping around with the center pole collapsed and most of the pegs pulled out, those girls had to be having a real cat fight. The situation was as interesting as hell. Even Shep was bouncing around, barking advice to them.

This must have gone on for two or three minutes and the noise was unbelievable. Every once in a while I could make out one of the girls screaming my name and to bring the gun and help. Well now, I was not about to stick my nose into that fight for any reason, not with or without a gun. It was amazing that so much hostility had erupted without warning in there that they wanted a gun to settle the accounts. Unreal!

One of them finally found the zipper to the tent door and when she got it open, all four of the girls came out of the tent in the same instant. I mean they just squirted out of there. What's more, everyone of them was in their birthday suits and with no concerns for modesty. I immediately realized that I was travelling with some damn good-looking women.

Once they were out of the tent they didn't seem to be fighting each other any more. Instead, they all turned on me, screaming about why I hadn't come in to help. Under the circumstances, that was a hard question to answer. The girls had run several yards out into the meadow, but within a few moments they started returning to the campsite but they were acting very wary, even though I hadn't made the slightest move to approach them. One of them walked right up to me, put her hands on her hips, and yelled in my face, "Well, aren't you going to get that goddamn thing out of there?"

Then it began to dawn on me that perhaps I had misjudged this situation. Perhaps the fight wasn't what it appeared to be. But even at that, there was still no sign of a bear.

I finally did take my eyes off that lovely parade and looked back at the tent. I noticed that Shep was very interested in it as well. I noticed a movement inside so then I knew for certain that there was more to this than what I had first thought.

I turned back to the girls who by then were standing right beside me and asked, "What the hell have you got in there?"

The cook, who seemed to be getting her cool back a bit faster than the others, said with an obvious tone of hostility, "Well Choate, if you would just turn your goddamn eyeballs back into that tent, you could get the answers for us." By then

I knew that they really were expecting me to do more than I was doing, so I walked over to the tent where I could see that the something was still in there. Whatever it was, it was not very large.

It can't be a snake, I thought, because there aren't any in this area. Maybe it's a wolverine.

But the wolverine idea didn't make much sense either, because if one had been bold enough to go into there, at least one of the girls would have ended up getting marked up. Not one of those girls offered to help me straighten up the tent so we could see inside and I wasn't about to crawl into it. For some reason even Shep was acting cautious. He would not put his head into the open door and that seemed odd because he had a reputation of being an aggressive dog, at least towards other animals. I ended up going to the back of the tent and began rolling it up towards the door. By the time it was about half rolled, we knew that the "something" was a small-to-medium-sized animal and by then Shep was taking pounces onto it from the outside of the canvas. The "something" was trying to fight him back, but for some reason was not growling or snarling like Shep was. I still suspected it was going to be a wolverine so I told the girls to stand clear because when it finally did come out of there, it could be capable of quite unexpected behaviour. I also nervously noted that the cook had grabbed my rifle and had it pointed in either my or its direction, which was only a difference of about three feet. Have you ever faced a naked woman who's pointing a loaded 30:30 at you? Well, up to then I never had either, but take my word for it, it does strange things to your heart muscles.

Well, after I got the "something" manoeuvred right up to where the door of the tent was, I stood up and gave the tent a big heave and a shake and out flopped one of the biggest marmots in the valley. Shep must have known what it was all the time but it was big enough that he refused to actually grab

Lunch time in Paradise Valley, just one short ride from Heaven.

hold of it; he gave it just enough room so it could run down another hole that was nearby.

After the excitement was pretty well over and the girls had retrieved their clothes, we all sat around our breakfast fire speculating on the experience from our various points of view. By that time we knew that the marmot had got into the tent by coming up through an old hole that we had set the tent

285

over. All that breakfast and most of the morning after, I had a difficult time keeping organized because every once in a while I was overcome with paroxysms of laughter. Sometime during that breakfast I made another social faux pas when I mentioned that I was going to look into the possibility of training a marmot into making this a regular routine. Perhaps I shouldn't have mentioned the possibility of trying to sell tickets to the show to the cowboys, because that was when one of the girls jumped up and grabbed a water bucket as she yelled at me, "Choate, you need a goddamn shower and this show is for free!" She then hit me with the water, bucket and all, damn near knocking me into the fire.

I still remember that trip often and I'm sure that if a man could have an experience like that at regular intervals, he could live forever.

Something else sort of on that same subject, is about a question that often gets put to me, almost always from men when they wonder aloud just how much "fun" does a guide have when he is out in the bush with a party of four or five pretty young women? Well, the honest truth is if you discount the teasing, then not a goddamn thing happens. I don't care if you believe that or not, because my wife still does.

CHAPTER 25

$\mathbb{A}$ROUND THIS PART of the country, 1973 became the year that was. The recently elected New Democratic Party put into effect some of the new ideas for managing resources that had been aired for the past several years. If these new people were really serious about land reform, then perhaps they were worth supporting. As soon as the NDP took office, I began writing letters directly to the new ministers, especially the Natural Resources Minister, Bob Williams. The objective was to try and make the new politicians stand on the platform that they had run on and as time was to go on, we were successful at that. Of course I tend to be a bit narrow minded, so I tried to keep their attention focused on the Gang Ranch country, which for many of those city people was an area of B.C. that they had never heard of before.

But before 1973 was over, many urban people came to hear words such as over-grazing, predator control, livestock neglect, grazing leases, grazing licences, water licences, and a whole bunch more that had always been the watchwords of rural life.

In March of 1973, *The Williams Lake Tribune* ran a story in their Outdoor column about the conflicts between cattle and wildlife out here in the Gang Ranch country. I'm still not sure how or who they received their original information from, but it may well have been from Harold Mitchell, the F&WB representative here. For a newspaper located in "Cowtown, B.C.," it was a strange column to have printed, because although the things that the writer, Peter Killick, said were true enough, at the same time it was a subject that very few people around here had ever shown much interest in before so it took us all by surprise.

Within a few days the large provincial newspapers from Vancouver and the radio and tv networks from across the country picked up on the story. What Killick had done was to research BCFS archives as far back as 1938, when it had been noted that the range used by the Gang was already badly over-used. The article also alleged that nothing much had been done by anyone to alleviate the situation.

For some reason it became an instant in subject and B.C. was saturated with news of the mismanagement that had been going on in the Gang Ranch country. On several occasions I was called into Clinton and Williams Lake to be interviewed, as was Chris (Cactus) Kind. He had been working on and off for the Gang over the previous few years, so was a good source of up-to-date information from there. Mitchell, as the public manager of wildlife for the area, was quoted dozens of times.

The one thing that surprised us the most and probably stunned the Gang Ranch and many other ranchers and government resource managers, lay in the fact that it was not a one shot news story like most environmental and resource exposés had been up to that time. The Gang Ranch story was on the front page and second front page of *The Vancouver Sun* several times throughout the months of March and April. It became a very popular subject in suburbia. That must have been the way that the new NDP government viewed the situation as well, because within a few weeks we were receiving confirmations from almost every ministry that was

Harold Mitchell holding a "pickup" set of bighorn sheep horns. The animal was probably killed by preditors or starvation. This Vancouver Sun photo, and the story that went with it, became the turn-around point to saving the almost last remnants of bluewheat bunchgrass in the Chilcotin.

named or involved, telling us that our message had been heard and furthermore, there was then going to be a whole series of resource investigations into this area. I even received personal letters from two cabinet ministers assuring me of the same.

So the tide had finally begun to turn, even though it did take a little manipulation to get it started. But once that had happened, we suddenly found ourselves right out in the forefront and expected to make suggestions and give advice on all sorts of resource subjects and issues of the day.

One of the most helpful people we were fortunate to be able to ally with was Moira Farrow, a resource reporter for

The Vancouver Sun. When I first met her, she did not immediately come across as the sort of person we were expecting to have as supporters, as she is an English gal, straight out of the city. I never did find out how she got mixed up in natural resources, but she turned out to be another one of those cases where looks can be deceiving. She was able to report on the issues from around here and also many other agricultural and resource problems from all over the province without ever getting her wires crossed. Lots of smokestack experts tried tripping her up and nit-picking her reporting but she was able to endure them all with flying colours. Right from the time of our first meeting with her, we knew that she had an inquiring mind, backed up with a natural ability to relieve people of little bits of touchy information that they probably had no intention of parting with. Some people are very good at the work they do.

One of the best interviews Moira did on the Gang Ranch versus wildlife issue, she got from the "acting" manager of the Gang Ranch, Irvin Sidwell, one of his sons who was working in the cowcamp, and some of the other hired hands. After the initial Gang Ranch stories hit the front pages of the *Sun*, she was invited out to the ranch to see and hear "the other side of the story." Her article, complete with quotes and photos, appeared in the March 17, 1973 edition of the *Sun* and probably did the Gang Ranch and many other ranchers more harm than anything that had been said by anybody else before. I still have those clippings and as I sit here and sort through them today, it seems more incredible than ever that the Sidwells were actually so insensitive to public opinion to say what they did.

This particular story was about cowboys killing bears. There is a large picture of two of Irvin Sidwells' sons, along with another cowboy, holding up the mounted hide and head of a very large grizzly. The picture and story take up two-thirds of the page, but the quotes by acting manager Irvin Sidwell make up the bulk of the story. Cactus, Mitchell, and I are quoted in it as well, but the real story concerned how the Gang rationalized the killing of that bear as well as wild or loose horses. The horse shooting system revealed a rather gruesome method they were using. One of their former hands had alleged that they had gut shot a herd of wild horses so they would then run off and die somewhere else. Hopefully out of sight, I guess. When Sidwell was asked to comment about this, he refused.

The grizzly skin that they are pictured with was estimated at being thirty-four years old and Irvin is quoted as claiming that it was responsible for killing twenty-eight adult cattle per year for at least twenty-five years of its life. Claiming that those cattle at that time were worth $400 each, he worked the value of the 700 as $280,000, but he was also quoted as saying that perhaps it ate only half that many. The message that he seemed to be trying to put across was how could this grizzly or even any grizzly be more important to B.C. than his cattle?

Over the following few months, he was to discover to his dismay exactly what people in B.C. and all across Canada thought about his priorities and values. Times were changing and he found himself a long ways out on a brittle limb, with very few friends offering to help. When Irvin offered such absurd figures for probabilities, it showed that he was either a very stupid person, or he hoped the people who read it were.

There was an amusing spin-off from that story that must have made some of the people in Clinton think that the real American Wild West had been resurrected. I was in town the day after that story came out. Cactus had come down to my house that morning where we both went over the story in detail, because we both knew that there could easily be some repercussions over it.

About midday we decided to walk over to the post office.

A Vancouver Sun photo taken in the Gang Ranch office in March of 1973. Pictured are Irvin Sidwell's sons along with another cowboy, Willie Rosette. This photo and especially the story and quotes by the Gang Ranch manager, did more harm to the GR than any other single writeup ever did. The story that went along with this was not only about the reason the bear was killed, but also about the gruesome methods the ranch used for getting rid of wild or free-roaming horses. This photo and accompanying story began the real downslide of the GR and quite possibly to some extent, the entire ranching industry of B.C.

As we were clumping up the board walk, who should we spot coming from the opposite direction, but Irvin Sidwell himself. As soon as we saw him coming I suspected that our meeting might become a bit confrontational, but in a town with dozens of witnesses handy, I didn't think that any serious trouble would erupt. When we first noticed him, he was still about a hundred yards up the boardwalk, but even at that distance I could tell by the way he was walking with his fists clenched and arms swinging, that he was angry about something. Big Irv is one of those Idahoans who, when he walks down a street, the town knows that he has arrived, if you know what I mean.

Irvin must have had his mind on something else, because he didn't recognize us until we were about twenty feet apart, but when he finally did see us, he stopped dead center in the boardwalk and bellowed as loud as a big fat man can, "YOU SONS OF BITCHES!" I was accustomed to his belligerence but for a moment I thought that Cactus might desert the cause by jumping over the hedge into Johnny Botterell's yard and making a run for it. Irvin just stood there, screaming curses, and putting on one of the most interesting temper displays that I have ever seen. It was a damn good thing that we had not brought our equalizers to town, or I'm sure that meeting would have ended up going down in some of Clinton's more colourful history. It must have been impressive to the other people on the street too, because I did take note that some of them were in a very obvious hurry to get out of our way. By then almost everybody in the town knew that there was bad blood between the Gang and Choate and some of them had already predicted that the situation had a high probability of ending badly. The only way I can now think of to describe the noise and jumping around that Irvin was doing is to suggest that you try to imagine the reaction of a grizzly bear if he were to get his nuts caught in a steel trap. If you can do that, then you have the sight and sound of big Irvin Sidwell on the boardwalk of Clinton on that March day, back in 1973.

Ever since those news stories had started coming out, I had suspected that there might be a show like this somewhere, but never for a moment expected it to happen in town. For the preceding few days, I had been travelling the range and roads fully armed, but that day in town the only thing I had was a sharp sliver of four-inch steel on my belt. However, Irvin wasn't armed either, so I felt comfortable enough to figure that the odds were mighty close to being even. Long ago, the paratroop instructor, Slippery Slick, had taught Steve Johnson and I quite a few close combat tricks, especially with knives, so this time it was going to be a broad daylight affair and strictly one on one.

He finally did calm down to a more rational level and even invited Cactus and I over to the Cariboo Lodge for a coffee. We accepted his offer as it didn't seem to make any sense not to. When we walked through the door, the owner, Freddie Hoad who knew us all, was right there like a maitre d' and ushered us straight through the restaurant into an empty banquet room. I knew Freddie quite well and when he did that, I smiled to myself, knowing that he wanted to make sure his front-end clients had no reason to panic and run out the door without paying their bills.

As soon as we had sat down, a waitress brought us in a round of coffee so the three of us began discussing the recent media stories. By then there had already been several of these stories and Irvin seemed quite upset that only one of them had given him or the Gang Ranch what he considered to be an even break. Cactus and I didn't think that he had even that many, so we asked him which story he was referring to. I could hardly believe my ears when he explained that his quotes in the SUN about the grizzly story had been in his favour. When Cactus shot me a side glance, we couldn't help it and burst out laughing. Irvin didn't catch on to what we were laughing about, but he wasn't exploding either.

Cactus must have started getting his nerve back a bit, because right about then he almost got both of us wiped out by asking Irvin how the SUN reporter, Moira Farrow, had got him to make those statements and get his boys to pose with the bear skin. That was the wrong thing to ask because suddenly Irvin caught on to the whole show.

Down came both of his huge fists onto the table, which sent our coffee cups flying and once again, right from the depths of his belly, he roared, "YOU SONS OF BITCHES!"

As my chair was going over backwards I noticed that the waitress, who had been more than obvious with her eavesdropping, was making a run for the door into the kitchen. Everything happened pretty fast so when I saw Sidwell coming up out of his chair, I deliberately kept forcing myself backwards and after hitting the floor, I rolled once before coming up again. I don't remember what Cactus did, but I can assure you that we were both doing whatever it took to keep out of Irvin's reach, because under the circumstances it didn't make the slightest sense to act any braver than was necessary. In the end, nothing really physical did happen, other than Irvin standing there waving his arms around while he ranted and cursed both of us, the newspaper, Moira, anyone else he could think of who was anti-Gang Ranch. He and I had been through ordeals like this before, so I wasn't really all that intimidated by him, but Cactus was still quite young and not very big, so perhaps all of Irvin's posturing may have been more for his benefit than mine. The last statement that Irvin threw at us was to tell Cactus that if he ever showed up around the Gang again, his ex-cowboy buddies would probably stretch his neck and he was so emphatic that I noticed Cactus's eyes took on a much rounder appearance than normal.

That was certainly an interesting coffee break and I do

hope that Irvin remembered to pay Freddie for the coffee, because I didn't.

Other things began improving as well; a short time later the BCFS circulated a letter stating that the local Livestock Associations would no longer control grazing permits or leases. Instead, they would all be decided by FS personnel only. We were quite certain that the letter's intent was to convince the rest of us that the FS was still capable of impartial decisions, but most of us on our side of the fence were still apprehensive about the possibility that there were still too many cosy friendships between the FS personnel and some of the industry people. But from that day on, especially if the FS began dragging their feet over their promise to act impartially, then we did finally have a letter of reference to fall back onto.

I liked their letter, but at the same time it still left me sceptical enough that I still kept a paper barrage going into the Victoria office until finally in May of 1973, the FS office at Williams Lake circulated another letter saying that from then on, they would begin recognizing wildlife as legitimate users of the land and forage. Even though many of us still had a difficult time believing the FS was serious about those written words, we did know that it helped to build a paper term of references that could become a valuable playing card when dealing with the government paper shufflers. Neither of these letters made my own business any more secure, but it did finally begin to appear that maybe the wildlife would not get pushed aside after all.

Even though I would be out of business if wildlife populations were to fall below harvestable numbers, hunting is not the only good reason to have wildlife. I am now completely convinced that having wildlife for close neighbours gives a person a warm, comfortable feeling of tranquillity, perhaps because these creatures are a living symbol or link between us and our original or supreme power. And furthermore, wildlife, because of its unpredictable behaviour, makes very interesting company — even the so-called "ferocious" types are far safer neighbours than some of the two-legged ones I have met and hear about.

CHAPTER 26

THAT YEAR THERE WERE ALL SORTS of interesting things happening around here. My diary reminds me that I was once again involved with another exploratory mining outfit, this time Noranda, who leased part of my home place to use as their camp and helicopter base. Since there was quite a large crew of them, they brought their own cook and equipment. All I did was watch how they operated and try to keep out of their way while doing it. Talk about changing times! I thought back to the CanPet people when we had to move their camps every few days with horses so they could camp right on the prospect sites, and compared that with how Noranda operated by staying in one location and helicoptering the crew out and back from the creeks every day. The new method is a pretty nice way to live and work.[25]

Something else that happened here in '73 that certainly did its share of helping to change the land and resource issues into more favourable channels, was when Harold Mitchell introduced me to a CBC film producer by name of Mike Halleran.

25 An interesting thing about these mining outfits that have worked this area over is that none of them has come back twice. That must say something about the mineral possibilities around here.

Halleran had been producing TV movies for a CBC series called *This Land* and as he and his family were all horsy types, he had a personal interest in wanting to do one right here in the Gang Ranch country. We finally did get our acts together and he did make a movie about me guiding their family through the high country on a three-week horseback trip. The name of that film was *The Long Ride*. Mike made several other films for the CBC, but I understand that the one he made here, became one of the most popular in that series and it has been shown across Canada on several occasions.

It turned out to be a bit of an exposé of the controversy over grazing cattle in wilderness areas as at that time the range had deteriorated to such a low level, it was impossible for even a greenhorn not to notice that something was drastically wrong. There wasn't as much of that sort of thing in the film as there should have been because the series was never intended to be an exposé. But all the same, the ranching industry was goddamn lucky that Halleran edited that film, instead of someone like me.

That was the first time I had ever been involved with commercial movie making and that part in itself was an experience too. We were in the hills for twenty-one days, which resulted in a film that was only thirty minutes long and to a non-media person, that must seem like an absurd amount of time, but every scene had to be taken from several different angles. I guess it's cheaper doing that, than having to come back at a later date to retake a scene.

The only bad part of that entire trip was the same as we most always run into and it was the goddamn flies. My horse herd is usually quite docile, but when they had to stand around waiting for the retakes, they became very fidgety from being chewed on by swarms of horseflies. We call them Bulldogs, because when they come for flesh, they seem to be capable of grabbing a pound or so to the bite. During the planning stages of the film, we had not taken insects into consideration, but once we were out on the trail, those little bugs became very big problems. The Bulldogs are at their worst during the heat of midday and to get the right lighting for the cameras, that was the only time of day we could shoot most of the scenes. On a normal summer trail ride, we deliberately get up very early so we can be a long ways up the trail before the flies hit their peak, but that doesn't work in the movie business.

So the poor horses ended up paying a high price to make a movie to entertain the armchair adventurers of Canada. Even as we made the film, we knew it was a tough trip on our buddies, but we rationalized some of it by telling ourselves that if all went well in the end, there would never be a shortage of feed again. I always hoped that the horses shared our optimism.

However, the film was finally finished and when it was shown on the national network the following spring, it created a furore among the ranching industry of B.C. Even though the story was based on and aimed at the Gang Ranch country, other ranchers in B.C. figured that they were being tarred by the same brush. We never intended to take on the entire cattle industry that way and told some of the ranchers so, but their hackles were up by then. Too many of them thought the wilderness was theirs to do with as they pleased.

I do not believe we ever tried kidding ourselves into believing that we started the crusade for saner forage allocations, as it had been tried by many others for as far back as thirty years, but for some reason the idea had never caught fire before, at least not like it did this time. No doubt that the government resource managers in particular figured that this was just another short term flare-up that they could easily put down from their positions of being experts. But this time it didn't work. In the natural resource industries, there are very few, if any, real experts. No question that there are people

Overused or over-grazed area near Gaspard Lake. Too many cattle for too long a time.

among us who understand the ecologies and issues better than others, but our educational system has not been examining such things for long enough to be truly creditable.

This particular controversy did not end in a week, like most people thought or hoped it would, but instead, it went on vigorously for months and this time the ranchers really did get their boat rocked, almost to the point of capsizing. At that time, many of B.C.'s largest ranches were owned by Americans or by people who were very recently Americans, so their south-of-the-border attitudes were very conspicuous in the local cattle industry. In 1973, that outlook was not really a social asset in much of B.C. and being the owner or leaser of large land holdings wasn't either, regardless of nationality.

If I had thought that we had been squeezed by the Gang Ranch in the past, then from the day after that film was first shown, I discovered what the wrath of an entire industry can be too. On many occasions I was advised by my rancher neighbours that they now considered me to be a piranha in their goldfish bowl. Up to that time, even though there had been a certain amount of contention between us, there had been several who were still friendly, at least, more or less, but after that exposé, there became a very noticeable thinning among their ranks. As one of my rancher friends who did maintain contact asked me a few years later, "When you got involved in this thing, did it ever bother you to lose most of your personal friends over it?" Up to that day I had never really thought very much about that angle, but my answer was, no it didn't, at least not very much. At some time I must have made a subconscious decision to go with what I knew to be the "natural right,"and if there were negative consequences, then that must be what real life is all about. It's hard to describe how or why a person makes decisions like that, but mine must have been forged between the ages of sixteen and eighteen.

So this became the beginning of the real grazing issue in B.C. and the more controversy it created, the more it attracted and it was not long before citizen organizations such as the BCWF became directly involved in the decision makings. This was probably at my instigation as well, but one thing it did result in, was the Fed (BCWF) decided to send a delegation through the higher elevations of the Gang Ranch country to check out the feasibility of the original wilderness park plan. There were several people in that group and they unanimously agreed that the area was still wild enough and that it needed some sort of special management that would keep commercial use to a minimum. The major reason they came to that conclusion was because the overuse by cattle was so glaringly obvious. It was also compounded by the fact that there was little evidence of the large wild animals that should have been here.

The behaviour of the young Gang Ranch cowboys towards these wilderness travellers also helped to reinforce our case. For some reason, at a time when you would think that the ranch would be trying to put their best boot forward, they remained their old belligerent selves and that attitude gave our case a great deal more credibility. The glares and the curses they greeted us with when we met on the trails were a disaster in their public relations.

One of the reasons the large game type animals became quite scarce in those days was because the scarcity of grass on the open meadows meant that the cattle were then having to wander off their traditional grazing areas and go up into the small remote pot holes and quiet places that the wild animals had been accustomed to have for themselves. When the cattle began doing that, then the cowboys and their dogs had to go there too, so the wildlife just started avoiding the entire area. Some of the problem was competition for feed, but I still think that it might have been because of continuous harassment, especially during the summer nursery months. We now know that many types of wild animals can only take so much of that before they start looking for safer places. The scenario is not a great deal different than with wolves. When they pack up, they are very capable of chasing their prey completely out of an area.[26]

---

26 Some people are now suggesting that wolf harassment is nothing more than a natural way of rotating the range, because when the prey is gone, the feed comes back and eventually the edible animals return for it because the wolves have long since left the area. This would make sense if we were living in the time before the white man arrived, but now that we are here, the unused ranges have become almost nonexistent.

Another consequence of wildlife harassment is the lower survival rates of the newborn animals. When animals are seriously disturbed, one of their first reactions is to abandon their young.

As the year began to wind down and cool off, one of the Gang cowboys who was still on friendly terms with us, came to visit and brought some interesting news to ponder. The Gang Ranch had said to hell with everybody and was selling out. The news seemed just too good to be true, but he assured us that the owners had a real live one on the hook and this time it looked like a deal was finally in the making. The idea that they wanted to sell was not at all new, as Bill Studdert had died in 1971 and his heirs as well as his partner, Floyd Skelton, had decided that they wanted completely out of the Gang Ranch operation.

For the past year or so, some of us on our side of the fence had been trying to get the provincial government to buy the Gang and turn it into some sort of experimental operation that would be better managed, but we were informed that the combination of tough economic times and the high asking price made such a proposition out of the question. We knew that there had been a few other nibblers too, but they had all backed off for various reasons. It's possible that the grazing issue or park proposal might have had something to do with it.

Another interesting or, more precisely, depressing situation this same cowboy brought to my attention on that October day was the news that the Gang had just moved 4,000 cattle into the valley above Gaspard Lake. This was not the entire herd, but it was still unusual for the ranch to bunch up so many of them that way and this on top of one of the driest and shortest grass years in recorded history. Why did they do it? Could it have been a decision based on taking one last belligerent swipe at the opposition in order to prove that they were still in the driver's seat? Someone was unbelievably stupid or crazy, or more likely, both.

As the year closed, some positive accomplishments were achieved. I was able to convince Harold Mitchell to

recommend an adjustment to the antlerless moose season. I
argued that by cutting off the non-resident harvest of these
cows, there would then always be a back country basic herd
that the resident hunters could not get to without horses. I
had another reason for wanting this that I never mentioned to
Harold. I figured that the moose population was going to nose
dive and I didn't want my business to be the scapegoat. If my
prediction came true, then the resident hunters and the F&WB
could reap their just rewards. So I was out of the cow moose
business and damn glad to be so.

In this part of B.C. during the 1970s, most of the environmental and wildlife arguments centred around grass or more
specifically, the lack of it. The ranchers were the ones who
had to stand and take the public wrath and perhaps justly so,
because if there had been a profit from "overgrazing," then
they were the people who received it all. They were easy
targets as they had no place to run or hide and, furthermore,
very few had any experience at fending off public criticism,
so we had at them, like they were ducks in a barrel. It also
helped our cause a lot knowing that they were guilty as hell
too.

But the people who were most responsible for the mess
the rangelands was in were the agrologists within the BCFS.
We were able to get to a few of them too, but most career
bureaucrats had become very adroit at passing the buck onto
others, usually people who had conveniently been transferred elsewhere or had already gone into the safety of
retirement.

Once we got our teeth firmly into the grass issue and
realized that it wasn't going to fizzle out anytime soon, I really
became hyped up and wanted to go for the throats of the local
bureaucrats in the FS offices at Kamloops, as they were the
ones I had tangled with in the past and I still figured they were
the ones most responsible for local problems. I was quite

certain that these agrologists were no brighter than the ranchers they seemed to be working for, so it was easy to imagine that they would be just as easy to knock off as well.

Our group had several quiet little meetings about that subject and our end decision was to let those birds set a while longer while we went after the head honcho who sat in his ivory tower in Victoria. We decided on the head of the grazing division of the BCFS, a man called Wilf Pendray. Although none of us knew much about him, we felt that if we could change the top of the heap first, then our long term objectives could be met much faster than digging out the entire foundation.

By the early spring of 1974, the BCWF had been able to set up a meeting with Pendray, so Bill Otway, the Federation's executive director and myself, as a committee member, went to Victoria to meet with Pendray. One of my objectives was to find out why the Grazing Division had made so many mistakes while managing the wild forage on Crown land. I was the junior member of our two-man committee, in both age and experience, so Otway carried most of the discussion from our side of the desk. It was a good thing he did too, because it took us only a couple of minutes to realize that Pendray disliked my being there and he did his best to cut me right out of the conversation.

On that particular day the discussion was quite broad, more in provincial dimensions rather than site specifics so I knew I was out of my league since Otway was much better informed about these things than I was. It was a good time for me to do more listening than talking.

However, the Gang Ranch and the Gang Ranch country were still very much in the news and Pendray could not keep the conversation away from them forever, so they finally did get around into my realm of knowledge. Up to that time and for a long time afterwards, one of the questions that was being

Choate standing amidst an all too rare "relic" crop of bluebunch wheat-grass. At one time, before white man's arrival here, all of the Chilcotin and Fraser benchland must have looked like this. This was the perennial gold that the ranching industry was built on. Mostly gone now.

asked by the range conservationists was, "Where has all the bunchgrass gone?"

There are several types of bunchgrass and most of them are super rich wild forage. However the one that is most prominent in the Gang Ranch country grows on the open sunny benches and is called bluewheat bunchgrass and I believe that it is the richest of all bunchgrasses. In this area of B.C. it is the preferred feed of all grass eaters. The early white settlers who came into the B.C. Interior built their cattle and horse empires on that perennial gold. In those days in some specific places around here, it had been in such luxurious growth that it was even mown for hay. But by 1970, it had been reduced to growing mostly on very rough terrain where livestock could not get to it, or in scattered clumps and much too small patches on the old traditional bench lands. In most places it was, to all intents and purposes, gone. There was hardly any questions about how and why it had disappeared, but there were still a few dinosaurs around who were quite prepared to use it right down to that last clump, and on that spring day of 1974, in the capital city of Victoria, Otway and I met and listened to one of the most classic examples of dinosaur thinking I have ever encountered.

After Pendray had made some comment about how he could not understand why the Gang Ranch had been singled out for such a blast of media abuse, I replied that it was largely because their cattle, that he was responsible for controlling, had overused the bunchgrass to such an extent that the wild bighorn sheep were in serious danger of running out of winter feed. By that time, everyone who had an interest in bighorns, knew that this particular type of bunchgrass is their major choice of feed and where there is no longer any bluebunch, then there is also very few if any California bighorn sheep. But the bighorns were not the only victims. Here in the Gang Ranch country, the mule deer have become very dependant on it too, especially during the spring green-up time when it is so rich that it gives them the extra nutritional boost they need then to shed the ticks they have accumulated over the winter. It also strengthens them for their coming migration to the high country where they will soon be fawning.

As soon as I got the conversation going into directions like this, I knew we were back onto home ground for me, so no doubt I began laying it on as thick as possible. Well, if it was home to me, it was alien country for Pendray and he tried to change the subject. But by then I was getting bolder and had the bit in my teeth, so I kept the conversation coming back to that topic until he became noticeably angry. He then dropped a bombshell by stating that if all of our arguments were being centred around the bluebunch wheatgrass around the Gang Ranch, then we were falsely accusing the Gang and the FS, because he knew there was no bluebunch in Churn Creek and furthermore, there never had been.

At that moment I couldn't believe my ears and I think it hit Otway about the same. I asked Pendray to repeat what he had just said and he surely did, but that time he spit it out to me. Holy Christ! Everybody else in the country knew that the original Gang Ranch had been built on bunchgrass. By then he was getting angrier by the moment and I figured the reason that he was losing his cool was he knew by then that he had jumped in over his head and was afraid to try back-pedalling for fear of exposing any more of his intellect.

Up to that time, Pendray was probably the highest ranking bureaucrat that I had ever dealt with and suddenly it became a case of "suspicions confirmed." If this was the type of person who really ran the government, then I began to really understand why the country has become as screwed up as it is. This fellow seemed to fit into that office so well that it became very easy to suspect that there were a lot more just like him, spread all through Victoria. It's a lesson that I've never forgotten nor ever will.

Since that day, I have met many other bureaucrats, some higher and many lower, and when we do meet I always remember to mentally wear my Wilf Pendray glasses to remind myself that these people might not have the only preserve on the right and best way of doing things. I've found that this makes it much easier to deal them.

Later on that day as Otway and I were returning home on the ferry, we went over that meeting and we agreed that one of our new priorities was to figure out a way to neutralize a very particular FS office. It took many more letters and more media exposure, but a while later, word came up the telegraph telling us that Pendray had gone into early retirement.

CHAPTER 27

By EARLY 1974, the rumours about the possibility of the Gang Ranch finally changing hands was the talk of the entire district. The ranch was still continuously in the provincial news and because of its size and past influence on this part of the country, everybody I met seemed to have opinions as to what should be done about it and with it. Up to that time, the most serious inquiries were from a group of Canadian promoters, calling themselves Columbia River Holdings and some of their people actually moved onto the ranch and started new buildings and began spreading their propaganda about how they were going to develop the ranch into some sort of huge subdivision of recreational ranches. That was rather alarming news, because what they were proposing would suddenly drop hundreds of new people into an area where there was presently something like 20. If this was to happen, then the wild Chilcotin as we had known it would be no more. There is nothing in this world that spoils wilderness faster than people. I also didn't care for their plan to keep Irvin Sidwell on as some sort of manager. Everything considered, this proposal didn't offer a very bright future for the Gang Ranch country.

However, sometime in June, Dr. Pat Studdert, who is Bill's son, entered the picture. Of course he was one of Bill's heirs and for some reason he didn't like this new subdivision proposal any better than I did, as I guess he figured there was not enough money in it for the heirs. Up to that time, I had never met Pat, but he came to my place with Henry Koster, a real estate salesman, and we had some interesting discussions about his late father, the present management of the Gang, as well as trying to agree about what should happen to the ranch in the future. It's unfortunate that he had not shown up around here years earlier, because he did not come across as being anything like his father. Before he left that afternoon, he told me that he was going to try and put a wrench into the subdivision deal and perhaps even move onto the ranch himself and try running it, but it turned out to be another dream.

Things were changing around here so quickly that it became almost impossible to keep up with. The new government was true to its word about trying to get a handle on some of the resource conflicts and in the case here, a special task force was formed to try and figure out what in hell had gone wrong. They were also instructed to make recommendations for future changes. The people that were sent into here were two agrologists who had been brought in from Alberta and a local forest ranger. My guess was then and still is, that the idea of hiring outside agrologists, was to try to get an unbiased opinion, because of the possibilities of too many personal friendships between the old government resource managers and some of the ranchers.

By midsummer the dam had burst completely. The old agrologists who had been working under Pendray were still being roasted. Their defence that they had been understaffed and should not be expected to be able to keep check on all of the open range of B.C. rang a bit hollow. If that had been the case, then why had they not been able to maintain any of the range areas? MLA Bob Williams was still the new resource minister and he must have been conned into believing at least some of their excuses, because he then doubled the the Grazing Division staff. No doubt his intentions were very good, but so much damage had already been done, we were soon told, that even with the new staffing, none of them were prepared to give us any assurances about how much of the damage could be rectified. We all knew that the range would eventually turn green again, but the question of whether the quality would ever come back was just as uncertain as ever.

Here in the Gang Ranch country, the task force spent about three months on the ground. The three of them moved right in with the cowboys and I hoped that their presence in the cowcamp, might tend to cool down the confrontational situation between the cowboys and me. The cowcamp crew was getting progressively younger hands all the time and they were demonstrating a very belligerent attitude.

In many ways we were all birds of a feather because I could still very vividly remember being their age myself and therefore was well aware that under the right circumstances, some small thing like a dare or just a careless word at the wrong moment could engulf our lives into an inferno. This is especially true when a bunch of strong, bold teenagers get together, since one of the last things they ever consider are rules, laws, or even common sense. Something else that compounded that situation here was the fact that uniformed law enforcement was always about 100 miles away and if that does not seem to be a great distance, it still meant that we only have police patrols out here about twice a year. So the law in remote areas like this, pretty well works after the fact. The only crime prevention we can rely on is the knowledge and threat of equalizers.

Even though the forest rangers were living with the cowboys most of the time, it did not take us long to realize that it was not going to bring the old Gang Ranch-Choate confrontations to a halt; if anything, they began to increase. In the past, very few of the cowboys had become involved in this conflict, but now that some of Sidwell's boys were employed in the cowcamp, their father's attitudes came along with them and seemed to infect a few of the hired hands as well. One of the reasons the cowboys were becoming more hostile was because I was being blamed for the nosey hangers watching over their shoulders so often.

They must have been getting advice from those rangers as well, because that was the first year that the crew ever tried controlling the cattle as they were grazing and this on a daily basis too. Before, the general practice had been to drive a herd of cattle into a valley, usually in herds of 1,500 or so, and then just drop them there so they could drift off on their own initiative. But that summer we often watched the cowboys split those large herds up into small bunches and even ride herd on them to keep the cattle from re-grouping. Sometimes a cowboy would stay with a herd all day, just riding around watching the animals eat. For Gang Ranch cowboys, this was a new method of work and they made it quite clear to us that they did not enjoy doing it. On several occasions when I rode by, either alone or with a party of trail riders, some of those cowboys would shake their fists at me and holler some very descriptive advice that they hoped I would follow. The Gang continued to prefer running true to their past, even though they had to have realized that times and conditions were changing very rapidly. All this attitude did for them was to anchor themselves more firmly than ever to their old problems. All of this suggests that their biggest problem was stupidity. There is no law against stupidity, but perhaps there comes a time when there should be.

But on it went and even with the reduction of cattle numbers in '74 and the new control methods that they were experimenting with, the range was still deteriorating to the extent that they could no longer maintain sustainable forage quantities, much less bring the range back to its former level.

My diary reminds me that the grass shortage in Lost Valley was the worst ever recorded and it was about the same in some of the other valleys as well.

After the grazing season was over that year, the rangers who had been doing the investigation of the forage problems in the Gang Ranch area wrote and published a report of their observations. I don't know how many copies of it were printed, for sure not many, but I received one and still have it and wouldn't part with it for a loaded gold poke. Well, I admitted then and still do today that it was a very fair report. The FS referred to it as the "Preliminary Report on the 1974 Range Survey of the Gang Ranch."

Sometimes lifting information out of a report like this one and then sticking it into a story where it then becomes a quote can be a dangerous or unfair system of passing on information because it might become sort of out of context. But in this case I do not believe that they do. Anyway, you have been warned, so judge for yourself.

"Among local farm labourers and cowboys, Gang Ranch has got the reputation of being a 'hard knocking outfit' that does not treat casual employees particularly well. This reputation may be the result of the particularly long working hours expected of employees, together with a 'work hard or walk to town' attitude."

On page 19 the report compares the interaction of cattle and cowboys with wildlife. This section is mostly true in the sense that the report often seemed to portray a rancher perspective towards the needs of wildlife, as most of us on our side of the fence were still opting for taking all cattle out of elevations over 5,000 feet. The rangers admitted on this page that they confirmed an out of season bear kill on July 4th, but they do not mention who actually killed it or if the ranch or rangers reported it to the F&WB. A line or two later they further confirm what I have previously mentioned here several times and the actual line says, "In previous years, ranch management has encouraged ranch employees to shoot predators, grizzly bears in particular." If you are still sceptical, then let's jump ahead to page 20 and quote the first paragraph in its entirety.

> "Criticism voiced against livestock grazing in the alpine areas presently used by Gang Ranch has been at least partially based on forage competition between livestock and big game. Judging from the degree of utilization in 1974 when approximately 2,600 animal units grazed the southernmost grazing units until September 30th, we can only assume that the effect of 5,600 animal units on this same range until October 31st in 1970 must have been traumatic. Because of the over utilization which took place in 1970 the grazing season in the high country was decreased by one month and the number of livestock permitted on the Gang Ranch west of the Fraser was reduced to 4,000 head. The previous five years use (1966 to '70) at 5,200 to 5,600 head per year would certainly have resulted in severe browsing on critical moose range in the Fosbery Meadow, Big Meadow, and Hungry Valley Units."

The report's major recommendation still did not come up to our no cows in the mountains goal, but it was still a great improvement over previous uses for the Gang Ranch country. It appears on page 26 under the heading of "Proposed Range Use Adjustments." In this section, the rangers recommended that the entire Gang Ranch herd west of the Fraser be reduced to 3,400 head. That figure I did and still do concur with, as after 100 years of overuse, that's probably all there should have ever been here since the forage began to change and diminish, around 1963. As far as I know as of this writing, the ranch has not exceeded that number since 1976. And if they have done, it wasn't by very much.

Something else ended up on a more encouraging note at that time too and that was Harold Mitchell, the government wildlife bio, finally had enough seniority to start cutting down some of the ridiculously long hunting seasons. Two weeks were chopped off the general moose season and the antlerless season in particular was finally reduced to half of what it once was. Considering how long it had been going on and the damage it had done, the only marks I would be prepared to concede here would be to say, better late than never.

In this area, 1975 started out with an ominous sound. Sometime in January I heard the roar of a logging operation starting up, about eight miles north of Gaspard Lake. That industry had been expanding across the Cariboo-Chilcotin by leaps and bounds as the government had recently licenced several huge saw mills in Williams Lake. The amount of trees that was being funnelled into them was becoming an alarming issue for those of us who lived within and were totally dependant on the standing forest. At that time, the logging operations and the extraction roads that go with it, had not bothered me very much, as the areas being logged were still down on low elevations that we seldom used for hunting or trail riding. For some reason I was still allowing myself the comfort of believing they would never locate commercial amounts of timber at the higher elevations, so we would therefore be able to coexist with logging.

One of the reasons for my complacency must have stemmed from the idea that with all of the recent publicity the area had received expounding the virtues of the beautiful scenery and wildlife, nobody would either want or dare to destroy these natural selections.

But the logging was rapidly approaching the high open areas in the Gang Ranch country. In '75 they were still selectively logging most of the sites, but we began to notice that there were also these other huge holes being created in the forest and they were being called "clearcuts."

We had all grown up with the old system of harvesting trees and, with a few modifications, we assumed that the industry would continue doing so, but this new system looked like it was designed by the same people who make their living by manufacturing nuclear bombs and Agent Orange. No doubt it takes a very special, educated type of personality to justify this type of progress.

My mind must have gone to sleep because even though the logging was right there to see and the future consequences must have been obvious, I postponed trying to do something about it for a ridiculous length of time. Imagine, I sat here and ignored the oncoming of what was to become the biggest problem of all.

Another interesting situation happened over that winter of '75 and that was when the law moved in on our closest neighbour, the Sky Ranch and took the owners to court for neglecting their cattle. This turned out to be a similar case to what happened on the Gang back in '56, but on a much smaller scale. A herd of their cattle had succumbed to what the Indians very descriptively call "being hungry sick." Gus Piltz had sold the ranch back in '59 and was now long gone, but the poor old ranch he had built had fallen on bad times and had been taken over by a series of real estate speculaters.

This most recent outfit was a green-horn family from Arkansas and they had just tried wintering about 400 cattle on 135 tons of hay. The court case went on for a while as these people were not offered the same comfort of a "quiet" magistrate's court that the Gang had been. This time all the information got flopped out on the ground for the rest of us

317

to examine. These people had also tried bailing themselves out at the last moment by bringing in feed from elsewhere, but it turned out to be too little and too late.

The part of this Sky Ranch case that I found very interesting was the way the Judge summed up the situation at the end of the trial. He was quoted in the local press as saying that he did not feel that some of the witnesses had given his court the quality of truth that was expected of people who had sworn an oath "to tell the whole truth and nothing but the truth." In the end, he did find the owners guilty and brought down a very heavy fine and not only that, there was a long probationary period where their operation would be monitored to be sure it never got into this type of trouble again. Perhaps it was just the changing times, but to my way of thinking, these people were not dealt with very fairly, especially when their case is compared to the old case at the Gang. Why was an outfit with very limited financial resources hit harder then Studdert had been when he had the feed, the experience, and had killed hundreds of cattle?

Sometime during the month of April, a message came over the local radio asking me to contact Harold Mitchell right away. It was such an unusual request from someone like him that I knew that something mighty important must have come up. Rather than discuss things over an open radio telephone, it seemed like it might be a worthwhile expense to drive the eighty-five miles into town and discuss things firsthand.

When I walked into Mitchell's office that day, he was reared back in his chair with his hands clasped behind his head and a big grin on his face. Even before I had pulled up a chair, he asked me, "Have you seen your big, fat neighbour lately?"

I knew he could only be referring to Irvin Sidwell, whom I had not seen recently, so I told Harold the same. He started to laugh and began to fill me in on all the latest telegraph. "Well, you aren't likely to see him out there again either, because we just received word that the owners have given him the boot, so he's packed up his familiy and all his belongings and moved to Kamloops."

For a few moments it was hard for me to believe what Mitchell was telling me, because even though it was one of the things we all wanted to happen, we also knew that the Sidwells had a ten-year contract to run the Gang Ranch and we had just assumed that they would probably stay there until the place was sold. It seemed too good to be true, but that's exactly the way it turned out.

When Harold finished telling me all he knew about the new situation out on the Gang, he was by then laughing so hard he had to wipe his glasses. He had no love for the Sidwells either and for good reason, as he had learned that the ranch had actually sent some feelers into the provincial capital of Victoria, trying to find a way of getting Mitchell fired or at least transferred out of the Cariboo-Chilcotin. They had not been successful, but Harold didn't appreciate their efforts. So for both of us, there was good reason for celebration. We knew that we had not won any wars, but it sure boosts morale to win a battle now and then.

CHAPTER 28

THE RELIEF OF NOT HAVING the Sidwells to contend with any more sure made life a lot more bearable, because several months before they left, the squeeze had been put on in a few new subtle ways. For instance, one of the girls who was looking after the home place heard the dog barking one morning, so she walked across the yard to investigate the alarm. As she rounded a cabin to get a better view into the bush behind, she came face to face with a young rider, sitting there on his horse with a drawn rifle cradled across the saddle, staring at her and the dog. There was only a few yards of distance and a barbed wire fence between them, but the rider never said a word. He just sat there, stared for about a minute, and then rode off into the bush. The rider never actually pointed the rifle at her or made any threatening moves, but she still felt certain that from his having drawn the rifle from its scabbard and the glare on his face the entire episode was intended to frighten her. Luckily the cook was not the type of person who was easily spooked by that sort of thing, but just the same, it did make her very angry.

It made me angry too, for even though I was getting used to their threats, I still did not like the idea of drawing others into a problem that had always been considered a strictly Gang

Ranch-Choate affair. We both knew who the rider was, but there was nothing we could legally do about it. It's not an easy situation to ignore, either, because confrontations like this could easily end up getting vicious. With incidents like this happening, it was probably a damn good thing for all of us that the Sidwells left because after putting up with them this way for twelve years, I was acquiring a very nervous trigger finger.

However, the Sidwell years were over and things did begin to calm down almost immediately. The next manager to take over the Gang turned out to be Floyd Skelton's son-in-law who arrived here from the States and that was how we first met Mike Fairless. He also brought with him from the same area, a new farm boss named Jack Issacs. I forget how we all met the first time, but it did not take long to realize that the primary job they had both been sent here to do was to try and cool the confrontations down. I think the real reason the owners wanted to do that right then was because the Gang was still very much for sale and trying to sell in the midst of such a well-known argument might have deflected potential buyers. They must also have been getting progressively worried about just how far the land-use controversy was going to go, because it was still a very popular provincial issue. I didn't care what their reasons for cooling things down might have been as long as it meant that I could finally go to the House of Lords and the horse pasture without having to pack an equalizer any more.

Both of these men turned out to be easy-going people and even though we did not always agree on some of the issues, at least I wasn't afflicted with shivers when I turned my back on them. In lots of other ways, the job that Fairless had taken on was not like any other new manager had faced, because the Gang was still being raked over by the news media and about all the Gang could do was learn to roll with the punches.

There was one meeting that we had right in the ranch office and it was sort of an official one as there was also a delegation from Goldbridge there. While we were on the subject of cattle grazing in the high country, the bunch of us finally did agree that cattle could use a wilderness area, but in a much reduced herd size than we had known in the past and for shorter periods of time. There was also a ranch promise to continue making the cowboys scatter the herd properly, too.

Something else that our side got out of that meeting was an admission from the Gang Ranch that the past complaints about bear predation on the cattle had been greatly exaggerated. Of course some of us at the table knew that was the way it had been all the time, but it was still nice to finally hear such a statement come right out of the Gang Ranch manager's mouth and into the ears of four witnesses. After we had discussed this subject for a while, Fairless even volunteered to try disarming the cowboys, and by God, he really did it too.

When the conversation got around to wild animals and the local hunting possibilities, Issacs asked our side about the history of the elk in this area, because he had it figured that it was some of the finest elk habitat that he had ever seen and he could not understand why there were not any around here. After we had discussed elk in general for a while, I mentioned to him that some of us had been lobbying for some time to have elk re-introduced into the Chilcotin, but so far had all of our efforts rebuffed by the ranching industry. That was when Issacs really proved that not all ranchers are of the same stripe, because he suggested that, from what he could see, the Gang had never done anything for wildlife other than kill it, so why not have the ranch truck a load of elk into here from one of Skelton's ranches in Idaho. The entire idea was a good-will gesture on the Gang's part, but that didn't seem to matter to the rest of us, as long as it put a viable herd of elk into here faster than they were presently moving.

During this conversation, I was on the edge of my chair and when we heard Fairless confirm that it might be a damn good idea, I knew it was just too good an opportunity to let go of.[27]

The word spread very quickly and it looked like the action was going to finally warm up too, but then the powers that be decided that we couldn't accept the Idaho animals. We would have to use our own stock from somewhere in Canada, probably the East Kootenay where there were elk to spare. For a great many of the hunters around here, the idea finally sounded so good and looked so certain, that we could almost taste those elk. But as you know, government never moves so fast that someone might get run over by unaccustomed haste, so we were told to sit back and let the right people do all their impact studies and whatever else the bureaucrats could conjure up in the job creating department. Well, beggars can't be choosers, so if that be the only way it could be done, we agreed to get out of their way and let them do their things.

Perhaps the Gang Ranch was willing to learn to live with elk as a public relations program, but we soon learned that many of the other ranchers were not nearly so eager to do so. There were a few exceptions but most of them considered the idea to be a step backwards, especially when they considered how much time and expense they had recently spent in getting

---

27 My interest was mostly out of concern that we would soon lose most of the moose herd to over-hunting. Habitat loss was a factor also, but that often occurs because of too many roads which make access too easy. And this comes right back to over-hunting. Moose are not as leery or as bright as elk are in avoiding people in vehicles. No doubt, elk can be over-hunted as well, but when it comes down to surviving from hunting pressures, they are far ahead of the poor old moose.

rid of the wild horses.[28] Some of these people did not feel that
it was fair that they had done all the work and now the grass
that they had won or stolen was going to be allotted to a
bunch of wild grass eaters again. God had made grass for cows
and every good man knew it. There were a few other reasons
the ranchers did not want to accommodate more wild animals.
Not only were they were still seething over the new park
proposals that were springing up all over the country, but also
the expanding tourist industry was asking for a share of the
beautiful grasslands. Through a rancher's glasses these things
must have looked ominous indeed. In this particular area of
B.C., Mitchell and I were considered to be the ones most
responsible for the cattle industry's recent reverses and they
damn sure let us know about it in every way they knew how.

I still had a few rancher friends who never completely
shunned me and they leaked us a little information from time
to time. One of those newsy items was to warn me that the
new owner of the Empire Valley Ranch was trying to organize
all of the ranchers into creating one massive squeeze against
me so to get the camp completely out of here. The idea had
a double edge as they hoped that by making an example of
me, it might also frighten off any other future trouble makers.
None of this really surprised me, but the one outfit that we
expected the most trouble from, remained very quiet on that
subject. That reference of course, is to the good old Gang
Ranch.

One of the things my rancher informants mentioned was
that what really bothered them was the fact that at one time
I had been one of them, so most of them still related to the
old adage of not wanting to have anything to do with a
turncoat. Hardly any of them ever accused me of lying; it was

28 In many cases, these had been Indian horses. The ranchers had
succeeded but it had been a very risky gamble on their part.

mostly a case of them wanting me to keep my mouth shut and mind my manners. If they really believed that such a thing would happen, then they were dreamers because I was born with a thick skin and social peer needs have never controlled my life. As for the ranchers who did sputter along with some devious manoeuvring, it ended up doing them more harm than it ever did me. We all have our Achilles' heels somewhere, but those ranchers never found mine.

Even though the new managers on the Gang never became noticeably involved in a new organized squeeze and we were still being civil to each other, that does not mean that this million-acre range became a neighbourly love nest, either. It's impossible for me to know what their thoughts on the subject were then or even now, but we were breaking some sort of new ground and it took us a while to create and adjust to the new circumstance. In some ways it was like people who marry late in life. We were both forced to share the same house, but we still wanted as much of our old ways as we could possibly retain. There were still disagreements, mostly about resource priorities, but there were lots of agreements too. Jack Issacs was still holding up as an agreeable sort, as he had it figured that if the cattle herd remained as reduced as it was, he would not be needing so much water out of the Gaspard reservoir, so then there would be more water for the fish to winter in.

An outfit like the Gang Ranch is not an easy place for a new manager to take over, no matter how much experience he has. That first fall that he was here, we witnessed one of the poorest cattle roundups in years and part of the problem was because Fairless had inherited some very sour hired hands, who did not enjoy having to be the ones who had to live up to all these new agreements of better cattle control. When those type of plans filter their way out into the cow-camp, it means longer days in the saddle for the cowboys and if there is not a really stiff ramrod for a cowboss, then it doesn't happen.

Once again during the winter of '75-'76 we had some of the fattest coyotes in the country.

Another old problem that came to a head again was when a new hand turned the valve in the Big Dam completely off and killed all of the fish in the lower creek. This was the third time this had happened since I had lived here, so warmer neighbours or not, I was goddamn angry.

For the new management at the Ranch, it happened at a bad time, because things like this were still contentious issues throughout B.C. and the government resource managers were still acting very sensitive from the continuous public flak they were receiving and therefore they had become much more receptive to suggestions of how to fix some of their past oversights. By 1975 it was public common knowledge that the politicians were trying to be seen this way too, so this time I took the Gaspard water problem right straight to them and let me tell you, it worked. Within only a few days, a meeting of all the interested or affected parties was conducted right there on the top of the Big Dam. There was the local fisheries biologist, a Water Rights representative, the Gang Ranch, and myself. Now that is the right system for resolving recourse conflicts, because when we stood right there, it became impossible for any of them to deny the problem or pass the buck any further than three feet, so it took only a couple of hours to come to agreement on final remedies to the old problems.

At this meeting the Gang finally offered to put that cleat on the bottom of the valve gate, so no one, for any reason, could shut the water completely off again. I don't believe the manager liked having to concede to doing that, but in front of so many witnesses, it must have been a bit embarrassing trying to defend the idea of wanting private control of all the resources, regardless of what the consequences might be to other users.

The valve wheel that works the headgate on the Big Dam at Gaspard Lake. The design never took into consideration the welfare of the fish and other aquatic wildlife that was dependant on a continuous water flow. The problem has still not been resolved to this day, as that screw and headgate can still shut the water completely off.

Another very positive thing for wildlife around here, actually begun the year before, was that the Gang Ranch had the northern portion of the ranch lying north of the Chilcotin River. We had always known that area as the Steer Ranch as that was what it had always been used for. Part of the Steer Ranch took in the land between the junction of the Chilcotin and Fraser Rivers and to us locals it's always been referred to as the Junction Country. Down in that junction area the Gang Ranch owned about 1,000 acres of range land and had a grazing permit that covered most of the adjacent land. This range had also been and to considerable degree still was, the most prime bluebunch wheatgrass country in the Chilcotin. For thousands of years before the first cow ever arrived there, a herd of California bighorn sheep depended upon that bluebunch. In the 1970s, they were still the largest herd of these animals in B.C. and not only that, they had become one of the most studied herds in North America. The sheep herd was estimated at about 400 head then, even though there had been some recent winter die-offs that Mitchell attributed to overgrazing by cattle from the previous fall, so he had been battling with the Gang and the FS over that issue for several years. However, the FS was dedicated to raising as many cattle on public land as possible. After all, their jobs were based completely on that principle because those good old farm boys had been raised and educated with the theories that civilization and progress equated into removing as many wild animals as possible and replacing them with domestic ones.

That little item right there was — and still is — the major stumbling block that is built into range management in B.C., as somewhere along the line, the teachers of these agrologists and other agriculture students have successfully instilled the theory that the open range is to be used to maximize the cattle industry on Crown land. One of the things those people indirectly taught us was that the minute some technocrat starts talking about maximizing the use of any natural resource, the only thing that seems to be a certain outcome is that wild or natural things become displaced or destroyed. This is especially true and becomes glaringly obvious when it happens to wild forage. Sometimes I wake up at night wondering if man was put on this planet by God or are we really the children of the Devil.

After the Gang sold the Steer Ranch to Riske Creek Ranch, Mitchell negotiated a deal with the new owner of the junction to trade that deeded land back to the government in return for some other Crown land closer to his home place. It was all quite complicated, but it did work out that all of the Junction area reverted into range for the bighorns and ever since then, the sheep have flourished and so has the bluebunch wheatgrass.

If anyone wants to see what most of the Chilcotin grassland must have looked like when whitey first arrived here, then the Chilcotin Junction Country is the place to go and visit, because it is now back to about as close to natural as any low elevation area there is in B.C. There is an all-weather road to within six miles of the core area and a jeep road right into the center of it, so it's quite accessible. The bighorns never leave the area and they are usually within easy walking distance of vehicles and it's a rare occasion that people go there and not see a lot of them. Don't get the idea that its just another Banff situation, because this is not a park of any kind and a limited amount of hunting is still permitted. The Chilcotin Junction truly represents an absolute showpiece of wildlife management.

The danger lies in the fact that the area is open Crown land and politicians could decide to lease or sell it in order to create revenue. What makes me fearful that something like this might happen is because of that old Yankee saying that goes something like: "Farmers don't want much; they only want what's next to theirs." That saying perfectly describes the cattle industry of North America.

CHAPTER 29

F OR SOME REASON both Fairless and Issacs must not have liked the job of running the Gang Ranch because by May of 1976 they were both gone and the manager's job went to Bob Munsey who had been ranching in other parts of the Cariboo for quite some time. The farm-boss job went to Willie Rosette, one of Augustine's older sons. Since Willie had already spent most of his life living and working on the Gang, it was a natural step for him. Times were changing all around us about then too, as almost all of the small ranches over around Big Creek began to change owners. Even the hunting lodges were changing hands. It seemed like there were no old timers left around here and it was a strange feeling to be alone in here with no one to relate to. I was becoming one of the old timers myself, but I didn't really feel like one; it was still too easy to remember the other people who really had been of that calibre.

The mid seventies were when two wildlire managers in the East Kootenay, Ray Demarchi and Dave Phelps were very active in organizing the Coordinated Resource Management Plans (CRMP) down there. This was a plan where all of the government resource agencies, the private resource users, and the organized recreational users of an area got together to decide how the land and the resources could best used for the benefit of the most people. They were so successful with it that Harold Mitchell was impressed enough that he became the major instigator in having the system spread northward into the Cariboo–Chilcotin country.

One of the more positive things that came out of the Gaspard CRMP occurred when the Lands Branch took back several thousand acres of grazing leases from the Gang because the land had been overused and was reverting into weeds. The ranch did not lose the use of the land; it was just a case that when it reverted back to public ownership; it also allowed the FS and the Ministry of Agriculture to reseed the area at public expense. This was not a new system as it had been done elsewhere as well. From our point of view, the real benefit was that it released the area from private control, back to where the public could designate it into other priorities if we ever chose to do so.

Now, all that area is once again open to public access. An agreement that I uneasily went along with allowed up to 2,000 cattle back into the mountains again. Even though we had recently received a verbal agreement from the Gang Ranch to go with only 1,000 head, they had since then reassessed that figure and decided that it would be unprofitable to go with less than 2,000. The FS was on their side, so the best that we on the wild side could get out of that agreement was that the 2,000 cattle would have more cowboys looking after them and those cattle would only be allowed up there for a maximum of two months.

I gravely feared that it was still too much of everything, but Mitchell cautioned us not to push too hard, in case the Gang or the FS just said to hell with public planning and walked away from the table. There was a great deal of mutual trust built into agreements like these and we were hopeful about that because it was an area where almost no trust had existed before. But it was still a wobbly situation because trust can evaporate for many different reasons.

What bothered me the most about the new alpine grazing agreement was the poor record the Gang had on cattle control and I did not believe that they would be able to keep their promises. For instance, Gang Ranch cow camp crews have a history of just up and quitting all at the same time, leaving the herd to fend for itself until a new crew could be put together, which sometimes took a couple of months.

I see another notation in my diary dated December 9th, that mentions that Mitchell had just been given tentative approval to bring forty elk into the Cariboo-Chilcotin and we were then having further discussions as to where the first drop site should be. Of course I was still stumping for it to be right here in the Gang Ranch country but Harold was beginning to have reservations about it, as Fairless was no longer manager of the Gang and the new fellow, Bob Munsey, was not favourable to the idea at all.

Mitchell suggested that, rather than take a chance of getting all bogged down on the very first load, perhaps we should settle for a less contentious area, such as over on the east side of the Fraser at a place called Skeleton Valley, as there was already supposed to be a very small herd of them in that area. This population had been sighted only a few times over a long period of time and for some reason their numbers were not increasing, so he had it figured that by pumping some new blood into the herd, it might finally take off and become a viable breeding herd.

His other reason for choosing Skeleton Valley as a starting area was because there are no ranches in the immediate vicinity and the present elk had never been known to cause a problem. The only problem he could spot centered around the fact that the area was known as a deep snow country and it could become a nip and tuck situation for elk survival. There was even a possibility that the deep snow was already the reason the herd had stagnated in numbers. However, Skeleton Valley still looked like it would be our safest bet to try, because if it did work out OK, we were quite sure that a new expanding herd of elk no matter where they were started, would eventually move around and locate their own preference of range.

We all knew that the natural elk herds throughout the Rocky Mountain trench have been on the move for the past several years and it was generally agreed that they are following the vast new logging slashes back out onto their former range. Mitchell was quite certain that this was happening, but as he told us then, there is just no way to know how long it will take them to come as far west as the Chilcotin. But he did convince us that the elk were on their way home and we all agreed that sooner would be better then later.

During the last days of 1976, we were so sure that the elk project was about to bear the fruit we wanted that it seemed like it was almost time to start warming up the roasting pans. God, we were even beginning to discuss the best locations and numbers for the second and third release sites. But as the year passed and the new one progressed, we soon learned that things were not going to happen as easily or quickly as we had hoped, as the ranchers, Socred politicians, and some nervous bureaucrats began to team up against the idea. A while later Mitchell was ordered to put the plan onto a back burner until more studies could be conducted on the subject, so once again the elk transplant was stalled off for at least another year. Do you think we were angry? I'll let the others speak for themselves, but for me it began to bring back thoughts of turning the tables and giving them a few "squeezes" in return.

The winter of 1976-77 also brought us other ominous sounds and that was from the ripping and roaring of the approaching logging industry. By that time, logging was nowhere close to being new in this area but what was changing was the increase in the size of their clearcuts which had jumped from about fifty acres to upwards of one hundred acres, and in some cases even much larger than that.

Something else that was beginning to make us nervous were the statements from the logging industry telling us that they might someday want to log the actual higher mountain valleys. That area was the core of our wildlife population and on which our business depended. Up to that time all of the logging was being done down in the flatter and less contentious wildlife habitat areas, so we had not been overly concerned about what our new neighbours were doing. Everybody in the country knew that the more mountainous areas were the last nursery and escape areas for the large wildlife and we just assumed that such places would become as sacred to the newcomers as they always had been to us, but we soon learned differently.

One important thing that the new CRMP meeting did for us was kept us informed as to what each industries long range plans were for the area. At that time there were only three industries using the land base: the Gang Ranch, which was about half of its former operation size and looked like it would stay about that way; the guiding industry (Garrard and myself), which had no plans of expansion except perhaps into more summer trail riding; and then this new timber cutting industry which seemed to have the intention of eventually grinding up every tree in the country. To us, they reflected an attitude that it was not to be a case of IF they took the trees; it was only going to be a case of when and how they did it. The possibility that any large area would be saved from their chop looked mighty remote and as it was such a huge and powerful industry, they sort of overwhelmed us into submitting to their ideas. From what we could see coming up the roads, if we had ever considered the cattle industry as being paternal or aggressive, it was a pussycat compared to what we were facing now. Somehow there is a difference between overusing a resource and that of grinding it up into oblivion.

We have always had some sort of law to control the enthusiasm of con artists and outright liars when they try operating out on the open street, but when they move into board-rooms and government ministries, for some reason we then begin to accept their actions as being respectable. A goodly number of those type of people have arrived out here in the Chilcotin bush as I was soon to learn, as they kept putting us country hicks through "continuing education" courses.

Let me tell you something else about that, they all came with a price too. My licensed outfitting area is made up of about 400 square miles of low elevation rolling timber and meadow lands and then there is another 400 square miles of much higher meadows, semi-alpine, and full alpine country. The lower portion was being logged right then, but I still believed that there was enough timber down there to satisfy any reasonable demand. Some people don't seem to learn things very fast and I guess I'm one of them, because eventually the overwhelming evidence revealed that we were no longer dealing with reason, but just plain old-fashioned greed, where rules, laws and ethics were only pawns to be played or sacrificed when necessary.

When P&T Mills and the Boards and Chips division of the BCFS first arrived at the CRMP meetings, they showed us on a blackboard a system of rotating cut blocks through the low country that wildlifers, trappers, outfitters and ranchers could learn to live with. I can still vividly remember how one of their members drew out on that board a long road with cut blocks marked off all the way along it. What they proposed to do was cut the first block immediately, then skip about four blocks and cut the next one, and so on down the road. Then in about thirty years' time, they would come back and cut the centre block and then on down the road to the next center block. After another 30 years they would be back for some of the other middle areas until the spread of time would be somewhere between 90 to 120 years, in which time they figured the first blocks should have regrown by then. At the same time they were showing us this system, they were also scratching off all the side roads that wouldn't be needed for the next thirty years.

Well, I didn't really want to see even the low country cut up that way either, but in an attempt to be compatible with our new neighbours, I did agree to endorse their plan. The Gang Ranch did too and so did the other outfitter. As a person sat back and took a detached look at their plan, it seemed like there was always going to be enough escape cover left over and we knew the cut blocks themselves would be producing plenty of new feed for wildlife.

The timber cutters even agreed to reshape some of the blocks into long zig-zags instead of the large squares and rounds that they had been doing. The idea of this was to slow down the velocity of ground winds and also to create more edge of forest feeding areas for wildlife. The co-ordination of our planning looked like it should work out so that almost nothing and nobody would lose very much. In some ways we thought there was a good chance that we could even end up winning more than we lost. Those of us on the wild side felt dead certain that with this style of logging and the impending arrival of the elk, we would end up with the richest wildlife area in the province.

There would be a few differences of course. The area would never be able to be classed as a wilderness again, but in reality, it had not been true wilderness since the ranchers had established an open range system over it a hundred years earlier.

One of our fears came to light when the Gang Ranch

reassessed the needs of the entire ranch and decided that they now had to have at least 5,000 cattle on it again to make it viable. One of the reasons for having to do this they said, was because the ranch was only getting a sixty percent survival rate from their calf crop which was a ridiculous situation even back in 1977, because most other ranches in B.C. were by then getting rates closer to ninety percent.[29]

The renege on the Gang's part came at an interesting time, because the taxpayers had just been tapped for about $200,000 to build all the new fences and corrals around here. Another thing that the Gang received through the CRMP was that the FS had taken over all of their old cowcamp cabins so they were now called range improvements and when they did that, the cabins became perfectly legal for the ranch to use and it also meant that they would never have to pay leases or taxes on them. Cozy.

Not everything was negative and the CRMP system did continue, but in a more subdued way. One of those things that helped both the Gang and the Gaspard fishery was when the ARDA money was used to remove an old holding corral that had been polluting the lake for years. We built them a new one not far away, not near far enough I figured, but it is an improvement over what had been going on earlier. Another part of the Gaspard fishery that had been verbally agreed to earlier got lost in the shuffle. The cleat that was supposed to have been put on the bottom of the valve gate at Big Dam was not installed.

---

29 As crazy as the sixty percent figure seemed to be, it was still an improvement from a few years earlier. I can remember a cowboss bragging that he had just broken the fifty percent mark, which means that there was a time that the ranch was getting less than that. I don't remember what percentage the ranch was setting back in the MacIntyre days, but I do know that it was a district joke among the other ranchers.

I see another notation in my diary from 1977. As mentioned here earlier, P&T Mills were frantically driving in all those new roads that had been approved the year before and I used to stop and visit with the work crews that were building them. One of the fellows I used to chew the fat with was a longtime contract logger named Leonard James. Leonard told me one day that the cut blocks that they were then harvesting were turning out to be approximately twenty percent short on the timber that the FS said was supposed to be there. This was at a time when the FS was still claiming that their surveys were within five percent accuracy. James went on to say that because the mills had been set up to handle the higher figure, they might now have to consider expanding the size of the cut blocks or perhaps speeding up the cut more than the CRMP had been told.

Another thing that got my blood stirred up again was when we located several bedding sites of a small herd of large animals on a timbered mountain near home. We had run across beds like these on other years too, so it began to reconfirm my suspicions that we still had a small herd of very elusive elk living quite close to us. This was very good news in one way but there was an approaching problem too. The mountain was beginning to be logged and since then the huge clearcuts that have become the norm have already stripped away about half the escape cover up there. Not only that, but the long range logging plans tell us that almost the entire mountain is to get the chop long before there will be any regrowth to speak of.

No question that these elk will have to move on and it makes me sad to realize that we had them here so close for so long, yet were never able to get to know them. As of this writing, there have been a few more sightings in the area, but the numbers are still below what is needed to be a viable breeding herd.

Harold Mitchell sitting in one of Choate's mountain camps after a long weary day in the saddle of doing an "on ground" survey of land and wildlife.

That was also the fall when I lost one of my oldest and most loyal hunting partners, as Old Blue failed to show up on the horse roundup. He was the finest horse I have ever owned or known and for a long time afterwards, heading into the hills without him kept bringing back an empty feeling in me. He had been with the camp as the old standby ever since Collins had started it back in '43, so by adding all of the years together, we figured that he had to have lived to forty-seven, which is an ancient age for a horse. He had only been semi-retired for three years as we still put small children onto him, so he could parade them around the yard. As far as we knew he was not blind and was still able to feed well as the last time I saw him he was still in good condition. Considering his age and the way he disappeared, we have always suspected that he made a miscalculation and walked into a bog hole or

339

quicksand because that is a very common way for old open range horses to go.

One time when I was discussing Blue's disappearance with Jimmy Seymour, a long time friend of both myself and Blue, Jimmy just shook his head and reconfirmed, "When they gets old, they gets stupid."

I believe that statement fits a lot more than old horses too.

CHAPTER 30

EARLY 1978 BROUGHT another change into these hills, at least from my perspective it did. During the previous winter I had booked a hunter who was to come up on a spring bear hunt, so therefore I needed a cook to come along with us. That year, none of my former cooks wanted to come out at that time of year, so I placed an ad in the Help Wanted section of *The Vancouver Sun* newspaper. This had been done on several occasions in the past and most of the people who answered it were young women between nineteen and thirty.

Men, other than actual cowboy types, are not that interested in horses, so men rarely ever replied for this type of work. There were a few old burned-out cowboys that had wanted it, but knowing these types as well as I did by then and the problems they had with the bottle, I gave the women the benefit of the doubt every time.

To this particular ad, there was a large response, just as there had always been and the age and gender spread was still the same too. After reviewing all the resumés, I reduced the number down to three, two young ones similar to the past cooks and then there was one who admitted to being a bit older, so for a change, this time I chose the older one. There was never anything wrong with having younger women for this job except that most of them came for only a single season, so that always left me looking for another one for the next year. Most of the women who came for this job had not really been cooks in the past, but rather they were young professionals who were taking a working holiday to get away from the city for a while. The reason I chose the older one this time was because she said that she was a cook and also had previous experience with horses. There was also the hope on my part that if she liked the operation, she might be more inclined to return another year.

So I gambled on a new hand and so did she. Margaret arrived here about a week before the hunt was to begin, with the mutual idea that it would give her time to decide if this was what she really did want and also to get the feel of the operation. After spending a few days wandering around the place and visiting, she decided that she was staying.

Margo was not just a bit older than the former cooks, but she seemed to be different in other ways too. She turned out to be a rather tall, red-headed Irish-Scot who was obviously mostly Irish. It did not take me very long to discover that red-headed Irish girls are different. Oh yes they are! Margo had a grown up family that was scattered all over the Kootenay country so there were not going to be any incumbrances that way and the isolation here seemed to suit her just fine, so it looked like everything was going to be coming up roses.

At the end of the trial week I went into town to pick up the hunter and there was a message waiting for me that informed us that he had decided to cancel out, so that was the end of the spring bear hunt. That was not good news for either her or me because we both needed the business but it put her in more of a bind than I was in because she had burned a few bridges to take this job. After we had discussed this new dilemma for a while, she decided to stay around for a while longer, in case some unforseen business might show up. Well, it was a damn good thing she did, because before the season was over, we decided that we were getting along well enough to make the arrangement permanent. So ended my seven year interlude of bachelorhood.

It did not take Margo long to step right into the operation, both business wise and that other omnipresent problem with our big neighbour. All of this made for a lucky choice for me, because the neighbour situation was one of those things that we had come to realize might keep recurring, perhaps forever. But Irish people are not noted for running away from a good scrap and Margo, in that field, runs absolutely true to genetic form. Apparently I had not only found I myself a new wife, but also a partner who seemed to have considerable useful talents for handling whatever fate might drop at our doorstep.

As the summer wore on, Margo and I used most of it to learn to live together and do a lot of the odd jobs that I had neglected for the past several years. One of those was to finish building a log house that had been started when Carol was there, and as I am a poor and lazy builder, it had never been finished. One of the reasons Carol left, she said, was because I had promised to finish it, but never had.

I made the same promise again, but I must have learned a little more about psychology, because this time it did get finished. It's not the best log house in the country, but it is comfy. Unfortunately by the time it was finished, it ended up with a four-inch slope to the floor and perhaps more to the roof. However, it does keep out most of the elements and all animals larger than a cat. The water still walks in, just like it always had, but it does run out. The propane lights are a lot better and safer than the old Coleman pressure lamps and a solar panel runs the radio phone. I guess by most people's standards today, it's still rough living, but it's the most practical house I've ever lived in and it's a lot better than moving in and out of the old cook house.

The house that Choate built at Gaspard Lake.

As I am still a firm believer that people should keep at least a few nostalgic ties with the past, the House of Lords is still outside and that walk at -40° is the same brisk waker-upper it always was.

1978 must have been a leap year, because that was also the summer than an old friend, Pat Guthrie, returned to the Gang Ranch and married the acting manager, Bob Munsey. Marvin Guthrie had died a while earlier, so Pat had been a widow for a few years. Personally, I was very glad to see this happen as we knew that they both had strong feelings for the old Gang, but most of all it meant that I could take the buckshot loads out of the shotguns. Unfortunately nothing remains the same for very long, at least the good things don't seem to, as Bob and Pat did not manage the Gang for very long.

Sometime that October the Gang Ranch was finally sold and it wasn't to the Sidwell faction after all. For the first time in its history, the Gang had just acquired its first Canadian owners as it was taken over by the Alsager family who arrived here from Alberta and Saskatchewan. Munsey then stepped back to become cowboss again and the various Alsagers took over the running of the ranch. The sale and circumstances were big news in the local area and it was even referred to in the provincial media out of Vancouver. I forget just what the family pecking order was, as there were lots of them. The ones at the top that we had most to do with were oldest brother, Dale Alsager, who became the head honcho and official spokesman for the outfit, his brother, Rick, who took on the job of farm boss, and finally a brother-in-law, Dennis Rivard, who became some sort of ramrod as well. There was also a younger brother named Oren. We got to know him the best as he seemed to live in his small plane and was an avid hunter, so we crossed trails quite often.

The Alsagers arrived here amid a great deal of hoopla and very quickly the rest of us realized that they were feeding the media bullshit by the scoop-shovel full. Some of it concerned who and what they all were and what they intended to do with the Gang in the future. Lots of those stories made me more than a little nervous, mainly because of the way Dale in particular came across. He appeared to be a very aggressive businessman. They moved into here in an overwhelming way: brand new equipment, two airplanes, plans to supply the cowcamps by helicopters, and all sorts of other ideas that reflected the power of wealth.

These were obviously very rich people, far more so than anybody we had ever dealt with before. Bill Studdert had been an aggressive millionaire in his own way, but we very soon had the impression that these ones had hard sharp edges to them as well. So while they were fellow Canadians, I felt a

345

growing certainty that they might not turn out to be the cosiest neighbours a person could wish for.

I can still remember the words that one of our informants offered us about Dale Alsager and it has since turned out to be the best and most accurate information and advice that we have ever received.

"This guy is a very sharp operator, so you might be wise to have as little to do with him as you can, but if you must have any dealings with him, then for God's sake make certain that every t is crossed and every i is dotted. Always!"

The way he emphasized that last word made it sound like life in the Gang Ranch country was going to remain as interesting as ever. It did not take Marg and I long to begin meeting these Alsagers personally, especially Dale. He turned out to be a zoologist who also owned a private fenced-in herd of elk over near Maidstone, Saskatchewan.

Let me tell you, after the Alsagers moved onto the Gang, things began happening mighty fast and some of them were not to our liking at all. We further discovered that Dale had at one time been employed by the Alberta government as a nuisance animal control officer, so if there was anyone around here who would understand how to manipulate the system, it would be him. There was still more information that told us that he was also considered to be an expert on the use of poisons. Wow, it was sounding like if there is such a thing as human versatility, this fellow might be loaded and I was becoming increasingly alarmed about what directions this new operation might take.

January of 1979 brought us the news that our other neighbour, the Sky Ranch had gone broke and was in receivership. Since Gus Piltz had sold it to a neighbour in 1959, the Sky had fallen on rather bad times, as poor management and the continuing drought had reduced its capacity to produce enough revenue to support the expensive life styles the newer generation of owners kept trying to maintain. One of the major problems of the Sky Ranch and many other recently purchased ranches was their debt burden as these new owners had agreed to pay far too much for them. Since few of these transactions were done for cash, all it took was one unlucky year and they could be financially wiped out.

Another thing that compounded that problem was the fact that most of these same ranches were being taken over by people who knew very little, if anything, about running a ranch. By 1979, with the exception of the Gang, hardly any wealthy people were buying cattle ranches any more as the word was out that there was very little profit to be made in the beef cattle industry. For several reasons, it had become very much like the gold mining industry and had become notorious as a place for losing expensive shirts. However, the land titles were still changing hands quite frequently, as every generation seems to produce its own share of people who get starry-eyed enough to risk everything for the opportunity to be able to strut around the Interior towns in their western hats with cow shit on their riding boots, in order to be able allowed to proudly declare themselves as Cariboo ranchers. Ego and vanity can do interesting things to us.

If that was a winter that was tough on the Sky Ranch, it was also one that was hard on our woodpile, because the thermometer bottomed out at -47°. One thing about those types of cold snaps and other nasty weather patterns is they create lots of time for writing letters. In 1979 I was still very much in the public letter writing business, but there were also times when I wrote private ones that weren't nearly as snarky. One of the longest private ones I ever have written was done that winter: a five-page piece I sent to the new owners of the Gang Ranch. As we were destined to be neighbours with these people, we decided that it would be a good idea to try getting along with them rather than revert to anything like the Sidwell days again. From the conversations we had already had, mostly with Dale Alsager, I realized that there were many problem situations that the former owners had neglected to tell the new ones regarding some operations on the Gang. Well, I have been a nosey person all of my life and over the previous twenty years, I had been paying particular attention to the many disasters that happen so regularly on the Gang Ranch, so we decided to share this information with the Alsager family. This letter outlined, among others, weak spots in the irrigation system, locations of bog holes that had killed almost uncountable numbers of cattle, and extremely sensitive grazing areas that had attracted adverse publicity to former owners. In the past, I had used much of this information as part of my counter squeezer, so in a way I was a bit apprehensive about sharing it with the Gang Ranch until we knew for certain how we were going to get along with them. The entire reason for it was to see if we could all start out again from a square one situation, so from then on it was another wait and see. They did acknowledge the letter and Dale himself thanked us for it.

Well, it was only a month or so later when someone brought us word that the Gang had brought in an entire breeding herd of forty-three plains bison, without bothering to take out a government permit. It sure seemed mighty odd that someone with Dale Alsager's long history of working within government bureaucracies would attempt to do such a thing without first going through all those well-known proper channels. In B.C., buffalo had always been classed as wild animals and, as far back as anyone could remember, people who wanted to keep them in captivity had needed some type of government permit or licence. He probably knew or strongly suspected that if he was charged, he could more than probably bluff his way through a court case and that was exactly what he did.

The F&WB charged him under the Wildlife Act and when

it went to court, he won, largely because of the weak case presented by the F&WB. It all got bogged down over whether buffalo born in captivity were wild or domestic. After the case was over, the Branch did end up giving him a permit to keep them under confinement and on private property.

We knew that we were not alone in our doubts about game farms as there were a great many people within the organized hunting fraternity and the F&WB who were mighty nervous about it too, even if for different reasons. I began a correspondence with many of these people and even though locally the F&WB seemed to be on our side, the higher up the ladder that we reached, the more accommodating they seemed to be towards game farming. I had always known that the former director of the branch, Dr. James Hatter, was very enthusiastic about its possibilities and it now appeared like he may have left a few protegés behind when he retired.

So when this herd of buffs first arrived, I still had mixed feelings about them; it was not so much that they were here, but more like, "Why were they here?" The news media from all over B.C. played up the buffalo stories and Alsager fed them all the information that they could absorb. The reasons the buffs were here he said, was to start a new meat and hide industry and he was also quoted as saying that thcy would never be hunted for sport. He fed the local media and even many of his neighbouring ranchers everything they wanted to hear, like how buffalo were going to take the place of cattle because they were much more efficient feeders and not only that, the meat could be sold for three times the price of beef.

Well, a great many people around here believed him but I was still from Missouri and Harold Mitchell and a few others still were too. Even though this was touted as being merely a new meat industry that would stay within the constraints of their permit, I was very doubtful that it was the truth, because we could see almost no evidence of the massive fence building program it was going to require to hold these animals onto private property. Shortly after the buffs arrived, the ranch did reinforce a pasture of about sixty to eighty acres to hold the forty-three buffalo. But since many of them were due to calve soon, how many buffalo would this confinement really hold? When we asked some of the hired hands when and where the larger fenced pastures were going to be, all they did was shrug and say, "Don't ask me." When we asked the Alsagers themselves, we were pretty well told to mind our own business.

As far as I was concerned, the situation was becoming more ominous all the time. If this was to become an expanding herd, which it obviously was, then without the larger fenced pastures that any dimwit could see must be built almost immediately, then there was only one other possible direction that they were headed for and that was the open range. I remembered an earlier conversation I had with Dale when he felt me out about the possibilities of locking off some of the roads through the ranch headquarters area, very similar to what the Sidwells had proposed many years before. With all of this, coupled together with the old telegraph system, the entire operation was smelling more and more like a West Texas-style game farm all the time. In this case we could see that Alsager was bright and devious enough to perhaps throw in a few new Canadian twists. For the time being there was nothing we could do about it until it actually became a provable fact, so we had to sort of sit back and watch.

Mentioning access roads again brings a shudder, as I read back through my diaries of 1979. The loggers were swarming all over the Churn Creek slopes and cutting up some of the finest mule deer escape cover and migration routes that exist anywhere. This became extremely depressing when we had to sit here and watch this happening without being able to do a goddamn thing about it. What made it all seem so much worse was knowing that we had been screwed by the BCFS who had reneged on closing those very detrimental access roads.

We keep being reminded that time won't pause for anybody and that spring I had to put another one of my old hunting partners down. Shep was twelve and something in his system went wrong as all of his teeth fell out, so it was better to be gone than linger. He had been a fine and loyal friend and he and I had shared a lots of trails, campfires, and bones together, so decisions like that are not easy to make or do.

The word must have spread that I was down in the dumps over this because a few weeks later one of the former cooks arrived here with a big, gangly-looking pup of the same "good part of town" breed. As soon as we saw him, his name could only be Snoodle, so it was back to training another partner again.

All of these things went on amid the anticipation of the return of the Chilcotin elk which had become part of the efforts of the special projects of both the outfitters and the resident hunter associations of B.C.

There was still rancher opposition to the plan, but they seemed to be running out of steam, so we were pretty optimistic about the final outcome. That's the way we felt until early summer when Dale Alsager jumped into the arena and woke us out of our little fantasy. He had recently joined the local Cattlemen's Association and had almost immediately been either elected or appointed as their elk expert and was busy firing up the old anti-elk campaign.

Why they chose him to do this was quite obvious as he was probably the most knowledgable elk person they had, as well as being a zoologist (whatever in hell that means), and having a Master of Science degree. All of that gave him a great deal of credibility, especially to those who never really knew him or about him. Several of us had strong suspicions that this

appointment had something to do with controlling the competition between his farmed elk and the wild herd that we
wanted. It was quite possible that he might view the two ideas
as not compatible. Alsager, we knew, was going to be a tough
adversary and the only way we could come up with to perhaps
quieten him down was to form an anti-buffalo campaign and
also to challenge the entire concept of game farming in B.C.

CHAPTER 31

A REAL ESTATE AGENT who claimed to have picked this item off of their internal grapevine, informed us that the new Gang Ranch operation was not owned free and clear as we had been told, but rather, there was a huge five-million-dollar debt against it. This seemed to be an incredible figure as it was higher than we heard that the purchase price had been.

During that winter another fish kill had occurred in Gaspard Lake and it was the largest one I had ever recorded since living here. By this time, I was almost dead certain that the valve in the Big Dam had been left too open and more water had been let out of the lake than was coming into it.

Considering the size of the kill that year, we were extremely angry, so we asked the Gang to explain why it had happened. They explained that because they were new here, they did not yet understand how everything worked, so they had made a simple mistake. Well, the story did sound sort of plausible, so for a while we gave them the benefit of the doubt.

But we kept hearing rumours that the Alsagers did not want us located in the center of their ranch. We knew, that like all the previous owners, they tended to consider everything beyond their front gate as theirs.

My feelings of apprehension continued to grow until I

reached the point of wanting some kind of semi-official meeting with Dale Alsager to find out exactly where we all stood on many of these resource issues. We had met on the roads and at CRMP meetings, but those were brief encounters that did not allow for enough time to discuss some of these things in the detail that seemed to be necessary, especially if we were really going to try getting along with each other. If we were going to be at loggerheads, then that was OK too, but I just wanted to clear up the rumours and find out from the source what plans the Gang Ranch had. I deliberately went to the ranch headquarters a couple of times for just that purpose, but for some reason Dale was never there. But finally, on August 19th, he, his wife Betty, and three of their children arrived at our house, so the time had come.

The first major thing I wanted to get straightened out was about the elk. Alsager reconfirmed that he was still dead set against there being a wild herd either here or anywhere in the Chilcotin. So on the first point we were nowhere near agreement and we went onto the next, which was the possibility of the Gang establishing a private captive herd of elk here. Dale advised me that they were preparing to do exactly that. This information came as no particular surprise, but it was interesting to finally hear him admit it and also confirm some other suspicions about why he was so down on the idea of having wild ones here at the same time.

One of his reasons for wanting an elk-free location was because he was quite sure the wild ones would be attracted to the tame ones and would then create problems. After we discussed this for a while, I then mentioned having personally seen those three elk in Gaspard Creek back in '64, not to mention the continuous sightings of small groups of elk by other people. He dismissed most of it by suggesting that these local elk were obviously so few in numbers and so widely scattered, that there should be no problem of them mixing up.

We also discussed the water problems at Gaspard Lake, predator control, the already present buffalo herd, and the rumours that the Gang might be turned completely into a game farm. He was quite candid about many of their plans and I had to admit that, from the way he promoted his ideas, they might be able to be made to work. However, in the back of my own mind, that thought was exactly what worried me most, because all of this was going to be happening right in the middle of my guiding operation.

There was more talk about locking and blocking access, especially to the resident hunters. He felt they didn't deserve to be allowed into the area to kill wild animals, especially for the small licence and tag fees that they were then paying. Let me tell you, Dale Alsager had some really new ideas and it was interesting as hell listening to him, as he is a very convincing speaker. Sometimes throughout that day I wondered if his middle name might be Carnegie, but I never did get around to asking him about that.

I still wanted to have a wild elk herd in here and told him so. Well, Dale still didn't want one so he tossed out a counter offer. Instead of having a wild public herd, he would be willing to sell me their excess and over-mature elk and buffalo and we could then truck them up to Gaspard Lake where they could be turned loose for my clients to shoot. Again I would be a liar to tell you that it was not a tempting offer, but after mulling it over for a few moments, it all came back to the same reasons we never agreed to some of the things that the Sidwells offered. In a single word the spoiler was "trust." Also the idea of pot shooting animals that have been raised in captivity and calling it sport has no appeal whatsoever to me, so I told Dale to count me out.

Dale gave me a dumbfounded look when I turned it down. He told me that they already knew how many hunters we took out each year and what we charged them, so they also

355

knew that we had not been making very much money from this business. By coming in with them, that could all be turned around. I was still not interested, so what I offered in return, was to sell them my outfitters licence and then they could simply do everything they wanted to and do it all their own way. He thought a moment and then shook his head and told me that the way they had the ranch financed, they could not do it.

That little statement about financing began ringing more bells in my mind as it almost confirmed the rumours we had been hearing earlier. It would have been interesting to have carried the meeting further, but it was supper time so we broke it off.

The only decision that I could see that came out of that meeting was that we were all going to continue on our separate ways, like always, but hopefully this time, we would avoid fighting over the public resource bases we both needed. That seemed such a simple and straightforward necessity that by 1979, with all the past mistakes that had occurred, we would surely now not be forced to repeat them.

By the time the Alsagers left here that night, there was one point that we all understood very clearly; if we ended up having future neighbour problems, the most likely reason was going to be from a three letter word spelled E-L-K.

As far as we were concerned things began to deteriorate very rapidly after that and one of the first things that happened was that they overused Lost Valley again. It was almost like it had been done deliberately since the valley had been hammered flat. I had suspected in the past and was at the point where it was easy to believe again, that the reason the ranch insisted on overusing that valley was because I had a cabin there so therefore they knew we had become very dependent on that area for most of our moose hunting.

If they were going to sort of accidentally squeeze us again, then that could be considered as a nice quiet place to do it. There are no roads into Lost Valley, therefore the agrologists seldom go into there to inspect the range and anyway, there is very little true grassland to inspect as its mostly a brushy valley, much more suited to wildlife than cattle and that was why I set the permanent camp up in there in the first place. If this was the beginning of what I suspected it might be, then one thing I had in my favour, was the ranch was still running true to its past form and if that really did turn out to be the case, then I had twenty-five years of experience in how to handle the situation.

About the same time as we realized something was still haywire with the cattle management, a party of local hunters arrived at our place to visit and having just come down out of Hungry Valley, they had an interesting, and depressing story to share. It seems that they had been visiting with the Gang Ranch cowboys up there and these riders told them that sometime during the past summer, they found a grizzly feeding on a dead cow, so they shot it, even though it was out of season. The hunters did ask if the grizzly had killed the cow and the cowboys had replied that they didn't know for certain, but they weren't taking any chances either. The bear was past history and there was nothing we could do about it.

It was only a few days after that visit by the hunters that I was driving along a logging road near Williams Meadow, when something flicked a pocket flap on my shirt and at the same instant there was a hell of a "whack" sound in the truck. I never heard a gunshot, but some instinct told be that I'd just been shot at, so I floorboarded the gas pedal and spun dirt all the way up and over the hill I'd been climbing. As soon as I dropped over the crest, I stopped the truck because I still was not sure just what had happened. Within a moment or so, it became obvious that there were no new holes in me, so I looked all over the inside of the truck and couldn't see anything

357

unusual. Just the same I still knew that the truck had been hit with something. I was looking for a bullet hole that something kept tellin me had to be there somewhere. But after examining the truck body for several minutes I finally had to laugh at myself for being taken in by my own imagination. So I climbed back in the truck and as I was snapping the safety harness together on my right side, I happened to notice a strange looking bulge on the edge of the window-well on the passenger door. So there it was!

After opening the door and inspecting it from both sides, it was easy to figure out that the bullet was still lodged in there, but as soon as that was confirmed, instead of digging it out, I decided that it might be useful as some sort of evidence if it was left where it was.

One more thing that needed checking, out and that was to figure out where the bullet came from and who might have fired it, so I then ran back to the top of the hill to get a better look into the small gully that I knew the shot had to have come from. But after watching the area for five minutes or so and not seeing anybody, I came to the conclusion that the marksman must have been on horseback. About a mile away the Gang Ranch have a pasture and cabin that is known as the Williams Meadow cowcamp, so all of the possibles and probables began spinning through my mind. Something else began to dawn on me too which made me angrier by the minute at myself. I had just been caught on the road again without an equalizer. When will I ever learn?

I stopped at the Riske Creek post office to pick up the mail and the very first thing I noticed that the only other vehicle there was an RCMP patrol car. I pulled up beside them and told my story. One of the officers had a small pocket knife which he used to probe for the bullet. It had disintegrated into several pieces, so we also knew without saying, that there was going to be no ballistics taken from it. He handed me the remains of the bullet for a souvenir, he said, and also closed the case by suggesting, "Well, it could have been a careless grouse hunter too."

By then I had also taken note that neither of them had bothered to take down any notes during our conversation, so I suspected that as far as they were concerned, that was the end of it. Perhaps for them it was, but I still had my own opinions and they were not cooling my mind, not one goddamn bit.

From there I drove on into Williams Lake where I visited the local gunsmith. He examined the pieces and looked at the hole in the truck door and then he handed me the bullet too, but his comment was, "If this was fired by a careless grouse hunter, then he is one who shoots grouse with some type of high speed .22." He was referring to a rifle that shoots a .222 or a .223 — rifles that only a greenhorn would use on birds, because if a grouse were to be hit anywhere but in the head with such a bullet, all the hunter would have for dinner would be a blob of blood, guts, and feathers. When I returned home I told Marg the story and the more we thought about it and discussed it, it seemed inescapable that we were heading back into the equalizer days again. From then on, in the truck itself, no matter how big the inside load might be, there was always room made for the old double and a rack of buckshot loads.

Here is another one for you. Several months later, some bureaucrat in Victoria leaked a document out of the Ministry of the Environment's office, that turned out to be a written proposal from the Gang Ranch to bring that private elk herd into here. I received a copy of it too and it was an interesting proposal. The document asked the tax payers of Canada to pick up the tab for transporting those elk from Saskatchewan, pay for 90% of the fencing on the ranch, and then pay the wages of two biologists to monitor them. *The Vancouver Sun* sent Moira Farrow up to Williams Lake and the Gang Ranch, which resulted in a full page story, complete with pictures of Alsager and myself as being the main antagonists over the elk issue. That story in *The Sun* was mostly about the elk, but it also mentioned things like the out of season bear killing and the draining of Gaspard Lake.

It was sometime in the early winter of 1980 when we received some very bad news about the elk transplant that we had thought was so close to finally happening. Apparently the decision to approve the plan was right at the top of the list and it made some of the ranchers so angry, that they made one last desperate attempt to stop it. What they did, was to draw the local MLA, Alex Fraser, into the fray on their behalf.

We had always known that there was this possibility and a few years earlier some members of the Quesnel Rod and Gun Club, which was Fraser's home town, had met with him to discuss the issue and Fraser had told them that he had friends on both sides of this fence, so did not want to become involved in it. Up to the winter of 1980, he had kept his word, but then we learned that the ranchers had sent a delegation to him and got him off the fence and into their camp. For us this was quite a blow, because politically, we had always known that we were weak. Ever since the Socreds had come to power in B.C., here in the Interior the words "rancher" and "socred" had become synonymous and everybody knew it, so now the ranchers were demanding payment.

Sometime that spring Alsager tried a new tack with his public letter writing when he circulated one trying to locate support for a new idea of his, which was to close all hunting and especially guided hunting in the Gang Ranch country. Even though he was probably serious about the idea, it now seems just incredible that he really thought that it might become popular enough to become a fact. No doubt it must have been attractive to the anti-hunters, but he did not seem to realize that they are nowhere near as numerous as the

Alsager's sign greets travellers on the road near Gang Ranch headquarters.

hunters are in B.C. Most people in Canada seem to be "non" hunters but not necessarily "anti," so he again miscalculated the effect of the 150,000 licenced hunters of the province. And not only that, he really goofed by underestimating what the BCWF, which is the most aggressive hunter organization in Canada, would have to say about his proposal. But as it turned out, I was very glad that he tried it, because what it did mostly was expose the Gang Ranch manipulations for what they really were. In many ways it backfired on the Gang and perhaps most of the smouldering game farming ideas in B.C. as well.

Alsager's next trick was to erect a large sign on the main road leading into the ranch's headquarters area. In large letters it informed travellers that they were to check into the Gang Ranch office as they passed through. Other signs began showing up on other roads, claiming them to be private property, when we knew it was a fact that they weren't. Holy

Christ, they even declared the old Chilcotin Road as being private too and it was the oldest road in the country! This sign campaign went on for some time, until somebody took spray paint to the big sign and wrote "BS" on it, which tickled me to no end, as it showed us that others were beginning to get fed up with their gall as well.

Perhaps Alsager finally began to get the message that he was not able to con as many people as he thought he needed to, because it was about then that he brought in an American ranch manager by name of Dan Patten. As soon as we met this new fellow, we came to the conclusion that he and Dale were very comparable in mentality and it didn't take long for the idea to become confirmed. I still don't know what Patten's official title was at that time, but it appeared that he had been brought in to manage the impending game farm, as we found out that he had considerable knowledge in that field as well. I met and talked to him on several occasions and there became little doubt in my mind that he might be the person that the ranch was going to use to squeeze us with. This thought became much easier to believe after the cowboys informed us that not only was the Gang going into the game farming business in a big way, but they were also planning to couple that operation into a really large scale dude ranch and trail riding business as well.

We were never alarmed by the idea that the Gang was going to go into the trail riding business, but it did raise our curiosity as to why an outfit as big as the Gang would be bothered with it.

The longer we watched their operation gear up in a small way, we were more sure than ever that it might be only another Gang Ranch bluff to put the squeeze on us, perhaps with the idea of forcing us to lower the price on our guiding area, which most certainly would compliment the game farm they were planning.

By 1980, I had studied the dude ranching industry of North America as deeply as probably anybody had tried to do and some of the conclusions I had come up with, are something like this. The major problem with this business, especially in this part of B.C., is that there is simply too much existing competition. The competition for the real money spenders is not here in Canada, but in the mountain states of the U.S. Down there, they have been in the business since early in this century and there were a lot of beautiful lodges built down there during the depression years when labour was cheap. Those lodges still exist and their business is well established and it is very unlikely that B.C. will ever be able to draw their clients away from them. Not only that, but there are vast areas in those U.S. mountains that are every bit as beautiful as those here. To sum these comparisons up, I suggest to anybody that is thinking of buying or starting a dude or trail outfit here in B.C., they had better check out what the logging industry has planned for that area first. As time goes on, we Canadians may wake up and come to our senses before we wreck it all, but who wants to jump up and say we will.

The BCWF convention was held at the University of British Columbia in Vancouver during the spring of 1980. One of the politicians who was there was the Minister of the Environment, Stephen Rogers. Even though Alex Fraser was on record as opposing the elk transplant in the Chilcotin, Rogers was the minister who had the official say in the matter, so one evening while at that convention, the Federation executive put Rogers and I into a room to discuss Chilcotin elk. We were not alone, but I was given full opportunity to represent the wild side of the elk issue. It turned out to be a good and candid discussion and what came out of it was Rogers told us that if we could prove that the old elk had really lived here, then he would allow the Regional Wildlife Manager to re-introduce them again. When we heard him say that, we already knew that Mitchell had boxes of evidence, so that meant that the elk were as good as being back home.

After Mitchell produced all of the evidence and then wrote up a new resume to be recorded within the system, he presented the whole package to his Regional Manager for signing, which had to be done due to their chain of command structure. The Regional Manager at that time was Ira Withler, whom we all knew as Zeke.

Just in case there might be a financial hang-up for trucking the elk, we had already arranged for about $80,000 of private pledges, which really was overkill. But the bagman who raised it, said that as soon as he spread the word that it might be needed, he was overwhelmed with offers that he knew were as solid as pure gold. One supporter who we knew could afford it, offered to put the entire amount up himself, no matter what it cost. That's nice kind of support to have.

Mitchell was the head honcho for the elk project and I guess he got tired of taking all of our flak over the Branch's inactivity on it, so he finally called a small quiet meeting of us civilian elkers. He informed us that he had made up the transplant application himself and presented it to Withler, just like we had already been told. He had been told that there was nothing wrong with the way the plan was drawn up, but he thought the entire elk plan was just too socially contentious for the Chilcotin to handle, so he was not going to sign it unless Victoria ordered him to do so. This situation was just as crazy then as it still sounds today, because he was mandated to represent wildlife and had been given every authority to do it. The bureaucrats tossed the ball back and forth until there was no hope of getting it signed that year.

It was not very long after that happened, when we discovered that the buffalo were out and running. To start with, they did not go far but mostly hung around quite close to the Gang Ranch hay fields. There still had not been any new fencing on the ranch, at least not anything that would seriously slow down a buffalo, so we began asking questions of some of the hired help and even Oren Alsager who often came to our place to visit. The only answer we ever received from Oren was a laugh and a shake of his head as he informed us that it was not his problem and he didn't know anything about it. One thing we did notice was, every time the buffs got out again, they were wandering further from the home pasture.

Even months later, the buffalo were still making news around here as they were often out onto the open range where people were making deliberate trips out here to view them. A couple of my old buddies who were still working for the Gang came to visit one day and they brought us some interesting news about those animals. Most people around the Chilcotin didn't know anything about buffs and you could tell from conversations that they were very curious about any information that could be picked up. We were no exception and these two cowboys were quite willing to share some of their recent experiences about trying to manage buffalo. One of the stories they told was just a short while earlier, someone on the Gang had crowded some of the buffs a little too close with a truck and they turned on the vehicle and proceeded to wreck it. The cowboys warned me to be damn careful around the buffs, with either a truck or a saddle horse, because the ranch crew was still at the learning stage about what could and could not be done around these strange animals.

That was not the only news these boys brought us, because there had been another odd thing happen down at the ranch, when a bank sent some representatives out there to look things over and the crew got the impression that it was not a social visit, because they just received orders that all cattle were to be brought to the hay field for a count. Well, that really had nothing to do with us, but it was interesting just the same.

The best information that the boys brought was to tell us that the scuttlebutt around the ranch was saying that the Gang was now prepared to sell off some of its satellite properties as that same bank was demanding more return on whatever their investment here was. That began to make us wonder a bit too.

Now if you think the bullshit has been getting deep or aromatic, then get out your rubber boots and a gas mask, because 1980 is not over yet and around these parts it went out with a real ripper. In a large quarter-page story in *The Vancouver Sun*, dated December 30, 1980, Moira Farrow told the world of the latest Gang Ranch-Forest Service fiasco. The story was about how the most controversial grazing licence in B.C. had just been written up and issued for ten years. What made this story and the situation leading up to it so newsworthy was because up to then, the licence had been issued on a year-to-year basis, so it had made the rest of us around here wonder what the hell was going on, so we sicked the media onto the case and Moira got the answers for us. God, did she ever!

What had happened was, the word had got out of the CRMP that the cattle control on the Gang had deteriorated to such a degree that the CRMP had formed a special task group to tour the range and check things out. When the tour was over, they made a recommendation to the Forest Manager, (head forest ranger) that a ten-year licence NOT be issued to Gang Ranch until the ranch could show better management. Right at that moment the licence was still in the works but had not yet been signed by the forest manager, so it left many interested parties absolutely dumbfounded when Forest Manager D.A.K. McDonald issued the license to Alsager regardless. Several of the people on that special task group were his own rangers, yet from his ivory tower in Williams Lake, he overrode everyone else's recommendations. Why?

When that information caught up to me, I could hardly believe our sort of good luck, because from past experiences with this ranger, I had acquired a very low opinion of him. I immediately contacted Harold Mitchell about it, just in case he knew more than some of the rest of us did, as the situation began to take on a very strange smell. What made this licence appear to be tainted was it represented the largest licence in the Chilcotin and not only that, it was compounded by the fact that it was still the most controversial one because of all the recent allegations about overuse by Gang Ranch cattle and furthermore, much of the licence area was covered by the wilderness park proposal that went back to 1973. Therefore it did not seem like an area that should be committed, at that time, to a ten-year grazing licence. After Harold mulled the idea over for a while, he decided to use his position as the official representative for wildlife, to find out what the conditions of that licence might be, but when he inquired about it, McDonald refused him access to it. For some of us, what made this particular licence and the circumstances behind the issuing of it stink the worst, was knowing what the financial worth that thing represented to the Gang Ranch. The question we asked was, why would a ranger as high up in the hierarchy as McDonald was, stick his neck out so far? We never got a satisfactory answer here, but *The Vancouver Sun* did.

Here is a quote from the last two paragraphs of a long interview between Moira Farrow and Denny McDonald, the story appearing on page A8, *Vancouver Sun*, December 30, 1980. His comment: "The damn thing (the licence) was promised to Gang by our agrologist last fall and I don't go back on my word." McDonald continued by stating that the Gang performance would be carefully watched and the licence was no longer "any business of the F&WB."

The demand for answers raced around the range and the media for quite a while and one of the answers the FS lamely tossed back was that they could control a ten-year licence better than a one-year licence. But it's unlikely that they ever conned anybody that didn't want to be conned. There were more questions than these ones and they all slowly but surely got lost and buried within the FS bureaucracy, so in the end, the Gang Ranch was able to retain that ten-year license. From the point of view of the wild side, the only good thing that came out of that storm was when a short while afterwards, Mr. D.A.K. McDonald went into the safety of an expected retirement.

CHAPTER 32

THE WINTER OF 1980-81 was one of the mildest and had the least snow fall that I have ever recorded.

By this time the buffalo were roaming further and further from the private land and they were on many occasions seen down in Churn Creek, which was out onto the bluebunch wheatgrass that we had so recently won back for the bighorns.

The government ministries were saying as little about those buffalo as they could get away with, and this at a time when the FS still put notices in the local papers that threatened to roundup or destroy loose horses found on the open range. If all of this went on long enough, we knew that there comes a time that the situation might become one of those irreversible mistakes or precedents.

The rumours regarding the Gang Ranch financial problems had been rife for months and that February, a couple of friendly ranchers came to visit and they were just bursting with all the latest facts and figures. The two most interesting pieces of information they revealed to us was firstly, the Imperial Bank of Commerce had just settled their own farm manager into the Gang and the word was that the Alsagers did not like it, not one bit. The other fact turned out to be that Dale's brother Rick had already packed up and left the ranch. For us, this was certainly interesting news, but we were still uncertain how, or even if, any of it would affect us or the resource issues that we were involved in. Whatever these new events might mean, there seemed to be nothing for us to do but sit on the sidelines and watch the show, so that's exactly what we decided to do.

If the early part of the winter was mild, then the latter part of it went out with a vengeance. Of course it began in March and the proverbial lion jumped onto us with a ferocity we will never forget. On the second day of the month, late in the afternoon, a big Canadian Forces Buffalo aircraft almost took our roof off. It circled the valley and made another run at the house so we suspected something was wrong, as we knew from the markings on the plane, that it was a search and rescue outfit. We had no radio telephone then, so Marg turned the regular radio onto the local station in Williams Lake and we were stunned by news we did not want to hear. The helicopter that Mitchell and Prediger were travelling in while doing that sheep study had failed to return home the night before. Bert Wartig, a pilot for Okanagan Helicopters was a personal friend too and there was a fourth man on it, another biologist from Vancouver that we did not know. Almost before we could digest this info, an Okanagan 'copter arrived here with a load of F&WB people, inquiring if perhaps we had heard or seen that lost 'copter the day before, but we hadn't. As soon as we had shared all the known facts, they took off again to join the air search that was by then in full force. There were helicopters and planes within sight and sound right up to dark.

Marg and I spent the following day with our ears glued to the radio waiting, but by that evening there was nothing new to report. The Canadian Forces Search Master was quoted as saying that the next day there would be more planes in the air and he was asking for civilian volunteers to come along as spotters. That night I said so long to Marg, loaded my bedroll into the truck and headed for the Williams Lake airport.

For the next several days I sat in an OK helicopter until there were calluses on my butt. Still we flew. By adding up the hours on all of the 'copters, it turned out to be the biggest helicopter search in Canadian history. One of Wartig's proteges put himself and his 'copter at my disposal and for a few days we flew where I wanted to go. There was probably a couple of reasons they did that, one being it was common knowledge that three of my best friends were on that 'copter and also I probably knew the ground better than anyone else around here. We knew that if it was mechanical failure, which we all figured it was, that it could have fallen into the Fraser River and it would never be found. The Fraser is a natural sight path that many pilots follow and we flew it high and we flew it low, but there was still no sign or signal. By this time all searchers knew that the electronic locator had for some reason failed to work and that was when we were told that they had always had a rather high failure rate. That was not very comforting knowledge.

For me there seemed only one other thing to do, so I gave up my seat in the 'copter and began walking the breaks of Churn Creek, because it too, was a possible flight path that they might use on their way home, because there are sheep scattered along its full length. So for several days the 'copter would come to our home in the morning, pick me up, and then drop me off along those breaks. We would have already agreed to a rendezvous spot further on, where they would pick me up in the afternoon. So then it was back to walking the ridges and gully bottoms and in the month of March, that can be tricky business as there is still a lot of ice under the mud, as I soon discovered by taking several toboggan rides down the clay banks, sometimes on my butt and sometimes on my belly.

Even though the area had been flown repeatedly by several different crews, there seemed just a chance that their 'copter might have impacted into a small pile of junk under a big fir tree or on the bottom of a deep gully. There is not much to a helicopter and as one of the paratroopers had told us on the first day, "Perhaps what we are looking for is just a small pile of junk, that looks nothing like a helicopter."

Well, I walked all of my old sheep hunting trails and located nothing but more sheep. Marg got tired of being left at home all the time and she came out and walked some ridges too. But it was all to no avail and sometime in early April the search was called off until the snow in the high country melted as there was always the possibility that it went under a snow drift or hit a glacier.

It was sometime in June when Gordie Wolf, one of the wildlife technicians, drove out to our place to inform us that Tom Arduini had finally found the missing 'copter on Shulaps Mountain, just a five minute flight from where Wartig had fuelled up at the little town of Goldbridge. There must have been 200 search flights that went right over top of that spot, because it was right on the most obvious flight path that Bert would use. It did turn out to be just a pile of junk; the biggest part they located was the cargo door. Several months later at the crash inquiry, we were told that it was almost certain that they hit a raven as parts of it were found imbedded in a body. When the 'copter hit the ground, it burned totally and then the squalling storms of that day and following night covered everything with snow. As it turned out, it was just a freak accident, but still and all, it was a mighty heavy blow to lose most of our best friends in one fell swoop. Well, life for the rest of us had to go on so I'm going to drop this subject before I start to cry again.

That spring at the CRMP review meeting we were presented with a new Gang Ranch proposal to increase the cattle herd by 350 head. Three field agrologists recommended against it, but the head ranger was all for accepting it. Mitchell's job had

Taken from the air over Gaspard Lake looking west, showing Choate's Place in the first point of trees and then the vast meadow land that lays beyond, which straddles Wales Creek.

not been filled yet but Marty Beets was standing in. I was a bit nervous about facing these agri-foresters without Mitchell's expertise, but Beets soon put that apprehension to rest.

Alsager informed us that if the Gang did not get that increase in grazing, he would appeal the decision to the newly formed agri tribunal. This group could not make firm decisions, but its recommendations went straight to the provincial cabinet. Cabinet decisions can be very dangerous to environmental concern, especially the cabinet of that time which was still Social Credit. There was nothing we could do but plan to attend the appeal hearing when it occurred.

That following summer we had a lot of visitors that weren't really the client type. It astounded us how many of these strangers came to just sit and talk about the problems and conflicts of the Gang Ranch. Some of these people came right out and identified themselves as representatives of the Bank of Commerce and a few others were obviously interested in the possibility of investing in the ranch as either partners with Alsager or were waiting to purchase it directly from the bank, as they were all in agreement that the Gang Ranch or Alsager were just about finished.

Some of them never did declare what their interest was, but Marg coffeed and cookied them all anyway. There was an endless line of word games with some of those people and I found it really interesting that all of those bank reps came to talk to us, because it was not our bank. Why bother with us? Almost everyone of those visitors left us with more questions than answers.

One of the visitors was the new farm manager from the Gang Ranch and even though we agreed on very few points, I'll give him credit for being candid and probably truthful. He brought three sets of figures with him, one was astounding and the other two alarming and absolutely unacceptable. The first set showed that the previous spring the ranch had lost close to 800 cows and calves, mostly at calving time. When we heard that, we then knew one of the reasons that the ranch was foundering.

The second set of figures he tossed out indicated that in order to make the ranch financially viable again, they were going to need at least 6,000 cows on it. He obviously came here with the idea of getting my endorsement to such a plan, but I flatly refused to even consider it. That many cattle allowed back into here under any circumstances was almost certain to spell wildlife disaster.

The third and final set we did make consensus on. That was over the value of the Gang Ranch. He reconfirmed that the Alsagers had paid about four and a half million for it, which at that time the bank had considered to be fair market value.

Since then, the bank had loaned them more money, bringing the total up to seven million, but the difference was accounted against other properties the family had in other provinces.

Even though the manager had been told that all of the money had been invested into the Gang, he could not see very much added value to what they had originally purchased. There were two new houses, one of which could be described as the proverbial mansion on the hill, that Dale had built for himself and another smaller one that his brother-in-law had built. There was some new machinery and a couple of new overhead sprinklers, but even at that, it did not add up to anywhere near a seven million dollar investment that would ever return so much as the interest on the loan, he said.

This fellow seemed to be about as knowledgable as anyone who had ever been on the ranch, so we asked him what we considered to be the ultimate question under the circumstances, which was, how much did he think the Gang was worth right then?

"Well, there has been a lot of discussion about that lately and the new figure is three million at the outside," he informed us.

That was exactly the same figure I had estimated for the past several years, so I had one more question for him when I asked, "If that's really the case, then how do they ever pay for it?"

He just shook his head as he replied, "It can't be done unless the cattle herd is doubled."

For me this was quite valuable information because now we knew for certain just how desperate they were, so that grazing increase application somehow had to be kept in check or it might throw open doors into God knows where.

The Gang Ranch did appeal the case and it was heard before a panel of three supposed unbiased farm experts. The panel included the ex-Liberal MP for Kamloops, Len

Marchand, who had been some sort of agriculturalist before getting into politics, and a rancher from the lower part of the province. This panel had only been called together on a few occasions in the past and those earlier cases had attracted little or no public attention, as only the aggrieved parties and the government expert had ever showed up. However, the hearings are always open to the public, so in this case we let every news reporter and rod and gun club in the vicinity know what was up and they responded in a swarm. Even Moira Farrow of *The Vancouver Sun* came up to Kamloops and reported on the proceedings.

It must have taken the judges by surprise, because I was there early and as the other interested parties began filing into the room, we could detect looks of disbelief on the faces of the judges. It was obvious to me that Marchand in particular did not appreciate so many people looking over his shoulder. Every time a new arrival came into the room, he seemed to just glare at them and I never saw him smile all day. The public presence seemed to upset Dale Alsager too, so naturally I began to feel the atmosphere as being more encouraging.

Actually the inquiry went very well and the witnesses seemed to be telling the truth. Dale admitted that it is near impossible to control large numbers of cattle in the high country. His cowboss expressed the problem best of all when he described what had happened the year before.

"The whole operation just fell apart and I don't know why," he told the panel.

In the end, common sense did prevail and the Gang Ranch lost the appeal. The decision did come to us as a pleasant surprise, but at the same time, we were still feared that it was not the end of the problem, because if it calculated out like the ranch manager had said, then the difference in the cash value of the ranch would likely attract continuous attempts to re-adjust that grazing licence. Apparently the difference worked out to be in the millions, so that alone had an ominous ring to it too.

It was not long after that when some friendly cowboys came to visit and they reported that the Gang was in such a bad way that there was not even money to buy salt blocks for the cattle.

These boys were pretty upset about something else as well, because they had just been informed that from then on their wages were going to be docked fifty dollars a month each for rent for the use of the range cabins. We found this to be just hilarious since all of those cabins are on Crown land and had become part of the range improvements of the Grazing Branch of the BCFS. The word was also out that the Gang had taken to renting those same cabins to tourists and that really angered Marg and I as at that point, they were coming into direct competition to us, but we had to pay leases, taxes, and maintain everything at our own expense. It seemed to beg a question like, "What happened to free enterprise?"

These cowboys seemed to treat the whole affair as a big joke and said they weren't working very hard any more as they expected to soon be working directly for the bank. They told us stories about how the Gang Ranch was already in the game farm business, West Texas style. Several hunters had already come to the ranch and shot some of the buffalo. The crew recounted side-splitting tales of how the buffs had been baited into the field, and then a hunter and his guide would drive up in a truck. The hunter would take a rest across the hood and pot his trophy while it was eating out of a feed trough.

By this time we were becoming more apprehensive about this local game farm situation because we also knew that they were hunting those buffs right out onto Crown land, which in essence meant that they were guiding hunters on my exclusive licence area. So we wrote a letter to the Minister of

Environment in Victoria, to see what was going on. We received a very polite reply direct from the minister, who was still Stephen Rogers.

My letter consisted of a list of questions and Rogers answered every one of them and very clearly too, but the first and third answers were of particular importance to me.

The reply from Stephen Rogers was numbered as MO 9764, October 21/81.

Question 1: Where are the farms to be located?

Answer: There has been no determination as to the location of the game farms except that they would be located on private land.

Question 3: Who will operate the game farms? Will a resident hunter have to pay for entry?

Answer: If the trial is authorized, game farms would be operated by private farmers under strict government control and inspection. The farm would be operated like a livestock ranch and the animals would be slaughtered by conventional methods. There would not be hunting of the animals on these farms.

The letter is duly signed by the minister and I still have it.

Since the Gang had no permit to have buffalo on Crown land, I decided to ask more questions to the F&WB Regional Supervisor in Williams Lake. When I confronted him with Rogers letter, he became flustered and babbled away about the problems of sufficient evidence. Holy Christ! Evidence? All he had to do was drive down the logging road between Big Creek and Gang Ranch headquarters and he stood a good chance of being chased off the road by the evidence!

By that time there were about twenty head of these buffs

out onto Crown land most of the time as the Gang had just about given up trying to hold them onto private land. Many times when travelling the road to Riske Creek we met what must have been the entire herd out and running. Just what does it take to make the higher echelons of government enforce even their own rules? I was beginning to get goddamn angry at those sons of bitches and tried everything we could think of to make them move, but all they ever did was shovel more paper.

There were a couple of positive events that fall, the first one being that Dr. Darryl Hebert took over Mitchell's old job and we could not have asked for or received a better replacement. And secondly, the cow moose season was reduced down to five days. But even that had a dark spot too, as it attracted so many greenhorn hunters into the meadows that week that it took a brave person to venture out on horseback. It was absolute bedlam in the low meadows where the new logging roads had opened up easy access.

One thing that I noticed that fall was that the natural meadows both close to home and up in the higher valleys were beginning to brush up at a very rapid rate. By comparing photographs taken in the 1950s to what we now saw in '81, it was easy to come to the conclusion that the grassland that I first saw in 1955 was beginning to disappear into the shade of the much higher willows, arctic birch, and encroaching evergreens. If these meadows do not catch fire soon, then the old cattle empire will fade from these hills for reasons other than wild-eyed environmentalists. If the present rate of brushing continues, then I think that, to all intents and purposes of commercial livestock feed, the high altitude grass will be finished by 2020. However, if that's the way it goes, it might be the best thing for wildlife, as they will get their old homeland back and have it all to themselves too. Sometimes history does almost repeat itself.

1982 started out about normal. Most of my previous winter had been spent writing letters to various government ministries trying to clarify the legality of the Gang renting these range improvement cabins, so at that review meeting the Lands Branch brought the answer I wanted to hear but perhaps not the same for my big neighbour. As it turned out, the Lands Branch then informed the Gang Ranch that if they were going to continue doing this, then they would now have to take out regular land leases and pay taxes, the same as every other business was having to do. Dale Alsager was there himself and he complained that if this became the case, then it would add about $20,000 a year to the ranch expenses. Even so, that still remained the government answer.

I also brought up the annual question about the buffalo which had by then become pretty much a free roaming herd and the F&WB told us that the Gang was still under orders to pen them up, but there was still no mention of enforcement if they weren't.

April 20th is my birthday and the present I received that year came to us over the local radio station when they read off a news release that informed the listeners that the Gang Ranch was once more officially for sale. For us that seemed like good news but there was a bit of a dampener added to it, when the announcer revealed that the owners were offering it at one of those Gang Ranch fire sale prices of only ten million dollars.

When we heard that figure, it also gave us our day's laugh, especially when we remembered what the ranch manager had told us just the year before. If they were serious about that figure, then it made us wonder how long it might take them to locate a sugar-plum who would really pay it. Perhaps we were going to be stuck with the present neighbours for longer then we expected.

On May 14th when the ice finally went out of Gaspard

Choate's Place on the west end of Gaspard Lake (taken from helicopter).

Lake, we discovered that there had been another massive fish kill under the ice. We rowed the length of the lake and estimated we had seen about 5,000 dead rainbows, most of them large adults. It was not a total kill but it was depressing to see, just the same. It was the same cause as usual; there had been more water going out from under the ice than there was coming in. The good water just ran out.

CHAPTER 33

LATER ON THAT SPRING, some tourists stopped by our place and brought us word that they had just been turned back by a locked gate down near the Gang Ranch headquarters. They were very angry at having to detour 100 miles around by Williams Lake and come in on the new logging road. We were expecting this to happen as we already knew that the Gang had built a large iron gate down there. It had been locked on an on and off basis, but there didn't appear to be any pattern to the closures, but now it was locked for certain. These people had taken pictures and they were angry enough that they assured us that when they got home, they would be writing letters to the government to find out what the score was.

I could hardly believe the Gang Ranch could really be this stupid because we knew that there were government records to prove that public money had been spent on these roads. The ex-game warden, Bill Fenton, had explained the entire situation to me back in 1955 when he had searched out those records for his old buddy, Bill Studdert. According to Fenton, Studdert had also considered locking the road off, but when he saw the public records, he thought better of it. If old Bill was afraid to try it back in the '50s, then it seemed ridiculous that anyone would attempt it at this late date. It may have seemed absurd to rational people, but these were the Alsager years around the Gang Ranch, so a person had to learn to expect stupidities. After these tourists left, I took my own camera down there and recorded that the lock was indeed there.

So now, what to do? In some ways the situation to us was as much amusing as it was alarming. We were not cut off from getting in and out of our home as the new logging road from Riske Creek was open by then and it not only came within a few miles of home, but it actually intersected with the old road above the Gang headquarters. But what was alarming was the thought that if they got away with this on a public road, they might try it elsewhere as well. Even the new logging road cut across Gang Ranch private land near the old Home Ranch and up to then, I had not thought to check the legal status of that road. There might be a possibility that the Gang and the loggers might collude to lock up everything.

It was fascinating to consider what repercussions would befall the Gang Ranch when the resident hunters began arriving in a couple more months. I personally knew many of the people who hunt this area and if they arrived at that locked gate in a rummed up condition (which would be about normal for some of them), then the possibility of sparks flying were very real. I had already decided that if the need to open the gate should arise, I would get a cutting torch and do whatever adjusting was necessary.[30]

However, the more we thought about it, the more it looked like a situation for other people to resolve instead of us. We decided it was time some of them got their feet wet too. So the torch would only be used as a last resort.

We fired off personal letters to all the government ministries that could possibly have an interest in this situation,

---

30 As a matter of fact, a businessman in Williams Lake offered to give me a complete cutting outfit to keep if I would do it right then.

including the R.C.M.P. The Lands Branch responded first, verifying that the Gang had no right to control those roads.

When confronted with this, do you think the Gang withdrew those locks? Not on your duff, they didn't. Again, we sent that information to the R.C.M.P. but still the locks remained in place. Our business was still able to operate without the cutting torch, and by then there was enough action along the road that it didn't need any more grease from us. Every time the Gang had a confrontation with a traveller, we had a new ally. What was happening down there was even better than if I'd planned it myself.

Some cowboys came to visit and to share the moccasin telegraph. One of them was Ray Rosette, one of Augustine's older sons, and he informed us that his brother Willie had just left the Gang Ranch after working there for twenty-three years, because he couldn't stand the bullshit any more. We all knew that the Gang would soon miss Willie because there was nobody else anywhere that knew the country or understood the operation as well as he did. Willie had served as cowboy, catskinner, cowboss, hay boss, and ramrod for just about everything that had to be done and that kind of experience is irreplaceable. Ray didn't think he would stay much longer either. It would sure be a different ranch without any Rosettes on it as I doubt if there had ever been a time in the past when at least one of them was not represented there. Times change.

Then the word came up on a different telegraph telling us that the F&WB had issued the Gang Ranch one more extension on the buffalo permit. Not only that, the Gang was now being considered for a legal buffalo farm licence. There were a few strings attached to the coming licence though, because they were also advised that this time the buffs must be contained on private property. The new permit and coming licence stated that if any buffs broke out, they must be recaptured within a certain length of time or the government would take posses-

sion of them. We could never understand why the government wasted their time issuing such a permit with those
types of strings, as it was common knowledge throughout
the district that the Gang was flat broke and the cattle fences
didn't even slow the buffalos down. Even as that permit was
being written up, the buffs were out and running most of
the time.

There is a long entry in my diary dated November 27,
1982. I had been into Williams Lake and returned home with
some interesting news. The bank had finally moved out onto
the Gang and ordered all cattle to be brought in out of the
hills, which was about three weeks earlier than normal. The
cowboys did a quick roundup and started the cows down the
road. One of them told us that the Gang had already shipped
out several truck loads the week before. Perhaps they were all
getting shipped, he didn't know and didn't care. We also heard
that Dale had moved off the ranch and had left his father,
brother Oren, and brother-in-law Rivard behind to salvage
whatever they could, since they had all put up personal
properties as collateral. Not only was the bank there for its
pound of flesh; the cowboys told us their cowboss of the past
summer, who had been working by contract, had pulled out.
Perhaps it was almost over. We hoped so.

Out of curiosity, on December 3rd I drove down towards
Gang Ranch to check out the locked gate situation. I thought
that if Dale Alsager had left, then maybe the roads would now
be open. We knew that the Gang Ranch had received a letter
from the government explaining the status of the roads and
asking the Gang to remove the locks.

However, when I arrived at the first gate, I found it shut
by two big brass padlocks. Not only that, but Dennis Rivard
had his pickup parked across the road and refused to let me
pass. We had a heated discussion about it. He admitted that
the government had asked them to open the road, but they

had decided to ignore their request. I had an equalizer with me, but decided to hell with it. After all, this was not really at the stage of a Johnson County range war, where people blew each other away for smaller disagreements than this, so I turned back the way I had come.

That little episode wasn't quite over yet. Several weeks later when I went into the cop shop in Clinton, the corporal said he was glad to see me and wished I had arrived a day or so sooner because he had a surprise for me. He told me that the Gang Ranch had laid a trespass charge against me and, until yesterday, there had been a warrant for my arrest laying on his desk. But the day before, the charge had been withdrawn. He would not tell me who had laid the charge, but that didn't matter because I knew anyway. Talk about gall! They had charged me with trespassing while I was on a public road. It made me goddamn angry but there was nothing I could do about it.

The long awaited news came over the radio on December 4th. The Gang Ranch was in receivership for defaulting on seven million dollars worth of debentures. Needless to say, we didn't really bother with the crocodile tears, but at the same time we wondered what the future might hold for the old Gang and especially ourselves, because there was no getting around it; both the Gang Ranch and ourselves had a tiger by the tail. But even with the vultures so close, we still felt that we had survived an important hurdle.

Though Dale Alsager was gone and a receiver had moved onto the ranch, things were not showing much sign of improvement, at least not from our perspective. This was driven home to us on February 3rd when an R.C.M.P. helicopter came roaring into our yard and disgorged three armed Mounties. We were standing outside in our bedroom slippers, wondering what the hell was going on, because when the first two jumped out, I noted that one of them had the flap on his pistol holster rolled back, something that they rarely do. The youngest one came striding straight up to me and asked, "Are you Choate?"

I had to admit that I was. He then he pointed to our truck and asked, "Is that your truck?" He was checking the licence number, so again I had to agree. He then informed me that he had a few more questions to ask me, so we invited them into the house.

Inside, the young Mountie opened his briefcase and pulled out a sheaf of hand written papers. An interrogation began. I was curious as hell and as Marg poured us all a coffee, her eyes had become very round. About then the pilot, an RCMP sergeant, came in and he was packing a small pistol too. I had flown with RCMP in the past, but had never seen one of their pilots armed. This was getting more interesting by the minute.

From the questioning, we learned that a Gang Ranch barn had been burned on Christmas Eve or morning. Not only that, but someone had reported seeing our truck down there at the same time. We hadn't heard anything about the barn but the truck was a different matter. Even though about two months had elapsed, we could still vividly remember every-thing about our Christmas because that year was a very open winter and we had five guests who had come to visit and had stayed a few days with us. Something Marg had begun when she first moved here was to establish a guest register book in the house and ever since then, she has had people sign it. That Christmas everybody who had been here had signed the book, so I had more than enough witnesses to testify where I and my truck had been at that time.

When the young Mountie looked them over and recorded the names, he gave his partner a curious look. The older fellow was the same corporal who had told me about the trespass charge a couple months earlier. After a few more questions that I noticed were beginning to get a bit softer, the young

Mountie put his (or is it my) file back into his briefcase and all three of them smiled and shook their heads. After that, he re-flapped his pistol and we had a much more social visit.

After the R.C.M.P. left that day, it raised another question in our minds. How would that case have turned out if we had not had guests that Christmas?

We had been looking forward the coming CRMP review that spring because it was almost certain to reveal what was going on at the Gang and perhaps suggest what its future might be. Well, it sure as hell did all of that. The Gang Ranch arrived in a very belligerent mood and was represented by Dan Patten, who had been elevated to manager, plus a farm expert representing the bank.

When they were asked about the new road status through the Gang Ranch, they stated emphatically that they were going to re-lock the same gates again that year and, not only that, they also intended to lock another road going into lower Churn Creek. Let me tell you, they were really aggressive and the rest of us damn soon learned that the bank was behind Patten 110 percent.

When we asked how they could rationalize that position in light of the government letter explaining the legal status of the roads, they replied that the Department of Highways had not ordered the locks removed, they only "asked" for them to be removed. Most of us could hardly believe what we were hearing, but that's the way it was.

At the same meeting the F&WB also gave notice that the regional supervisor had finally fallen off the fence and was ordering all the buffalo to be rounded up and shipped out of the province or else slaughtered. He further stated that there was not going to be any more yearly permits to keep them here, because there was no evidence that the Gang was going to control them. This seemed to make Patten even angrier: the old Gang was still in a fighting mood.

The entire tone that day was pure Alsager and the reason for that may very well have originated with Dale, as he once told us that public relations had no cash value to a rancher. We already knew from our conversations with potential buyers that a locked-up ranch was worth more to them than one that's criss-crossed with public roads.

It was no secret that the bank expected to get the seven million plus the accumulating interest, which would bring the price up to about ten million. The cowboys told us that even the Mormon Church was looking it over again. They had considered it once before too. Darryl Hebert and I tried encouraging some of my old sheep hunter clients into coming up and taking it over, but it was the same answer as before: too many uncertainties. We even offered to help pave the way for them, as we figured that, knowing as we did about the operating problems of the Gang, between us, we could work out a true and fair resource use plan that should alleviate most of the past problems. It still didn't work.

I tried interesting Ducks Unlimited into buying it, using their land use knowledge to put it together differently so that, after it got going again, they could resell it with a clean slate, but they wouldn't try it either.

Different answers did begin falling into place in late April when the Department of Highways finally released the outcome of their investigation into the road status throughout the Gang Ranch area. The Gang Ranch was sent a letter from them, that stated in part that this had been a recorded public road going back to at least 1894 and noting that the government had begun spending public money on it in 1900 and continuing for at least twelve consecutive years. Therefore the Wycott Reservoir Road Number 85 is covered by Section 4 of the Highways Act and it is sixty-six feet wide.

The letter goes on to describe how the road intersects with various other surveyed lots and notes that in those original surveys the already existing road was deleted from the private land.[31]

What really burned me up, now that all of the evidence was in, was that no one at the Gang Ranch was being charged for deliberately obstructing public roads. They got away with it, off and on, for about a year and a half, but there was no penalty for doing so. I asked the R.C.M.P. about that and they had no answer. The only satisfaction we received came from the last paragraph of that three page letter signed by J.C. Jensen, District Highways manager, stating, "Failure to remove the locks will leave us no alternative but to have the complete gates removed from the road permanently."

In my opinion, all of us who live or travel in the Gang Ranch country owe J.C. Jensen a vote of thanks, because that letter is the most positive statement that I have ever seen a bureaucrat sign his name to. When I received my copy, we had a hundred more photocopied and sent to every rod and gun club that we knew of, just to ensure that the old records don't become "lost" again. The locks were duly removed and have never reappeared since. It took a while, but another round had been won.

Another round that had yet to be resolved was our attempts to get those wild elk into here. Hebert had taken up the torch from Mitchell on this issue and he began devoting much time and effort to it. When he first arrived here and looked over the past records for the elk proposal, he noticed that there was still one very important thing that the Cariboo-Chilcotin resource use plans lacked and that was an actual forage allocation for wildlife. Between 1973 and 1976, when the FS started getting all the flak about overgrazing by cattle, they made and printed statements saying that from then on, wildlife

31 I also found it interesting that, in the early days, Churn Creek had been known as St. Mary's Creek.

would be considered in their grazing plans, but nothing was really said about how much of the feed wildlife could have. Was it to work out to one blade of grass, or was it to be more?

I was worried that the Gang Ranch, under whatever new owners, would try to rebuild the cattle herd up as far as the total feed resource would allow. We needed a firm forage allocation in the worst way, but under the present FS administrators, it did not look like it was going to happen any time soon.

For the next little while, the old land and cattle empire slowly continued to dig its own grave until it dwindled away. The receiver began selling off the satellite ranches on the east side of the Fraser until only the core area was left. The Alsagers tried unsuccessfully to bail it out but the real end of their tenure here was when the R.C.M.P. laid over thirty charges on Dale Alsager: theft over $200, theft of cattle, criminal breach of trust, and fraud. As *The Vancouver Sun* wrote it up, "The Crown alleges during 1981 and 1982 Alsager stole and sold 1,672 head of cattle belonging to Alsager Holdings Ltd. and kept the proceeds for his own purposes. Alsager is also charged with stealing approximately $650,000 from the company." Of course he pleaded not guilty.

If the Alsagers were finally gone, the Gang Ranch itself was still very much here and the manager and receiver kept up the pressure regarding road usage until the Dept. of Highways must have decided to hell with Gang Ranch and the trouble it was creating. Highways just moved in and re-surveyed the old road into its original location and built a gravel highway right through the middle of the headquarters area. All of the gates have been by-passed with cattle guards, so now the travelling public can roll right through and connect with the new logging roads from Williams Lake. This new highway absolutely assures the rest of us that the chances of new owners ever being able to lock up the Gang Ranch country are now over. Highway Number 85 can be said to be the real coffin nail to the old Gang as we used to know. In the end, as it was all winding down, there was still a lot of unresolved bitterness but perhaps that will evaporate with time. It's hard to say.

Well partners, all stories have to end somewhere and as our fire is burning low, this seems like as good a place as any to end this one. Even though the Gang Ranch is still here and so is the hunting camp, an era of the Chilcotin has certainly closed. It can never be the same again, especially with the huge clearcuts and the logging roads that are encroaching from the north.

As time goes on, there will probably be another joker played in the land and resource issues around here and I believe it will show up as another over-commitment by the BCFS when they set the Timber Supply Areas and the Annual Allowable Cuts. If we thought the forage problems of the past were an environmental issue, then by comparison, overcutting will be sheer devastation. Don't ever let them con you into believing that silviculture is the answer, because if the powers that be used common sense, we would not need silviculture. We wait and wonder.

Most of my life is over and looking back on it now, it brings to mind a recent conversation I had with several other outfitters at an annual convention. We were sitting around a table in the bar, swapping the past year's telegraph and I had just told of the most recent happenings between the Gang Ranch and Choate (my version). After the laughter and head shaking were over, a woman at the table raised her glass and said, "Do you people know what I believe? I believe that Choate and the Gang Ranch deserve each other."

This has gone on long enough. Let's break camp, saddle up, and take another ride up through the high country before Smokey wrecks it all. The last one to mount can piss on the fire.

Chilco Choate gazing across his dreamland in the upper watershed of Big Creek. Photo taken from Dash Hill, looking sw. Choate is probably contemplating the park proposal of whether to "park it or log it," because all the trees seen here have been catalogued for the Williams Lake Timber Supply area. As a high- ranking forest ranger told Choate, "It doesn't matter where it is, it's all good wood." He was referring to chips.

Into the smoke and flames
Of a thousand campfires
The old man swore an oath,
That somehow and some way
In a brighter day
This land will once again
Become what God originally intended.
A wildlife range —
The only use that makes any sense.

The very head of Lost Valley, or as it's listed on maps, Dash Creek. This is park proposal country.

Powell Creek in the Snow Mountains but now more commonly known as the South Chilcotin Mountains. This is within the park proposal area.

EPILOGUE

THIS STORY ENDS IN 1983. Here is an update.

Big Dam on Gaspard: still unresolved. The promised cleat to be fastened onto the headgate has never materialized.

CRMP: a few years ago, the FS used their mandate to dissolve it into a system that they can easier manipulate. Now we are continually reminded that the District Forest Manager reserves the right to make final decisions. And by God, around here they do, too.

Forage: recovering since the cattle numbers have been reduced but nowhere near the mid-fifties amounts. In too many areas, weeds have replaced quality grass feed.

Forest allocation for wildlife: on December 16,1987, the Regional Forest Manager for the Cariboo Forest Region, John Sauer, stated in a letter that, from then on, the open range is to have at least thirty to fifty percent left on it at the end of the summer grazing season by livestock for the benefit of wintering wildlife. If we don't remain vigilant, we run the danger of the open range reverting into maximum range use all over again.

The proposed park or wildlife area: still unresolved. Parks Canada has recently declared an interest in establishing a national park that would run from the junction of the Chilcotin River to south almost to Goldbridge, which would take in both sides of the Fraser River and then west towards Taseko Lake.

Forest cutting: the low country has already been extensively logged and now they are chopping away right at the foothills of the alpine, telling us that they want to go all the way up. With the new chip mills in Williams Lake boasting that they can utilize trees down to three-inch butts, you should be getting the message.

Road closures and leave strips: mostly reneged on by the BCFS. Only a few token roads have been closed and then only recently. The cover strips that were supposed to be left at the open roadsides have never materialized. The clearcuts come all the way down to the road edges, leaving game animals only a minimal chance from long-range rifles. The zig-zag block cuts have rarely been implemented. The FS justifies this discrepancy by trotting out the old bogies of the need to eradicate bark beetles or mistletoe. This conveniently allows them to road or cut wherever these are detected, never mind the numbers. I wonder if they have ever considered that these have always been part of the forest ecology. Ah well, never mind. Smokey knows best.

The Gang Ranch: has changed hands three times since the last page of this book. It is now owned by Saudi Arabian interests. The telegraph says that they paid over seven million for it. They don't live on the ranch and seldom visit. The ranch is back to a straight cattle operation and the herd is under 3,000 head, which is about right. All of the satellite ranches were sold off after the Alsagers went broke, so now it's only a shadow of its former size. It still has that grazing licence that covers about 1,100 square miles. Considering the size of that licence and the type of land that it covers, I hope that you will watch very closely because the ranch has had a long history of being able to make profitable blunders.

ANIMALS

Buffalo: to all intents and purposes — gone.

Grizzlies: probably no more than fifteen left in the entire Empire Valley and the Gang Ranch ranges combined. If these magnificent animals are to be maintained, then ranchers' grazing licences should be held accountable. That would go a long way towards preserving these animals.

Elk: A few sporadic sightings but no herd. We still lobby and pray that the politicians will eventually relent and allow an experimental herd to arrive in government trucks.

Moose: now greatly reduced in numbers. In much of the lower elevations, where new logging roads have opened up easy access, they are not in huntable numbers even though there is still a two-month hunting season on them. If the Forest Service carries out their plan to road every watershed, then the only way the moose can survive is for all moose hunting (including Indian hunting) to be by limited entry.

Wild sheep: the one bright light for the wildlife in this area. Numbers are now in the 500 range and still rising.

Wolves: a stable population of under thirty animals which is just the right amount. For the time being, hunters seem to be bagging just enough of them to keep the population in an acceptable balance.

PEOPLE

Alsager, Dale: after leaving the Gang Ranch under a cloud of criminal charges, he went to trial and, after a lengthy trial, he was acquitted. He then taught at Okanagan College for a while. What did he teach? Would you believe Agriculture? It could only happen in Lotus Land.

Arduini, Tom: still flying helicopters.

Beets, Marty: went up the F&WB ladder and is now supervisor for the Cariboo-Chilcoton area.

Bishop, Jim: After leaving the Gang Ranch, he cowboyed on the OK Ranch and several others until age forced him to retire.

Choate, Carol: after leaving the Gang Ranch country, she went nursing for several years. She has remarried and now lives in the Okanagan.

Choate, Chilco: has recently sold the guiding business but still lives on the shores of Gaspard Lake with one dog, four horses, and six cats. The home place is still in business for tourists and travellers. He also calls himself a "Resource Consultant" for the Gang Ranch area of the Chilcotin.

Choate, Margo: When the guiding business was sold, Mother Goose returned to her flock in the East Kootenays.

Clara: stayed with the Gang for several more years and died in Ashcroft at a fairly young age.

Hebert, Daryl: retired from the F&WB and is now tinkering with private enterprise.

Kind, Cactus: now resides in Clinton.

Hatter. Dr. James: retired from F&WB and was/is involved in

game farming, and then, out of the clear blue, he was allotted a guiding licence in southern B.C.

Munsey, Bob and Pat: moved to the Merritt area where they are still ranching.

McCabe, Jess: transferred to the Kootenays where he became the Regional Protection Officer.

Piltz, Gus: sold the Sky Ranch to Dick Church around 1969 and died shortly thereafter.

Rivard, Dennis: returned to Alberta.

Russell, Jim: changed his name to Davies and has retired to a cabin near Big Creek.

Rosette, Alex, Ray, and Willie: all of the boys are still working on ranches around the Cariboo.

Sidwell, Mel: returned to the U.S.A.

Skelton, Floyd: died in the U.S.A.

Sidwell, Irvin: after leaving the Gang Ranch he developed a hay ranch at Walachine, B.C. and has since left that to operate a quarry operation in southern B.C.

INDEX

Quesnel Rod and Gun Club
360

Rafting; *See:* Whitewater
rafting
Railways 22
Rainbow Trout; *See:* Trout
Ranches; *See:* Canoe Creek
Ranch; Chilco; Church;
Douglas Lake; Empire
Valley; Gang; Home
Valley; King; Maindley;
OK; Old Home; Riske
Creek; Sky; Steer
RCMP; *See:* Police
Relay Creek 125, 227-228
Rifles; *See:* Guns
Riske Creek 30, 33, 328, 358,
379, 383
Riske Creek Ranch 328
Rivard, Dennis 345, 385, 399
Rivers; *See:* Campbell;
Chilcotin; Columbia;
Fraser; Nicomecel; Salmon;
Serpentine
Robison, Wayne 215-216,
218-221, 224, 227-228
Rocky Mountains 47-48, 333
Rogers, Stephen 363, 378
Rosette, Alex 87, 399
Rosette, Augustine 34-36, 40,
52, 87, 99, 206, 330, 384
Rosette, Augustine Charley 35
Rosette, Jimmy 130
Rosette, Lilly 34-36
Rosette, Ray 384, 399

Rosette, Willie 35, 292, 330,
384, 399
Royal Canadian Mounted
Police; *See:* Police
Russell, Jim (Davies) 41-42,
60-61, 64, 69, 71, 73, 105,
130-131, 203-204, 207,
230, 399
Rustling; *See:* Cattle rustling

Salmon 102
Salmon River 90
Sanford, Bill 111
Sanford, Murray 4
Saskatchewan 345-346, 359
Sasquatch 280
Saudi Arabian interests 396
Sauer, John 395
Sawmills 188, 316, 396; *See
also:* Forestry
Schooling; *See:* Education
Scotland and Scots 24, 342
Seattle (Wash.) 31, 102
Serpentine River 3
Seymour, Jimmy 340
Sheep, Domestic 48, 61
(Sheep Flats), 119-121,
124-126, 150, 219, 270
(Sheep Camp); *See also:*
Bighorn sheep
"Shorty"; *See:* Watson, Shorty
Shulaps Mountain 372
Sidwell, Blaine 197, 199, 215,
225, 237-238, 244
Sidwell, Irvin 197, 199, 215,
225, 237-239, 244-245,